Museum Texts

What is an appropriate level of complexity for a written label?

Why do some choices in language make a more direct relation with visitors?

Is there a correct way of representing a particular view of content?

How do design practices contribute to the overall meanings being made?

Louise Ravelli provides a set of frameworks to investigate the complexities of communication in museums. The frameworks enhance the way we critically analyse and understand museum texts: both in the sense of conventional, written texts in museums, and in an expanded sense of the museum as a whole operating as a communicative text.

The book uses a wide range of examples, and demonstrates that all communication needs to be understood in relation to its social context. Importantly, it argues that communication is an active process of meaning-making, and in this way, communication issues can be seen to lie at the heart of institutional practices, contributing in fundamental ways to what a museum is, who it relates to, and what it stands for.

Louise Ravelli is Senior Lecturer in Linguistics at the University of New South Wales, Australia. She is interested in the relationship of communication to its social context, especially in the domains of museum communication and academic writing.

Museum Meanings

Series editors
Eilean Hooper-Greenhill
Flora Kaplan

The museum has been constructed as a symbol in Western society since the Renaissance. This symbol is both complex and multi-layered, acting as a sign for domination and liberation, learning and leisure. As sites for exposition, through their collections, displays and buildings, museums mediate many of society's basic values. But these mediations are subject to contestation, and the museum can also be seen as a site for cultural politics. In post-colonial societies, museums have changed radically, reinventing themselves under pressure from many forces, which include new roles and functions for museums, economic rationalism and moves towards greater democratic access.

Museum Meanings analyses and explores the relationships between museums and their publics. 'Museums' are understood very broadly, to include art galleries, historic sites and historic houses. 'Relationships with publics' is also understood very broadly, including interactions with artefacts, exhibitions and architecture, which may be analysed from a range of theoretical perspectives. These include material culture studies, mass communication and media studies, learning theories and cultural studies. The analysis of the relationship of the museum to its publics shifts the emphasis from the museum as text, to studies grounded in the relationships of bodies and sites, identities and communities.

Also in this series:

Museum Texts

Communication Frameworks

Louise J. Ravelli

Routledge
Taylor & Francis Group

LONDON AND NEW YORK

First published 2006
by Routledge
2 Park Square, Milton Park, Abingdon, Oxon OX14 4RN

Simultaneously published in the USA and Canada
by Routledge
270 Madison Ave, New York, NY 10016

Routledge is an imprint of the Taylor & Francis Group

© 2006 Louise J. Ravelli

Typeset in Sabon by
Florence Production Ltd, Stoodleigh, Devon
Printed and bound in Great Britain by
TJ International Ltd, Padstow, Cornwall

British Library Cataloguing in Publication Data
A catalogue record for this book is available from the British Library

Library of Congress Cataloging in Publication Data
Ravelli, Louise.
Museum texts: communication frameworks/Louise J. Ravelli. – [1st ed.]
p. cm.
Includes bibliographical references and index.
1. Communication in museums.   2. Museums – Social aspects.   I. Title.
AM125.R38 2005
069–dc22
2005017300

ISBN10: 0–415–28429–5 (hbk)
ISBN10: 0–415–28430–9 (pbk)

ISBN13: 9–78–0–415–28429–5 (hbk)
ISBN13: 9–78–0–415–28430–1 (pbk)

To the memory of
two extraordinary women:

my aunt and fairy godmother, Miep;
my mother and guiding light, Nancy.

Contents

Illustrations

Figures

Plates

Tables

Acknowledgements

All communication occurs in context, and as a result of a complex set of interacting frameworks, which enable meaning to be made. This book is no different, and the context for it arose because of the vision and enthusiasm of Carolyn MacLulich, former Director of Education at the Australian Museum, Sydney. It was Carolyn who saw the need for more knowledge about texts in museums, and the potential for informed linguistic advice. Her invitation to me to work with the Australian Museum in developing language guidelines opened up a new set of frameworks for me, and she has continued to be a source of both inspiration and practical help throughout.

My professional frameworks include a group of generous and active scholars who continually push forward the boundaries of text analysis, in all its senses. My formal debts to them will be evident throughout the book, but I must especially thank Anne Cranny-Francis, Ann Hewings, Jim Martin, Clare Painter, Geoff Williams, and the Multimodal Discourse Analysis Group at Sydney University for their interest and support. Special thanks to Clare again and to Gay Hawkins for the extra time they have taken to provide feedback and guidance.

That the framework of the book has gained flesh and bones is thanks to the encouragement and hard work of many people, and I would like to extend my gratitude to the Series Editor, Professor Eilean Hooper-Greenhill, for her constantly generous advice and boundless enthusiasm, and to Eilean again and Flora Kaplan for their practical feedback. My thanks to the publishers and especially the editors, including Julene Barnes, Polly Osborn, Catherine Bousfield, and finally Mathew Gibbons, who has seen it through to the end. And not least, I thank the many museum professionals who have generously given their time and expertise to share their ideas about communication with me – some of these have moved on from the institutions which are cited from the time of our discussions, but I thank: Dominique Botbol (Cité des Sciences et de l'Industrie, Paris); Jane Bywaters (Museum of London); Richard Cassels (Queensland Museum); Giles Clark (Natural History Museum, London); Julie Ewington and Thérèse Burnett (Museum of Contemporary Art, Sydney); Roland Jackson (Science Museum, London); Penny Morrison and Carolyn Meehan (Melbourne Museum); Carolyn MacLulich and Linda

Ferguson (Australian Museum); Louise Oakley and Oliver (New Art Gallery, Walsall).

The materialisation of the book has been dependent on institutional frameworks, and I gratefully acknowledge the generous support of the Humanities Research Program at the University of New South Wales for a Teaching Release Scholarship which enabled this book to be completed.

Most importantly, this book is also a product of my personal framework. Thank you to my husband, Rob, who has supported me all the way, guiding me through the quagmire to a little clarity, and who through example has helped me understand what it means to integrate work with the everyday living of life – not that I have always been able to achieve that! And to our beautiful son Jeremy, whose very presence brings us so much pleasure.

Illustration and text sources

I would like to thank the following for permission to use their photographs:

John Nicholson: Guggenheim Museum at Bilbao, Spain

South Australian Museum and the Parkes Radio Telescope: exhibits

South Australian Museum and Deb Jones: entry panel (*used on cover*)

I thank the Australian Museum for permission to reproduce examples from Ferguson *et al.* 1995.

Unless otherwise noted, all examples are authentic, from actual museum exhibitions. I gratefully acknowledge the many institutions who have allowed me to re-present their communication in this way, and I trust I have done justice to their communication efforts. The institutions are:

Art Gallery of New South Wales, Sydney

Australian Museum, Sydney

Australian National Maritime Museum, Sydney

Cité des Sciences et de l'Industrie, Paris

Guggenheim Museum, Bilbao

Melbourne Museum

Museum of London

National Museum of Australia, Canberra

Natural History Museum, London

Parkes Radio Telescope

Powerhouse Museum, Sydney

Queensland Museum, Brisbane

Royal Tyrell Museum, Alberta

Smithsonian, Washington

South Australian Museum, Adelaide

Tasmanian Aboriginal Centre, Hobart

Museum of New Zealand Te Papa Tongarewa, Wellington

**Exhibits at the first museum
of natural history were few.**

1

Introduction

Texts, frameworks and meanings

Communicating in museums

This book is about communicating in museums, especially through written texts, but including also some broader senses of communication. Communication within a museum potentially encompasses all of an institution's practices which make meaning – from the pragmatic effect of whether or not there is an admission charge (which makes meanings about what the institution is, and who may enter it), to the overall aesthetic impact of the building, to the organisational layout of the galleries, to the written texts pasted on walls or written in brochures, which support exhibitions. This, of course, is the broadest possible definition of communication, and it would be impossible to address all such facets of communication in equal detail in one book. However, what I aim to do here is to provide a set of frameworks for understanding communication in a generalised way, with a primary focus on language, especially written texts, and a secondary focus on the way in which these frameworks can be extended to some of the broader senses of communication.

This book, then, is about museum texts. There are at least two ways in which this phrase can be understood. The first is that of *texts in museums*: the 'texts' with which visitors, and museum professionals, are very familiar. These might be called labels, extended texts, wall texts, catalogue entries, brochure descriptions. This book is primarily concerned with these kinds of texts: the language produced by the institution, in written and spoken form, for the consumption of visitors, which contributes to interpretative practices within the institution. These texts are an intrinsic part of a museum's communication tool-kit, sometimes being placed on a par with exhibition material (Ekarv 1999), and having a fundamental role to play in the conceptualisation and design of exhibitions (Serrell 1996), and in the responses that visitors make to exhibition content (McManus 1989a, 1991, 2000; Screven 1995). While meaning should not be seen as residing 'within' the text (Witcomb 2003), texts themselves are a powerful communicative resource, and need to be understood as fully as possible.

At the same time, 'museum texts' could mean *museums as texts*: the way a whole institution, or an exhibition within it, makes meaning, communicating to and with its public. *Texts in museums* contributes to a sense of *museums as texts*; in this way, the book addresses both senses of the phrase. More explicitly, however, the communication frameworks proposed here, largely to account for 'texts in museums', in the sense of the language used within them, are extended to include a much broader sense of communication – the ways in which elements of design, layout, content selection and so on contribute to the overall impact of an exhibition or institution. This enhanced sense of communication is taken up in the last chapter of the book, and is used to highlight the potential for a more extended application of the frameworks beyond language, to other forms of communication. After all, exhibitions are 'one of the principal ways that a museum or institution communicates with its public' (Spencer 1999: 156), and they are constructed of a complex variety of resources, including, but not limited to, language (Kaplan 1995). The 'experience' of an exhibition or an institution is a powerful communicative tool, and is one of the defining features of museum visiting.

Within the primary focus of the book, that of *texts in museums*, emphasis is placed on *written* language – the labels, explanatory texts, brochure and catalogue descriptions, because of their intrinsic contribution to the communication agenda of museums. I am not particularly interested (here) in the more pragmatic aspects of signage ('*this way to . . .*'), and nor do I give extended attention to other forms of texts, such as the content of guided tours, or the recordings in an audio/CD guide, or the public lectures given by specialists, or the hypertexts which may be found on an institution's web site. These are all relevant and potentially significant texts in museums, and given that they are all constructed in language, then the communication frameworks proposed here will be applicable to these as well. However, each medium of communication also has its own unique features, and it is beyond the scope of this book to address each of them specifically. I will, thus, concentrate on a generalised use of language, and illustrate the issues with texts deriving mainly from written sources.

The motivation for this book arises from the important role that communication plays in the agenda of contemporary cultural institutions. The overall function of such institutions, including museums, art galleries, heritage parks and related cultural sites, has changed: from their early role as cabinets of curiosity, or the privileged face of learned societies, their responsibilities to the public, and their definition as 'public' institutions, are now well entrenched (Saumerez Smith 1989; O'Neill 1999). The overall relation of institution to visitor has also changed: there is a much-increased awareness of the diversity of visitors and, at the same time, intense competition for their interest. Museums today are much better placed to evaluate visitor demographics and responses, and to adjust their practices accordingly, and their fundamental social role and purpose continues to evolve (Belcher 1991; Hein 1998; Falk and Dierking 2000). The fundamental relations between museums and their visitors are changing, enabling more dynamic encounters, and more diverse interpretations (Bennett 1998b; Witcomb 2003). At the same time, the approach to knowledge within museums has changed: the emphasis has shifted from curatorially defined exhibitions of the past, highlighting individual disciplinary-based knowledge, and presenting authoritative views of the subject matter at hand, to thematically focussed, inter-disciplinary exhibitions, which may problematise and critique received wisdom in any given domain (Hooper-Greenhill 1994, 2000; O'Neill 1999; MacDonald 1998).

These seismic shifts in overall function, relations with visitors, and fundamental approach to knowledge provide both challenges and opportunities for museums. Communication needs to be more explicit and more reflexive – to bring implicit assumptions (about what is important, for instance, or about particular facts) to the surface; it needs to be more diversified, to accommodate the needs and interests of a variety of visitors; and above all, it must be *effective* – that is, actively contribute to and enhance an institution's aims and objectives, and similarly meet the needs and demands of visitors. Museums have the opportunity to reflect on their communicative practices, and use diverse ways of communicating to reach out to visitors and communities, to construct powerful messages, and to critique and reflect on their own social positioning. This book aims to contribute to some of these processes.

Why museum texts?

Museum texts, especially exhibition texts, are important because they form a central component of a museum's communication agenda. Indeed, it is the development of the thematic exhibition, with its strongly educational goals, which has placed the role of exhibition texts at the forefront (Samson 1995; McManus 2000; Schiele 1995; Jacobi and Poli 1995). In the past, a curatorially driven agenda, developed with an audience of peers in mind, could function successfully with just minimal labels, noting such details as the date, scientific classification, and source of a specimen, for instance. Minimal use would be made of extended text, and if used, it would be directed largely at fellow scholars, and few other interpretative strategies were drawn upon. However, a thematic, open, educationally oriented exhibition, aiming to appeal to a wide range of visitors, needs to make use of extended texts, which contextualise an object, and which make explicit the basis for its interpretation. Indeed Bennett links a concern for 'clear labelling' with the late nineteenth-century move in museums to educate, and 'civilise', the mass public (Bennett 1998b). Today, a wide range of text types may be invoked to support these goals, and other interpretative strategies, such as teacher-led tours, or web-based resources, may be drawn upon.

In such ways, communication has become an essential part of the contemporary institution's agenda. And communication is important because it is largely about making meanings – constructing, sharing and interpreting a range of content, attitudes and values. However, communication is not a straightforward or transparent phenomenon: it takes a complex range of skills for either an individual or an institution to be an effective communicator, and there can be debates and contestations over both what should be communicated, and how. Communication in museums often falls short of what might be expected

– visitors are frustrated by texts which are overly complex, debates rage within the community about what 'should' have been presented in an exhibition, extensive time is spent writing and re-writing texts, and a specialist who has been able to write a successful doctoral thesis may be unable to write a simple explanatory text for an exhibition (MacLulich 1992). Despite the enormous interest in and appreciation of communication within museum contexts, it is still the case that communication can fall short of what is desired, leaving the question remaining: 'How is it possible that so many competent and dedicated museum staff around the world write labels that do not work?' (Screven 1995: 125).

Yet at the same time, while all such failings are manifestly evident in many museums, the success of an enormous range of communication practices goes largely overlooked. Many exhibitions work magnificently, creating interesting and engaging exhibitions, providing texts which balance accessibility with interest and challenge, making meanings which inspire and move visitors to respond. Just as communication failures remain difficult to overcome, successes, while appreciated, are largely left unexplained. The communicative success of an exhibition is likely to be attributed to fortuitous circumstances ('everything just came together'), or else, to the 'gifts' or 'talents' of a particular writer or writing team. Communication, however, is not a gift: it is a skill. Gifts are available only to those who have received them, whereas skills can be taught to anyone. To see communication as a skill, and not a gift, requires some change of perspective, and some shared knowledge base about what communication is, and how it works. This book aims to contribute to that knowledge base.

It is important to recognise the nature of the contribution of a book such as this, and the likely reactions it might provoke. Any book which claims to cast some light on communication processes is essentially giving some form of guidance or advice about language – and where issues of language advice are concerned, there tend to be contradictory reactions. One reaction can be to bow down unquestioningly in front of any authority who gives a definitive rule, such as 'avoid the passive voice', or 'keep your sentences short' (cf. Cameron 1995). A contrary reaction can be to rise up in protest if told 'how to write' or 'what to say', as if the very basis of communicative freedom has been threatened. One museum curator described debates between scientific and educational staff in his institution as 'bloody battles'; and in the text production project at the Australian Museum, which first drew me into this area (MacLulich 1992; Ferguson *et al.* 1995; Ravelli 1996), our work was described by some in the institution as that of the 'text police'. These latter reactions point to the significance of communication in general, and language in particular: meaning is a valuable commodity, those who trade in it might be regarded with awe, or suspicion, and there are strongly vested interests in communicating some meanings, rather than others. In other words, there are strongly vested interests in *controlling* the meanings which are made: no wonder 'bloody battles' arise. We *should* be vitally engaged in debating, critiquing, and evaluating the meanings we make, as well as the meanings made by others. Notably, battles are most bloody when the weapons are crude, or non-existent – where there are only our 'intuitions' or 'values' to go on. Where, however, there is a little more knowledge, it is possible to stand back and re-evaluate; battles can become debates. I hope the focus in this book will lead towards this more middle ground. The book does include some specific language advice, especially some thorough debunking of a few precious 'rules' – to highlight them for the fallacies they are. At the same time, the book also provides more generalised descriptions of how language works, in multiple ways, and provides a means to enhance a general understanding of communication, rather than specific advice as to how or what to communicate. I hope that the book can thus contribute to informed debate and critique about language and communication in museum contexts, and that it can be one of the resources which enables museum professionals to enhance their own practices.

Most importantly, the information provided here should be part of *institutional knowledge* about communication. While it can be appropriate to have particular areas of expertise, that is, individuals or groups within an institution who have special responsibilities for communication, it is not enough for an institution to palm off its responsibilities to such people. Some basic knowledge about communication – how it works, its effects, its significance – must be a shared institutional resource, and of concern to all. I believe contemporary institutions are deeply concerned with these issues, and I hope that the time people invest in this book will be rewarded with new perspectives and insights into this area. This book will not answer all questions about communication; it will not stand on its own without reference to other current work on communication in the museum context; but it should be a useful part of an institutional 'toolkit', one – informed – contribution to the debate, one more reason to be vitally engaged in reflection on communication, and one *less* reason to be engaged in fruitless battles.

An approach to communication:

There are potentially many ways to understand and explain communication. In this book, some of the key ideas are that communication is an active, social process; that meaning is understood in relation to issues of choice; that it is complex in nature, and always embedded in context. These notions are explained further here.

. . . as an active, social process

Here, communication is understood as a fundamentally *social* process – that is, as always embedded in a social context, arising from the need for social beings to interact with each other and to engage in and with the world. Museums and related cultural institutions are no different: their engagement with communication is a way of enacting their role as social, and socialised, institutions, creating relations with their visitors, and engaging in the world by finding ways to re-present it. At the same time as arising from the social context, communication feeds back into that social process, helping to construct actual relations between people, and to construct particular ways of engaging with and representing the world. It is the process of communicating itself which makes meanings. Meanings are not a pre-ordained 'given', which are then simply transmitted through channels of communication; meanings are actively constructed in and through the use of communicative resources, such as language. In other words, communication is also a *semiotic* process, that is, a process of *making meaning*. A *social-semiotic* view of communication (Halliday 1978; Hodge and Kress 1988) focusses on communication as a contextualised, meaning-making resource. As meaning always arises in relation to the contexts of social use, the relevant focus of study is real text, instances of actual communication in use, not decontextualised extracts or hypothesised forms.

. . . where meaning relates to choice

Within this social-semiotic approach, the notions of both 'meaning' and 'context' need some further explanation. Meaning arises wherever there are *choices* in communication (thus at the simple level of a word, '*hot*' has meaning because it contrasts with something like '*cold*', or '*warm*', or '*lukewarm*'). In an exhibition, one relevant contrast in meaning is the way in which information is presented to visitors. For example, if an exhibition label says:

> Arrangements of belts and pulleys like this are known as 'line shafting'

then the language of the label helps establish one kind of relationship between an institution and its visitors – one where the institution is positioned in a relatively authoritative way, somewhat distant from its visitors. In contrast, if a label says:

> How have the anatomist's knife, the x-ray machine and the microscope changed the way we live and the way we view ourselves?

another kind of relationship is established, closing the distance between institution and visitor, and constructing a less formal presence. The choice in presentation here is a choice in meaning, creating meanings for and about the institution, the exhibition and the visitors engaged in the exhibition. Thus, wherever there are options – different ways of saying things – there is meaning. But what are these meanings? How can the contrast in the examples just cited be said to be an issue of meaning?

. . . where meaning is complex

Meaning is typically understood in terms of representational content: that is, that one of the functions of communication is to 'refer to' or 'represent' things:

objects, people, places and abstract concepts. Dictionaries are generally seen to be a resource for explaining this aspect of meaning: we look up words to see what it is they represent. This understanding of meaning in *representational* terms is certainly important: it encompasses the meanings we make in order to engage with, understand and refer to our world. It reflects the fact that all communication is 'about' something (even if that 'something' can be very vague or abstract), and that part of the purpose of communicating is to convey some kind of 'content' in this sense. But this is only a very partial view of meaning. There are other ways of making meaning, less obvious and less widely understood, but equally important. Consider the following scenarios. If a museum was choosing their next exhibition focus, and deciding between an exhibition on transport, and an exhibition on spiders, the resulting exhibitions would obviously have to make very different meanings, because the 'content' would be different. Let's say they choose transport – there are still countless ways in which the exhibition could take shape. Of course the general term 'transport' doesn't begin to account for the actual focus of the exhibition: it could be a comprehensive view of the history of different forms of transport, or a critique of the environmental impact of particular forms of transport – or many other things. This is one domain of meaning that needs to be considered in the exhibition – the representational. The examples cited above, about 'belts and pulleys' and 'the anatomist's knife' are different in their representational meaning, as their subject matter is different. At the same time, other options of meaning arise. Will visitors be invited to try out different modes of transport for themselves? Will they be presented with a vast array of information, and expected to absorb it? Will the museum present an authoritative view on the subject matter, or open the subject up to debate? Such choices of meaning are not necessarily about 'content' in the representational sense, but are a way of *interacting* through the communication process, whatever the content. This then is another important facet of meaning: that communication includes *interactional* meanings, and that this is one of the main functions of communication – to take up roles, construct relations and convey attitudes. Again, the examples about 'belts and pulleys' and 'the anatomist's knife' contrast in this regard, the former presenting information to be absorbed, the latter engaging the visitor in a more explicit response. And there are still further options: is the exhibition content to be presented largely via written texts? Are those texts to be very brief, or quite long? Or will the information be presented through a guided tour? Or on the net? There must be some way of *conveying* the communication – the representational and interactional meanings will only be effective if they are shaped or *organised* in an appropriate way, and different forms of organisation are themselves a form of meaning-making. The particular organisation of a text enables some meanings to be foregrounded over others, and contributes to the coherence and unity of a text. *Organisational* meanings – to do with the way the text is organised, not the meanings of the 'institution' as an organisation – enable similar messages to be conveyed in different ways. The examples about *'belts and pulleys'* and *'the anatomist's knife'* contrast in this regard also, the former being organised in a way more typical of written language, and the latter being more conversational in its style.

. . . where meaning relates to context

Meaning, then, is neither straightforward nor simple. It is a complex phenom-enon, made up of the complementary strands of *representational, interactional,* and *organisational* meanings. These frameworks of meaning were proposed by Halliday (1978, 1994)[1] in his analysis of language. I will be using these frame-works of meaning to account for both *texts in museums* and *museums as texts* – that is, communication via language, and communication via a broader range of resources, such as elements of design in the physical layout of an exhibition or gallery. A distinguishing feature of Halliday's social-semiotic account of language is that meanings are seen to relate explicitly to issues of social context. Part of this context includes the *Field*,[2] or subject matter that is to be communicated; when the Field changes, representational meanings change also. So, the choice of topic is part of the context of communication, which has an evident impact on the text. It is the need to communicate *about something* in the social context which motivates some of the meanings made in texts. Another part of the context is the *Tenor*, or roles and relationships between the interactants in the situation: these roles and relationships give rise to interactional meanings.[3] It is because we communicate *to someone* in the social context, that some of the meanings made in texts are motivated. Finally, another part of the context is the *Mode*, or nature of the communication taking place, which gives rise to organisational meanings. It is because we need to communicate *in a particular way*, that texts have some of the distinctive meanings they do.

At the same time as context influencing text, text also impacts upon context, that is, choices made in the process of communication feed back into an under-standing of context, and help construct a view of what that context is. For instance, if a museum consistently chooses impersonal forms of language in their exhibition texts, then this will contribute to a sense of distance between the institution and its visitors. The social distance may be 'there' in the context, but it is also *constructed by* the choices made in text. Thus, meanings relate 'upwards' to issues of social context. At the same time, they relate 'downwards' to actual communication choices, in that there are identifiable communication resources – in language, or in other semiotics, such as visual elements – which connect with particular meanings. Thus, any explanation of meanings should be able to be related to an *explicit* analysis of text. As a result, the explanation of meaning provided by this approach is more than just an elegant hypothesis about how communication works; it is an explanation which makes *explicit* connections between context and communication, thereby enabling explan-ations of meanings in text to be grounded with reference to actual textual analysis, as well as to actual interpretations of context (Halliday 1994; Halliday and Matthiessen 2004).

An additional question remains about meaning, and that is, how do we know what something means? Meanings must be interpreted within a broader discur-sive framework; the social and cultural conditions within which texts are made; the complex networks of communicative practices which shape and influence interpretation. It is the overarching set of discourses which give significance to particular communicative choices. It is well recognised that 'a' text can have multiple meanings, depending on the discourses within which the text is interpreted (Hooper-Greenhill 2000), and this is an important way in which polysemy, or multiple readings of a text, can arise. Meaning therefore needs to be interpreted in relation to the networks of which it is a part. In addition, however, when the complex nature of meaning is stressed in this book, it should be noted that this also refers to the *multifunctional* nature of meaning – its simultaneous organisational, interactional and representational facets.

The frameworks of this book

The communication frameworks introduced in this book are those of the organisational, interactional, and representational meanings, and these are addressed in two ways. First, the organisational, interactional and representational meanings are examined in terms of how they operate in language, and Chapters 2–5 focus on these frameworks in relation to language in detail. Second, the frameworks are extended beyond language, to include a broader understanding of communication, and how it is realised through other communicative resources, such as layout and design. This perspective is addressed in Chapter 6, which outlines some of the ways in which each of the three frameworks can be seen to operate within this enhanced sense of communication.

The exploration begins in Chapter 2 with *organisational* meanings, partly because this is a less obvious place to start (as opposed to the more familiar domain of representational meanings, for instance), and partly because it is the issue of organising texts which poses some of the more challenging communication issues for museums. Organisational meanings are described as impacting on text in two ways. First, different choices of organisation can contribute to quite different organisational effects in text, leading to potentially quite different meanings. It is thus a powerful and creative resource for communication. Second, problems in organisational choices can lead to a breakdown of meanings, and potential confusion. It is thus a resource which needs to be more fully understood, to maximise its potential, and avoid its pitfalls. Chapter 2 examines organisational meanings at a range of levels, from the macro-level of the whole text and its overall generic purpose, down to the micro-level of the organisation of sentences.

Organisational meanings are also addressed in Chapter 3, which takes a focussed look at issues of accessibility and readability in texts. In order to understand these issues in more detail, Chapter 3 provides extended discussion of the notion of 'complexity' in language, explaining the different ways in which complexity can be understood in written and spoken texts. This enables a number of widely circulated 'myths' about good writing practices to be thoroughly debunked, and the simplistic views of 'Plain English' approaches to be rejected.

In Chapter 4, the focus is on interactional meanings, and the ways in which the roles and relations constructed by an institution, with its visitors, are an intrinsic part of meaning-making practices. The variety of roles and relations are related to specific resources in language, and additional interactional issues, of the general style of communication, and the overall stance created towards a subject area, are also examined.

The last of the three core frameworks, the representational, is introduced in Chapter 5. This chapter deals with those aspects of meaning related to more traditional understandings of 'content', or what a text is 'about'. This can include a very micro-level perspective such as how to address issues of technicality in text, and also macro-level issues, such as how a whole taxonomy for a subject area is built up through choices in language. In particular, the significance of the representational framework for museum communicators, is that multiple pictures of the 'same' subject area can be created through the choices made in this framework; it therefore has a major impact on the communication agenda of museums.

The focus of the book shifts significantly in Chapter 6, moving away from language, and the issues of 'texts in museums', to address the ways in which meanings are made through visual, physical and discursive resources. This extended use of the frameworks is used to explain how it is that 'spaces', such as exhibitions, and indeed whole institutions, can be read and experienced as meaningful texts. As each of the three frameworks are addressed within this chapter, the picture provided is that of a condensed snapshot of the potential of this approach, introducing some of the main ways in which visual and related communicative resources contribute to meanings at this level.

The final chapter, Chapter 7, addresses ways of integrating these two perspectives, that of 'texts in museums', and 'museums as texts', arguing that they operate as a unified communicative resource. It is also stressed here that every text is a product of each of the three frameworks, and that they need to be understood as operating together, and influencing each other. The frameworks come together then, from both perspectives, as a way of enabling both the critique and understanding of the complex and diversified state that is communication in contemporary cultural institutions.

A little bit of architecture

The communication frameworks developed in this book derive from Halliday's *systemic-functional linguistics* ('SFL'; Halliday 1978, 1994; Halliday and Hasan 1976; Martin 1992; Halliday and Matthiessen 2004). As already noted, this is a social-semiotic approach to language, which accounts for language and communication as meaning-making resources within a social context. It complements other approaches to language, such as critical-discourse analysis (for instance, Fowler *et al.* 1979; Fairclough 1995; Chouliaraki and Fairclough 1999), which also critique communication in relation to issues of social context. SFL has also been a strong influence on multi-modal discourse analysis (for instance, Kress and van Leeuwen 1996, 2001; O'Toole 1994; O'Halloran 2004), which attempts to account for communication resources beyond language, such as visual aspects of communication, and this is a particularly important resource in the latter part of the book.

The overall approach to communication in this book is informed primarily by SFL theory, and will use some of its terminology and theoretical 'architecture', but the book is not in itself a linguistic textbook, and technical terminology will be kept to a minimum wherever possible. In fact, in all the areas covered by the book, the linguistic detail could be extended considerably, and I will point readers to further resources as relevant.[4] However, it is still the case that *some* technicality is absolutely essential: in order to interrogate communication and language as 'objects', there needs to be some way to stand outside of them, and examine them critically. This requires a *metalanguage* – a way of talking about language, and thus, some technicality. The point for readers of this book is not to memorise all of the terminology, but to understand the ways in which the terminology is functional: how it helps to explicitly identify a meaning-making pattern in a text, for example, and how it functions as a resource for sharing knowledge about language. It is the absence of a shared metalanguage which leads to many text-writing problems in museum contexts (Ravelli 1996). Any technical terms will be explained as the book unfolds, but there are a few basic concepts which it will be useful to explain here.

One of the key distinguishing features of SFL and related approaches to language and communication is that language is seen as a *resource* – that is, a potential for making meaning. Language is not a formula or a list of rules that simply needs to be implemented for communication to take place; the picture is more complex than that. As a resource, which can be drawn upon in endlessly creative ways, it is then not relevant to speak of 'correct' and 'incorrect' versions of language. Language always occurs in context, and so must be evaluated in relation to that context: some language is appropriate in some contexts, but not others. Thus, the approach in this book aims to see how language is functional (or not) in its context, rather than trying to provide a definitive view on what is 'correct' or acceptable.

An additional feature of SFL and related approaches is that the primary object of analysis is *text*: that is, authentic examples of communication, which have some purposeful function in the context, and which make some meaning (Halliday and Hasan 1976; Halliday and Matthiessen 2004). Texts may be long or short, ephemeral or carefully preserved, private or public, serious or fanciful. The analysis may focus on tiny building blocks of these texts – a word, a grammatical structure – but the point is to understand how those building blocks contribute to the meaning of the whole. An understanding of the building blocks themselves is a means to an end, not the end itself. A general theme of the book will be to consider text across a range of levels, including individual sentences, but also whole texts, and even the way in which the texts and other communicative resources within an exhibition can be seen to work together to create a 'genre' for that exhibition.

In Chapters 2–5, where language is the primary focus, a number of different levels of language will be considered. As noted, texts can vary in many ways, and can be of different 'sizes' – sometimes a 'whole' text may consist of a single word ('Stop') or a single sentence ('Do not touch the display!'), sometimes the text may spread over several paragraphs, or even be a whole book. Given this variation, there needs to be some way of breaking a text down into its relevant parts – what are its basic building blocks? To understand this, the book will see 'text' as being made up of units at different *levels*[5]: the text as a whole is one level, at the top of a hierarchy; at this level we will examine the overall shape and structure, and purpose of the text. At the bottom of the hierarchy are *words*, being the smallest building block,[6] and we will see that of course individual words can have quite an impact on meaning in texts. In between words and text are two other levels. *Clauses*, which may occur on their own, or together with others in a *clause complex*, are at the level immediately below text; these are largely equivalent to *sentences*. In this book, the term 'clause' will generally be used instead of sentence, as a sentence may refer to either a clause or a clause complex. In turn, clauses are made up of *groups* (clusters around a word, such as noun groups and verb groups) and by focussing on groups and clauses we will be able to see some of the ways in which the various structures of clauses contribute to meaning, across each of the frameworks. The main levels that will be referred to in relation to the language of museum texts can be illustrated as follows:

Levels in relation to language
Text
Clause complex
Clause
Group
Word

This way of describing the building blocks, however, captures only the basic *form* of each element – whether a word is a 'noun' or a 'verb' for instance. It is even more important to address issues of *function*, that is, issues of meaning, and to identify the role these elements can play in creating a meaningful text. Each of the chapters on the organisational, interactional and representational frameworks will demonstrate some of the ways in which these basic building blocks contribute to meaning in text, that is, how they take up different roles in relation to each framework. Every text will be seen as being multi-functional, and every component of every text potentially makes multiple contributions to the meaning framework. So, a text such as 'How have the anatomist's knife, the x-ray machine and the microscope changed the way we live and the way we view ourselves?' constructs a certain representational content, that is, a sense of what the text is 'about'. At the same time, it positions visitors to respond in a particular way, inviting them to actively interact with the text. And it is organised in a particular way to convey a reasonably conversational tone. Throughout the book then, in any one chapter, the focus may shift from the text as a whole, to one of its components (and back again); and across the book, some of the same examples will be revisited, to draw out some of the multiple ways in which one text can make meaning.

In Chapter 6, when the focus shifts away from language to broader senses of communication, the notions of text and levels are slightly adapted. Here, the top level is the 'institution', within which exhibitions, or galleries, are seen to be meaningful units, in turn made up of exhibits or displays.

Expanded sense of levels
Institution
Exhibition/gallery
Exhibit/display[7]

Exhibits and displays, in turn, are made up of a wide range of communicative resources, including both language, as used in exhibition texts, and resources of visual design, spatial layout, item selection, and so on. These complex relations will be addressed further in Chapter 6.[8]

Contextualisation

It is important to compare the approach adopted in this book with other possible approaches to communication. Most importantly, the social-semiotic approach to communication adopted here contrasts with linear, transmission models of communication, but has some similar concerns to those of social-constructivist approaches, and to those which attempt to account for the role of visitors in the communication process. The overall approach presented here is not intended to be a prescriptive, 'how-to' guide, but rather to be a reference point for deeper understanding and further exploration. These points are expanded on below.

The social-semiotic approach contrasts strongly with linear, transmission models of communication, which show messages being passed from 'sender' to 'receiver'. Such models present a fundamentally flawed view of communication (Hooper-Greenhill 1994). No matter how complex or sophisticated their presentation, such models basically capture only the mechanics of communication: the physical fact, that there is some auditory or graphic material created by one person, which is indeed 'received' by another. However, these models are not able to explain what is fundamentally going on with communication: what is it that is being sent and received? How is it that the physical material makes meaning? How is it that senders and receivers can make and understand such a wide range of meanings? Transmission models are part of the modernist museum's conceptualisation of communication (Witcomb 2003), and are unable to account for the intricate nature of actual communication processes which take place in museum contexts.

In this book, I am going to resist the generic requirement to present a visual model of communication, as such visual presentations almost invariably invoke a sense of directionality which replicates the errors of transmission models. Instead, it is important to note that the social-semiotic approach incorporates an inherent sense of interactivity in its model, whereby interactants in the communication situation – such as museums and their visitors – are mutually engaged in the communication process (McManus 1991, 2000). Meaning is 'forged through social and cultural frameworks' (Hooper-Greenhill 2000: 50). At the same time, the social-semiotic model represents communication as being inherently *constitutive*, rather than reflective. That is, communication does not simply reflect or transmit a pre-existing reality, but actively constructs and contributes to a sense of that 'reality' (Reddy 1979).

In this way, the social-semiotic approach complements a social-constructivist view of communication, whereby social context has a profound impact on communication. In writing theory, writing is viewed as a contextualised social act which takes place for a specific audience (Hewings 1999; see also Johns 1997). In education theory, social constructivism foregrounds the conditions for learning (Hooper-Greenhill 2000), and in generalised learning theory, the learner is seen to be actively engaged in processes of making meaning (Hein 1996, 1998, 1999). The fact that learning is also a fundamentally social experience (Falk and Dierking 2000) means that it is highly appropriate to adopt a model of communication which is socially contextualised. While the focus here is not on learning as such, the analysis and critique of texts and their meanings provided here contributes to an understanding of some of the conditions which impact upon learning in a museum context.

One of the substantive developments in museum research in recent years has been the expanded depth and breadth of visitor research, placing visitors at the centre of the communication agenda (Durbin 1996; Hein 1998; Falk and Dierking 2000, among many others). Both text and visitor need to be accounted for in a complex model of communication (Hooper-Greenhill 1995; Serrell 1996; McManus 2000), and a 'text only' focus in fact ignores the very nature of communication itself: that it requires two parties to be engaged in the process. It is important, then, to account for visitors' roles in the communication process, and the potential variety of responses to a given text. Close observation of visitors reveals the complexity of their learning in a museum environment: two individuals visiting together can learn, remember, and value quite different aspects of the 'same' experience. A focus on texts alone presents only a partial view of what goes on in terms of making and understanding meanings in museum contexts (Falk and Dierking 2000: 7). A crucial part of understanding visitors is to *evaluate* their responses, in terms of front-end, formative and summative evaluation (Belcher 1991), and to incorporate these into exhibition processes. A text may be carefully prepared, thoroughly critiqued and evaluated internally, but potentially have quite a different impact on visitors from that which was intended. Such evaluation is a critical part of contemporary museum practice.

In this book, I do not wish to replicate the errors of a 'text only' focus, but I do wish to concentrate on texts, to bring in detailed and specialised knowledge about their nature and function. I will foreground texts as being centrally important, while recognising that they are only part of the picture. I do not claim here that close textual analysis will reveal 'the' meaning of an exhibition, nor that close textual analysis on its own can account for the multiple ways in which the meanings of 'a' text can be inflected. It is not the case that the attention paid to communication in this book aims to 'perfect' the medium of communication, nor that the medium of communication is 'all powerful' (cf. Hooper-Greenhill 1995: 5). But, I am claiming that close textual analysis will reveal *some* of the meanings which are constructed in, by and from the text/s in question, and I am claiming that, by and large, these meanings are systematic products of a communication system. While being firmly embedded in a social-semiotic approach, and while foregrounding and prioritising 'text', I do not see this as being at odds with recent cultural critiques of the post-museum, which emphasise the polysemy of meaning, the role of visitors in the production of meaning, and the complex and often competing discursive frameworks which influence the production and interpretation of meaning (Hooper-Greenhill 2000; Witcomb 2003). On the contrary, the purpose of text analysis from within a social-semiotic perspective is to cast additional light on the social processes which are an intrinsic part of communication, and to understand some of the ways in which these are inflected in text. A text-based approach should not be a confining one (Witcomb 2003), but one which addresses communication as a meaning-making resource, a creative potential, itself multi-functional and multipurposeful, and always socially situated.

While the focus in this book is primarily on texts, visitors are implicated in the process in two ways. In the first instance, the fundamental explanation of communication presented here *includes* visitors as part of the model: a text is a way of interacting with another party, a way of constructing a particular view of the world for another to engage with, and is in itself a way of enabling communication. That is, without the other party, there would be no text, so a 'text' focus, from a social-semiotic perspective, includes some inherent account of visitors. At the same time, there can be differences between 'producers' and 'receivers': even though each may be engaging with the same set of communicative resources, used to produce a particular kind of text, the intentions and understandings deriving from that text can vary. Receivers can take up different reading positions in relation to a text – the reading position of the text is 'the positioning constructed for the reader at which all elements of the text make sense' (Cranny-Francis 1992: 184, following Kress 1989). While responses to text can be as varied as the visitors engaging with them, reading positions are negotiated in three typical ways. A *compliant* position accepts the constructed textual reading position, and negotiates it unproblematically. A *resistant* position is one which rejects the position that is offered, and a *tactical* position is one which makes an 'opportunistic' use of the text (Cranny-Francis 1992: 183). The reading position of any one individual in relation to a particular text may be a combination of these variables, given that subjectivity is constantly re-negotiated. Thus, the second way in which visitors are implicated in this model is through their reading position in relation to a given text. 'Receivers' are, at the same time, 'producers', and make use of texts in different ways. In this book, it will be largely the compliant position which is accounted for, although it is always possible for resistant or tactical readings to take place.

The readings which I give of these texts will be from my (broadly western) cultural perspective, influenced by my subjectivity, and others might interpret them differently. This does not mean, however, that the communication frameworks proposed are weak because of this: rather, it is a feature of the frameworks that they must be contextualised, within a particular cultural and social context. Multiple readings of a given text may arise for a number of reasons, including variation in the dominant reading position, as just described, but also because of the multiple meanings co-existing within any one text. The organisational, interactional and representational frameworks described in this book will demonstrate that every text is a complex of meanings, and while the frameworks operate simultaneously, it is possible for one of these to be foregrounded for a particular reader on a particular occasion, accounting for the fact that with the 'same' text, we may attend to different things.

This book, then, aims to provide a set of communication frameworks which will enable more detailed reflection on texts in museums, and on museums as texts, and which will enhance a generalised understanding of communication. The book is not a 'how to' guide (though there may be some pointers of that kind along the way), and is not intended to function as a manual (but see Ferguson *et al.* 1995 for a manual using the same frameworks as presented here). It is not about the practical or physical aspects of text production in museums – such as the appropriate height at which to hang a wall label, or how to factor writing into the planning processes of an exhibition team. It is certainly the case that such practical issues are important for museums, and they can impinge directly on issues of meaning, and as such, they will occasionally be mentioned, but without being a primary focus.[9]

In many ways, this book is very simple. It is just a framework: a reference point, a guide, the skeletal structure on which flesh and bones are built. And as such, it is just a beginning. But to provide a solid foundation, a framework must be multi-dimensional, and sufficiently robust to allow complexity to be built upon it. Thus, aspects of this framework will appear to be quite complex: there are *three* ways to look at meaning, not just one; there is a *metalanguage* for talking about language; and there will be no simple 'rules' to follow. This, however, is appropriate: communication itself is inherently complex,[10] and to treat it otherwise, to treat it simplistically, is to fail to account for it at all. An appreciation of the importance of communication is clearly on the agenda of contemporary cultural institutions; this book aims to contribute to an appreciation of its complexity – why it is so challenging, why it is endlessly creative, where it can go wrong, and how it can succeed magnificently.

2

Organisation as a way of making meaning

Using language to organise, shape and connect

Introduction

Discussions of meaning tend to focus on issues of representation, some actual 'content' that is referred to. Thus, the favourite question, 'what does it mean?', is usually answered by trying to explain what something 'is', or what it is 'like'; what is being represented or referred to. But meaning is more than just representation: a meaning-making system needs to do more than just refer to content; that content must be organised in some way, and the organisational framework[1] is an intrinsic part of meaning-making. It is an 'enabling resource' (Halliday 1978), bringing together both representational and interactional meanings into a coherent whole.[2] Any text, whether it be a sentence, a wall panel, or a whole exhibition, needs to be effectively organised, so that its individual components are able to function together, working as one unit. Consider the following example, with no obvious structure:

isn't has if content meaning organised no it

Each word here may be comprehensible, but the example has no meaning; its organisation has been lost (the version I was aiming for was: 'If content isn't organised, it has no meaning'). Such an extreme example as this is obviously a fabrication, but even minor problems with the organising framework will create a potential point of breakdown in a text, and while visitors may be able to circumnavigate one or two such points, consistent problems will lead only to confusion. Thus, the organising framework is critical to achieve coherence, and an effective organisation is essential for the successful function of a text as a whole.

At the same time, however, the organisational framework is more than just some kind of glue that holds other significant elements together. There are usually multiple ways to construct any one text, and different effects can be created with different organisations. In other words, different types of organisation can contribute substantially to the particular meanings of a text. Compare the following examples:

TEXT ONE	TEXT TWO
Museums provide an important range of experiences. For children, they can be a place of fun and learning. For adults, they provide an opportunity to reflect and explore. And for families as a whole, they provide an opportunity to enquire about the world.	Museums provide an important range of experiences. Both fun and learning are especially appealing to children, while the opportunity to reflect and explore appeals to adults. The opportunity to enquire about the world is important for families as a whole.

While these examples are not absolutely identical in their representational content, they are more or less the same; importantly however, their organisation is markedly different. They each begin in the same way, but then the first text revolves around the different groups (*children*, *adults*, *families*) who benefit from museum experiences. The second text revolves around the experiences provided by museums (*fun and learning*; *the opportunity to reflect and explore*; *the opportunity to enquire about the world*). The different organisational focus of these examples creates quite distinctive effects, and means that each text makes different 'points'. Thus, the organisational framework is an important part of meaning-making.

This chapter thus addresses issues of organisational meaning in the language of museum texts. The chapter is organised to move from 'macro' issues of organisation, affecting the structure of a whole text, down to 'micro' issues at the level of clause (sentence) organisation. Organisational meanings apply to the notion of 'text' at different levels: at the level of a single clause, a section of a text, the text as a whole, and at the level of a set of texts in relation to each other. The organisational framework is addressed in this chapter as both a *resource*, that is, something with creative potential, where there are distinct choices of meaning available, and as a *requirement*, that is, something which must be used effectively, in order to avoid breakdowns in meaning. Choices in the organisational framework both arise from and contribute to the context of situation, particularly the *Mode* of communication, and different organisational effects are appropriate for different Modes.

It will be seen in this chapter that the organisational framework encompasses both explicit and implicit resources for achieving organisational meanings and effects.[3] Explicit resources include such devices as literal organisation within a museum, such as signposting at the entry to a museum: what is there to see? where should visitors go? what is new? In language, explicit organisational devices include such devices as headings, to signal important points of structure. Organisation certainly includes these overt and explicit devices. But organisation also includes less obvious ways of signalling and prioritising, such as the overall generic structure of the text, or particular patterns of grammatical structure. These are the subtle yet fundamental ways of signalling organisation in language, which – while less obvious and less explicit – are no less powerful. It will be seen in this chapter that the organising framework operates in a number of ways to guide visitors: from point to point, making sense of the connections, and to relevant highlights. Visitors access organising clues in different ways: through drawing on predictive devices in text, to make sense of what is coming; through making connections between successive points, to see patterns flowing through a text; and through accumulating meanings as the text unfolds, building up an increasingly detailed picture of what is represented in the text.

Macro-level organisation: genre and the shape of texts

What is it that draws visitors to meanings, patterns and connections in text? How do they use such frameworks to predict, scan and accumulate meanings? And what are the structural features of language which enable such processes?

One of the major organising devices, and perhaps the most subtle, is the choice of *genre* for the text at hand. A genre is a text type, and text types are differentiated according to their overall purpose, and according to the overall structure which supports that purpose (Martin 1992; Eggins 2004). Thus a basic text type such as a *Procedure*, which is found in instructions, recipes and so on, has a very particular purpose, to enable a reader to reproduce that which is outlined in the text. It also has a particular structure to support this purpose, namely, a list of elements required to complete the task (such as ingredients or materials), and a sequenced set of instructions, typically in the imperative voice. In contrast, in order to fulfil the social purpose of 'telling a story', *Narratives* begin with an organisation which places the story in a particular time or place, followed by a complication which sets the main protagonists on a particular path, which is ultimately overcome in the resolution of the story (Labov and Waletzky 1967; Rothery and Stenglin 1997). These generic frameworks are culturally defined and familiar for members of a particular culture. Recognising a generic framework in operation enables readers to predict the structure of the text to come, and thus, to attend to the overall patterns of meanings to be made in that text, and in particular, to attend to the social purpose of that text.

All instances of communication fall into some kind of generic pattern, because every act of communication serves some kind of social purpose, and has an appropriate structure to facilitate that purpose. This notion of genre has some parallels with the notion of 'scripts', which are also used to explain the ways in which people share sociocultural knowledge (Falk and Dierking 2000), and which are closely related to stories and Narratives in structure. Here, however, genres are interpreted as *textual* phenomena, without making claims for any mental representations they may invoke; and the notion of genre here includes but also goes beyond stories and Narratives, to encompass a wide range of other communicative forms, in the personal, professional, and everyday realms (Eggins 2004; Christie and Martin 1997; Martin and Rose 2003).

19

It is useful to identify the key and basic genres operational in a particular culture, for example, the key genres which are typically deployed in museum contexts, but it is important to also remember that 'genre' is not a fixed concept. It is a meaning-making resource like any other, and thus open to innovation and renovation. Equally importantly, genres are culturally defined, and thus that which is obvious and basic to members of one community, may be strange and unfamiliar to members of another. (And clearly this is true for semiotic systems other than language, for example, that which constitutes 'music' or 'art' for different groups. It can be quite challenging to interpret, accept or appreciate the validity of culturally unfamiliar text types.)

The key to understanding genre is to clearly identify the *purpose* of the text, and to identify the *structure* which supports that purpose; 'Each piece of text should have a specific function and should be part of the system of communication as a whole' (Hooper-Greenhill 1994: 133). Bearing in mind the cultural specificity and potential diversity of genres, it is useful to look at a few of the text types which are most often to be found in museum contexts. The aim here is not to catalogue all possible text types, but to exemplify a few key genres, as a model for examining and understanding other types.

One very common genre found in museum texts is that of the *Report*. The social purpose of a Report is to 'describe the way things are' (Ferguson *et al.* 1995: 57; Martin 1993). It helps fulfil the classic museum function of cataloguing and reporting on knowledge. Reports are structured with an initial, general classification, stating what is being reported upon. The body of the Report is then a description of the object, article or phenomenon, and may be subdivided into thematically coherent sections (such as describing the body parts, eating habits, and behaviours of a living creature). Distinct genres are all characterised by specific language features; Reports tend to be written in the present tense, do not have temporal sequences, focus on processes (verbs) of *'being'* and *'having'* (which enable classification and description) and discuss general groups of things rather than individuals (i.e. *'dolphins'*, rather than *'my pet dolphin'*). The two texts shown on p. 21, about 'Satellites', work together as part of a larger Report.

These two texts are part of a sequence of seven texts in total, all on the topic of 'Satellites', within an exhibition called '*Space – beyond this world*'. The first text begins with a general classification in answer to the question, 'What is a satellite?' The remainder of the text, and the subsequent text, function to describe the features of satellites in a number of different ways. These texts have the characteristic language features of a Report, such as use of the present tense, classification with 'being' and 'having' verbs, and organisation around thematically linked sections (rather than, say, temporal sequence). At the same time, however, as a large part of the description is in terms of how satellites are made, and what they do, there is a fair proportion of 'doing' verbs (*are sent, carry out, are developed . . .*). Other texts in the sequence as a whole deal with *geophysical satellites, remote sensing satellites, weather satellites*, and so on. As a cluster then, the set is primarily oriented to the function of reporting – giving an overview of this general Field and describing some of its details.

Generic structure: *Report*	**What is a satellite?**	Text features
general *classification*	A satellite is an object which orbits another larger body. The moon, for example, is a natural satellite of the Earth.	*focus on general groups of things (a satellite; satellites)*
description: *– artificial satellites*	Artificial satellites are sent into orbit around the Earth to carry out a variety of tasks.	*– 'being' verbs (is)* *– present tense (is, are)*
– size	They can range in size from a few metres to as big as a house.	
– appearance at night	Satellites travelling in low orbits can be seen at night as bright, fast moving points of light.	
	What are satellites made of?	
– construction	Satellites are made of light, strong materials and contain the latest in miniature electronics. They *have* their own power sources – solar cells or small nuclear generators.	*'having' verbs*
– additional features	Reliability *is* extremely important because satellites are expensive to build and launch and difficult to repair. Many technologies and materials are first developed for military satellites and are later used for other, more 'down to Earth' purposes.	*'being' verbs (is)*
	Powerhouse Museum	

Another common genre is that of the *Explanation*. Explanations explain how things happen, or why things are as they are, and are important in museums in order to capture events and phenomena, as opposed to just 'things', or objects. Like the Report, Explanations have a simple two-part structure, however, the nature and purpose of these parts is different. Explanations begin with 'a general statement to position the reader' (Ferguson *et al.* 1995: 58; Martin 1993), that is, something which alerts the reader to the process which is about to be explained. This is followed by an Explanation which outlines the sequence 'involved in why or how something occurs' (ibid.). Explanations also tend to be written in the present tense, but unlike Reports, are characterised by temporal sequences (i.e., time is used to structure the text), and the processes (verbs) tend to focus on concrete 'doing' actions. Again as with Reports, participants tend to be generic. The text on p. 22, 'The fetus: from one cell to billions', is an example of an Explanation.

Generic structure: Explanation	**The fetus: from one cell to billions**	Text features
general statement	The fertilised egg *drifts* into the uterus. There the egg *attaches* itself to the uterine lining, which provides nourishment.	*'doing' verbs* *present tense*
sequenced explanation	The cells of the fertilised egg continue to divide. Within about 2 weeks it starts to look like an embryo. *The embryo* floats in a protective sack of amniotic fluid.	*generic participants*[4]
	*At 8 wee*ks the embryo has developed into a fetus. All the organs have formed and the heart is beating. Nutrients circulate from the mother's blood to the fetus from the placenta. The umbilical cord connects the placenta to the fetus.	*temporal sequence*
	By 40 weeks, the baby is about eight times bigger than it was at 12 weeks.	*temporal sequence*
	A baby is ready to be born.	
	Melbourne Museum	

In this text, the opening, general statement needs to be understood in relation to preceding texts, which have established the general topic. This statement provides an orientation which marks the starting point of the sequenced explanation which follows. This text is structured by time, is oriented towards 'doing' verbs ('drifts', 'floats', 'circulate'), and uses the present tense.

In addition to simple Reports and Explanations, museums typically have other agendas. One agenda may be to 'put forward a point of view or argument' (Ferguson *et al.* 1995: 6), and the genre typically used to achieve this is that of the *Exposition*. A conventional Exposition has three key parts to its structure, beginning with a statement of the argument, and an outline of the key points; the body of the text then includes each argument in turn, listed and elaborated, and organised logically, and the text is concluded with a restatement of the argument. Closely aligned to Expositions are *Directives*, which attempt to influence people's action or behaviour, as opposed to simply influencing their opinion, as is the case with Expositions (White 1994). The text on p. 23, 'Ecologic – creating a sustainable future', represents an interesting blend of both these types.

This text is the entry panel for the exhibition. On the one hand, it appears to be structured as an Exposition – opening with an argumentative statement (*Sustainability is . . .*), which is followed by supporting arguments. These arguments are then followed by another statement (*It's time to think differently . . .*)

Generic structure	Ecologic – creating a sustainable future
statement of the argument	Sustainability is about the future of life on earth. It's about meeting our own needs in a way that leaves enough resources for future generations.
supporting arguments	The environment supports us. We can't have a viable society or economy without a healthy environment.
supporting arguments	Right now we are using up natural resources faster and faster. We are reducing the diversity of living things, and we are polluting the earth with toxins. Human population is increasing and so is the amount each of us consumes. We use energy, water and materials to make almost everything.
restatement/new proposition	It's time to think differently and become more efficient about the way we use our resources. It's time to be creative and imagine our future. This exhibition shows that anything is possible . . .
	Powerhouse Museum

and a prediction 'forward', to the remainder of the exhibition. It is clearly the case that the second argumentative statement is a proposal: the desired response on the part of visitors is not simply to acknowledge the relevance of the opening argument, but to actually change their own behaviour in their daily life. This text functions, then, as a Directive, as does a large part of the exhibition which this text introduces. As discussed further in Chapter 4, Expositions and Directives position visitors to respond in different ways, and the blend of styles here is interesting.

Another genre very relevant to the Museum context, and related to the persuasive genres of the Exposition and Directive, is the *Discussion*. Unlike Expositions and Directives, which prioritise one major argument, Discussions are more likely to canvass multiple sides of an argument, and may end with a recommendation, or leave the conclusion open (Ferguson *et al.* 1995; White 1994).

The descriptions given here of genres reflect tendencies; not absolute rules. Genres sharing the same or a similar social purpose are likely to share the same organisational and linguistic patterns. However, examples of the same genre need not be identical; there might be variations in structure and/or language features. One way in which variation is incorporated structurally, is through the *obligatory* versus *optional* nature of structural parts. For example, while a restatement of the argument at the end of an Exposition may help strengthen the overall argument, it is not essential for the successful function of the text; it is an optional element in the text structure. The arguments in the body are, however, essential for the text to achieve its purpose (we usually expect a point of view to be backed up in some way!) and so they are obligatory elements. Thus, two Expositions might have some differences in their overall structure,

Generic structure: Exposition	**Battered fish: Australian fisheries in crisis**
statement of the argument	Each year, billions of fish are caught off Australia's coast. The problem is that too many fish are being caught. Most fisheries here and around the world have collapsed from overfishing.
supporting arguments	Our fisheries could last far into the future if we manage them well. Fish are a renewable resource.
predictor	If we are going to have enough fish in the future we need to learn from past mistakes.
predictor	What are some lessons we should learn?
	Australian Museum

yet still achieve the social purpose of putting forward an argument. The text shown here, about 'Battered fish', illustrates this point.

This text is in fact the introductory text to the exhibition, which functions to draw attention to the crisis in the fishing industry, and to advocate change. Thus the exhibition as a whole can be seen to be an Exposition, as is the structure of this particular text, arguing that 'too many fish are being caught'. Some 'evidence' is provided to support this statement (paragraph 2: 'Fish are a renewable resource' – and so, by implication, overfishing is not an inevitable outcome) and the subsequent paragraphs (in this case, consisting of single lines of text only) point forward, to the exhibition, and to the ways in which overfishing might be avoided (*by learning from past mistakes*). Thus, while not a 'classic' Exposition in structure, this text is arguing a point, and pointing forward to the remainder of the exhibition to substantiate this point.

Genres may also vary because the language features of a basic model are adapted in some way. The following text (p. 25), 'Are you a responsible cat owner?' is an example of a Procedure, but it is metaphorical, because instead of being presented as a list of instructions, the information is presented as statements 'of fact'.

A characteristic language feature of Procedures (instructional texts) is the imperative voice, that is, the use of commands (such as 'be a responsible cat owner'; 'desex your cat'; 'keep your cat at home'). In this text, however, the commands are disguised as statements. It could be said that this text functions only as information – a checklist against which visitors can answer the question 'Am I a responsible cat owner?', however the text also operates as a Procedure, even if indirectly. Thus an 'uncharacteristic' language feature can be used to subtly adapt a more typical genre. This example will be revisited in Chapter 4, in relation to its interactional meanings.

It would certainly be interesting to catalogue the major text genres operating in contemporary museums, although that project is beyond the scope of this

Genre: Procedure	**Are you a responsible cat owner?**	
typical text features	Do you know . . .	*Actual text features*
commands: imperative voice 'desex your cat'	*Desexed cats that aren't allowed to roam live longer and are cheaper to keep.* They don't need treatment by a vet for injuries from fights or road accidents.	*statements: declarative voice*
'don't let them roam'	*Keeping cats at home improves relations with the neighbours.* They won't be complaining of cats trespassing on their land, scent marking, fighting and killing 'their' wildlife. (and so on: text continues for 3 more paragraphs) Australian Museum	

book.[5] Even without such a catalogue, however, the value of understanding genre is the opportunity it provides to reflect on the effectiveness of macro-level organisational patterns in texts, and to reflect on some of the implicit assumptions behind the structure of some texts. At the Art Gallery of New South Wales, for example, two annual, co-occurring exhibitions each have distinctive generic patterns for the explanatory texts accompanying the artworks in the respective exhibitions.

The first of these exhibitions is the Archibald Prize, an annual and very popular portrait exhibition. In 2003, the accompanying explanatory texts followed a broadly similar structure: first, the subject of the portrait is introduced (the subject is supposed to be someone of public renown). This is typically from the 'voice' of the institution. Then, the relationship between the artist and the subject is explained (perhaps how they met, or why the artist found the subject interesting); there may be some reflection on the process of completing the painting (whether it was enjoyable or easy, for example) and (although rarely) some reflection on technique. These latter steps are always in the voice of the artist, presented either directly, through quotes, or indirectly, via reporting of their comments. These texts usually conclude with some further background about the artist (their origin, previous success in this particular exhibition, and so on). This last step is again in the voice of the institution (see p. 26).

In contrast, the Art Express exhibition is an annual display of outstanding artworks from the previous final-year school examination, the Higher School Certificate. Explanatory labels accompanying these texts, always written by the students, include some reflection on what the work represents, and/or on how it was made, or how the student felt, and some discussion of relevant artistic influences.[6] Most of this is a requirement of the curriculum, that students be reflexive

Generic structure		Text features (voice selection)
	2003 Archibald Prize Exhibition **Art Gallery of New South Wales** Written by Jo Litson © Jo Litson and AGNSW	
identification: artist, subject, medium	Branca Uzur, Sandra Levy oil on canvas	
background to subject	Sandra Levy was appointed Director of Television at the ABC in June 2001, rejoining the network with a long and productive list of production credits including *A Difficult Woman*, *True Believers*, *Police Rescuer*, *Secret Men's Business*, and *GP*.	*voice: institution*
explain relationship between subject and artist	Branca Uzur saw a photograph of Levy in the newspaper "when there was some big noise about the ABC" and was really attracted by her face. Keen to paint her, she approached Levy who saw some of the Uzur's paintings and really liked them. "So it was smooth sailing."	*voice: artist*
reflection: process	Uzur admits she was very surprised to see what Levy looked like in real life. "She has a very sparkly face, very beautiful eyes, very much alive. We did one sitting, chatted, and that was it. I was then on my own with my photos and drawings." Asked about the bold colour of the portrait, Azur says that Levy's face had a very Middle Eastern look for her. "Somehow I saw her in those golden days of Alexandria. I pictured her as a noble woman behind the shutters in some beautiful space in Alexandria – I was listening to [Lawrence Durrell's] *The Alexandrian Quartets* CDs at the time, which probably has something to do with it.	*voice: artist*
background to artist	Born in Zagreb in 1954, Uzur was educated in Zagreb, Belgrade and Helsinki. She has had numerous solo and group exhibitions in Croatia, Finland, Austria, Spain and Cypress. She came to Australia in 1992. She has previously been a finalist in the 2000 Archibald Prize with a portrait of film writer Paul Byrnes and in the 2001 Archibald Prze with a portrait of renowned chef Tetsuya Wakuda.	*voice: institution*

Generic structure	Art Express Exhibition 2003 **Art Gallery of New South Wales** Written by Corinne Paoloni © Corinne Paoloni	Text features *(voice selection)*
Identification: artist, *high school,* *title, medium*	Corinne Paoloni The Illawarra Grammar School "Infatuation" Photography, 9 pieces	
reflection: *– representation &* *interpretation* *– technique*	My work explores the different stages in a relationship; the way it can change from complete obsession to rejection and isolation. I chose to display it as three series of three photos, each series focusing on a different emotion.	*voice: artist*
– influences *– technique*	The idea for my work originally came from the Greek myth of Narcissus and from the different emotions in the story. This progressed into how I could use composition and colour to enhance my original photographs.	

of their own artistic processes and acknowledge their overt 'sources', and the text displayed in the exhibition is in fact a shortened version of the text students are required to submit with their work for examination (see above).

Within each exhibition, the generic patterns of the explanatory texts are remarkably consistent. Thus for the exhibition designer, or the student artist, conformity or otherwise to the basic patterns provides a first point of evaluation of the text's organisation (has anything important been left out? did I mention my sources?); for the visitor, the consistency provides an opportunity to scan for and reflect upon the relevant sections. In addition, however, knowledge of these basic but consistent patterns provides an opportunity to reflect upon them critically: why is the student required to mention their sources and explain their techniques, and why is this virtually absent in the voice of the 'mature' artist? Technique is certainly not irrelevant to the Archibald, and can be the focus of much discussion,[7] but generally it is elided. The visitor may bring their own knowledge to bear on this, but on the whole, the exhibition does not provide it for them. Whether this is appropriate or not, is a matter for additional debate; the point to be made here is, that the generic patterns of the texts reveal implicit values behind the exhibition, and some recognition and understanding of the patterns enables them to be interrogated further.

Understanding the genres being used in text production is also relevant for another reason. Most importantly, a vague notion of 'topic' is not enough to provide an effective organisation for a text. Every text must have an explicit and clear purpose, otherwise there is no organisation *against which* to evaluate the final text, and writers will be working in a 'vacuum' (Screven 1995). An explicit and clear purpose corresponds to the 'big idea' which underpins – or should underpin – all exhibition and label development (Serrell 1996). For example, in an exhibition on the role of dolphins in marine warfare, a particular text within the exhibition might have the purpose to:

– explain the process by which dolphins are trained for marine warfare
– argue for or against the use of dolphins in this context
– retell the story of one incident where a dolphin saved the lives of a naval crew.

Each of these organising frameworks should clearly result in a quite different text – each with a different purpose and a different structure to meet that purpose. Being able to articulate the purpose and function of a text enables the multiple producers of an exhibition (subject specialists, designers, educators . . .) to compare and evaluate the intention against the outcome. Without such an explicit framework, there is no way to judge the final text.

The same principle applies to an exhibition as a whole, which is, after all, a 'mass communication media in its own right' (McManus 2000: 98). What is the guiding purpose of an exhibition, that is, its *narrative design* (Pang 2004), and how do the components of the exhibition serve that purpose? The exhibition can be seen as a kind of *macro-genre* – a 'super' text, which includes a range of elemental genres within it (Martin and Rose 2003). For instance, it is possible for a whole exhibition to be driven by a persuasive argument, as demonstrated in the text above from *'Ecologic'* (see p. 23), where one of the exhibition goals – as realised in the structure and texts of the exhibition itself – is to persuade people to change their behaviour. Thus, *'Ecologic'* functions as a macro-Directive. In contrast, other exhibitions may be presented more like a macro-Report, where information about a topic is canvassed, but where no particular persuasive argument is created about that topic. This is a very common macro-genre in museum exhibitions, where one general topic is the central focus, and aspects of that topic (such as 'Steam Engines' or 'Computers') are canvassed in different ways. Or, an exhibition could be structured as a macro-Narrative, retelling a 'story', and so on. Few exhibitions today would proceed without a clear statement of exhibition goals, including communication objectives, but these tend to be stated in the abstract, and it requires an additional step to recognise the explicit connections to generic structure. For example, the first communication objective for the forthcoming Aboriginal and Torres Strait Islander Cultures Centre, at the Queensland Museum, is as follows:

Aboriginal and Torres Strait Islander visitors from Queensland will feel that their experience and perspectives have been expressed.[8]

Such a goal necessarily demands a renovation of conventional museum genres, as it is the conventional genres which have effectively excluded Indigenous groups in the past (and some such renovations are canvassed further in Chapter

4). At the same time, such a generalised goal – while being absolutely critical to the conceptualisation and design of the exhibition – leaves open the many possible ways in which the exhibition and its components could be constructed. The key to understanding genre is to understand that it focusses on *meaning* – overall purpose and direction. While the notion of a 'storyline' may be a familiar one to museum communicators, it is important to recognise that it needs to be more than just a blueprint for layout, for example, something which records the exhibition title, sub-titles, main texts, and objects (cf. Dean 1994: 103). Such a blueprint does not reveal the *meaning potential* of exhibitions, and any one such blueprint could relate to any number of genres, in the sense used here.

For visitors, recognising the genre of a text – whether that of a text panel, or of a whole exhibition – enables them to predict aspects of the text to come: stories should have a resolution; Procedures should have a final step. This is not to say that visitors use or require an *explicit* knowledge of genre, but they do recognise the *implicit* and familiar patterns of generic structure. 'Measuring the new against the expected' is one way in which people 'make sense of what is happening in their world' (Falk and Dierking 2000: 112). Predictions made through the implicit recognition of generic frameworks provide a background against which the meanings encountered in the text can be made sense of. In the words of Jacobi and Poli (1995: 66): 'Whenever visitors read a text, they seek [such] closure: the beginning of the reading is stimulated by the foreseeable end.'

However, given the cultural specificity of genres, it is important for museums attempting to broaden their cultural base and be inclusive of diverse visitors, to consider the genres that might be relevant, or irrelevant, to different communities. What ways of speaking are valid? What counts as 'informing'? What counts as 'entertaining'? Are the forms of presentation of objects or knowledge appropriate and permissible? Genre studies are not yet sufficiently extensive to account for or describe cultural differences comprehensively; the only possible way forward here is for genuine and extensive community consultation. A clear example of this can be seen at the Melbourne Museum, in the Bunjilaka Gallery, which showcases Indigenous Australian culture. As discussed further in Chapter 4, priority in this exhibition is given to texts which express the actual voices of Indigenous Australians, allowing them to tell their own knowledge. Such personal texts have not in the past typically carried great authority in museum exhibitions. The more authoritative voice has been the impersonal, institutional one, speaking 'for' or 'about' the subject. Such institutional texts also exist in the Bunjilaka Gallery at the Melbourne Museum, but the inclusion and prioritisation of Indigenous voices within the Gallery tells visitors, who may be unfamiliar with the authority of this genre, that these texts have the same status and weight as any other. In this way, the Melbourne Museum is renovating – giving new values to – our understanding of what types of texts, with what purposes, can be considered to be valid and important.

For non-Indigenous visitors, exposure to new ways of meaning introduces them to more 'insider' views of that culture. The danger is, of course, to see such

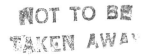

language patterns as being 'deterministic' of the culture, and thus to ghetto-ise particular exhibitions. Just as an un-reflective use of genre closes down access to some groups, so too would an over-differentiated, over-determined use of genre. If radical text forms are to be used, their use, purpose and motivation needs to be mediated by other means: explained to visitors, so that they have a way of accessing what might otherwise be an unfamiliar genre. In a non-linguistic example, the Art Gallery of New South Wales managed to reconcile the museum practice of public display with the presentation of Indigenous cultural objects – traditionally the domain of specialised knowledge circulated only among women of the culture. The Art Gallery reconciled these conflicting practices by presenting these objects in a separate alcove, and explaining their significance and cultural status on entry to the alcove. Thus, this presentation, which is 'odd' in terms of standard practices of open display, is explained for the visitor, and the display goes some way towards acknowledging the cultural value of the object.

The issues and examples here have pertained largely to the written texts that would appear as exhibition labels, or perhaps in brochures and pamphlets. Yet clearly, museum exhibitions today involve other manifestations of texts in exhibitions: audio-guides, voice-overs, digitally based texts. While each new manifestation will have its own particularities, on the whole, the fundamental issues discussed here apply in these more diverse domains also (cf. Schiele 1995: 42). Essentially, to consider genre is to consider the focus of the text. The focus of the text relates to an overall social goal, which is met by an appropriate organisational structure and relevant language features. Few museum professionals would approach exhibition design without extensive reflection on overall goals, and it is important that this reflection extends down as far as the social purpose and structure of the texts, in whatever form they come.

Mid-level organisation: pointers and signals

The macro-level of organisation relates to the overall shape and purpose of the text; within that framework, most texts will be made up of multiple stages – there are few texts that make their point in just one move! These stages are incorporated structurally – part of the nature of the language of the text. Thus, a Report has two key parts, the opening classification, and the body describing the relevant aspects of the subject (which may in turn have its own sub-stages). These are an inherent part of the structure of Reports, and the language of the relevant stages is distinctive, in order to support that structure.

When a text does have multiple stages, and multiple points to make, it can be useful to have some kind of *guide* for the visitor as to what are the relevant points to note, when to attend to a shift in the structure, and so on. These pointers to 'mid-level' organisation can be in two forms: linguistic and visual. Linguistic pointers are ways of using language to signal important aspects of text organisation, and may include *headings* which summarise key points, and *topic sentences* which predict the major points of a following section (Ferguson *et al.* 1995: 22). Headings and sub-headings are truly 'pointers'; their content alerts visitors to what to expect to find in a text or in a section of text. Visitors can therefore quickly scan a text for what interests them (or ignore the text altogether!), and breaking the text up with sub-headings may make complex content more easy to digest. This is a very simple, but usually effective, way to alert visitors to the key organisational points of an exhibition and the texts within it. In Plate 2.1 the headings are in fact the key steps in a *procedural* genre: a 'how to' text, explaining to visitors how to 'listen to the stars: sort frequencies; scan sky; time pulsars; compare results; avoid interference'.

As always, any device can be used creatively, and Plate 2.2 shows the same heading repeated in multiple languages, signalling that the exhibition will appeal to visitors of various language backgrounds.

Organisation can be signalled in other ways, however, and the main linguistic device for signalling changes in structure is that of *topic sentences*. Topic sentences are those sentences which function to predict the structure about to come; they may be paragraph-initial, but do not have to be. When a text will encompass a number of major points, a topic sentence[9] acts like a guide-map for those points; when they are encountered, the reader understands that they are there for a reason. Without such signalling, the structure of the text may seem unmotivated or disjointed. In the text 'UV damages your eyes'

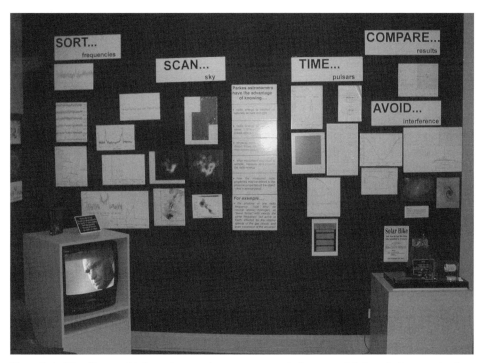

Plate 2.1 Headings which point to the structure of the text, Visitors' Centre, Parkes Radio Telescope, Parkes, NSW, Australia

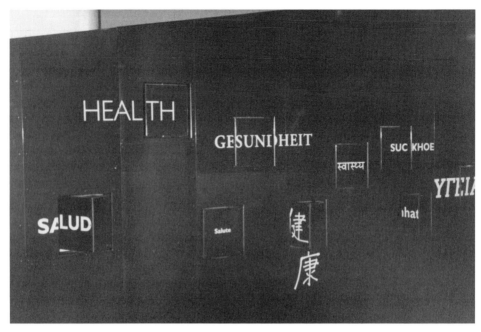

Plate 2.2 Headings which point to the appeal of the exhibition, Cité des Sciences et de l'Industrie, Paris

(p. 33), the underlined sentence is the topic sentence, and comes at the end of the first paragraph. It predicts the major points to be covered in the remainder of the text.

Thus, the topic sentence is a linguistic signal of the organisation of the text, and helps make sense of the structure which follows. The same organisational principle can be extended 'upwards' to the level of the exhibition, where the introductory panel of an exhibition functions to signal the organisation of the exhibition as a whole,[10] alerting visitors to the main points or experiences they can expect to find there.

Pointers to mid-level organisation in text may also be visual, that is, aspects of layout and design can be used to signal or reinforce other organisational meanings within the texts (Dean 1994: 119). After all, in museums, 'Text is intended not only to be *read*, but, first of all, to be *seen*.' (Jacobi and Poli 1995: 51). The basics of this field are dealt with in existing literature, especially in terms of the use of spacing, typography, and material presentation to enhance the text and make it as (literally) readable as possible (see, for example, Dean 1994; Serrell 1996; Belcher 1991; and many manuals, such as Blunden and Slam 1997). In terms of the concerns of this book, these elements of design are significant because they also contribute to *meanings* in text. Layout and typography impose a structure on texts, and this is a first step in comprehension: 'The visitor uses this structure to organize the assimilation of information' (Jacobi and Poli 1995: 53).

Heading	**UV damages your eyes**
topic sentence: *predicts key points*	UV Rays injure the eye's protective outer layer (cornea) and lens. Much of the damage which leads to eye diseases occurs when we are young. <u>Diseases caused by UV include cataracts, pterygium and conjunctivitis.</u>
1st key point	<u>Cataracts</u> usually develop with age. Currently 1.34 million Australians are affected. Cataracts make the eye lens cloudy.
2nd key point	<u>Pterygium</u> is a growth which begins in the corner of the eye and spreads across it.
3rd key point	<u>Conjunctivitis</u> causes the eye to become irritated and swollen. In serious cases, the cornea develops small, cloudy lumps.
	A drop in ozone levels by 1% is expected to increase the cases of cataracts by around 21 000 and of pterygium by up to 52 000.
	Australian Museum; cited in Ferguson *et al.* 1995: 23

An interesting marriage between visual and structural organisation is the use of three-level texts as a feature of text presentation (Belcher 1991; Dean 1994; Ferguson *et al.* 1995). The first level, in largest and most prominent font, may simply be a heading or label; this provides the most basic focus for the exhibit. Titles and sub-titles are included in this level, and these can help the visitor, '. . . regardless of attention level, follow the flow of information and relationships between objects.' (Dean 1994: 109). The second level is an introductory paragraph, in a medium-size font, giving basic or introductory information, which provides a more extended organisation. The third level, in the smallest font, provides more detailed or background information. Clearly the intention is that the multiple layers will cater for differing attention spans or degrees of interest, and as visitors are 'compelled' to be selective in their attention (Falk and Dierking 1992: 67), this is important. This is a very simple organising device that does enable differences to be catered for, and it is too often overlooked in the display of exhibition text. Plate 2.3 shows the way in which the three-level layout is used in an Explanation text, which is then re-presented in Figure 2.1 in terms of its levels and generic structure.

In Plate 2.3 and Figure 2.1, a complex text structure can be seen. The panel as a whole includes actual fossils, with labels, on the left, and an information panel on the right. This information panel itself has a complex structure, with two key levels. The first is for the exhibition as a whole, to which the heading and sub-heading apply: 'Clues to the past – Fossils can tell us a lot about the way the world used to be.' The second level is for the first explanatory text in the exhibition, in this case, appearing immediately under the exhibition heading. This text has labelled diagrams on the left, and information on the right. The text on the right explains how a particular process (fossilisation) takes place.

33

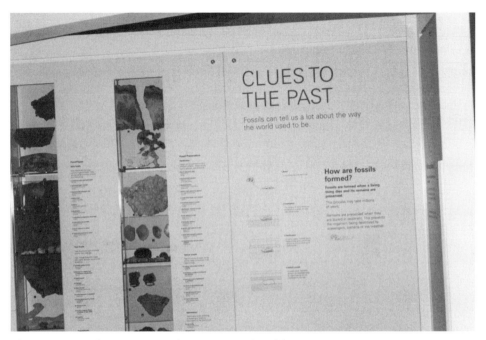

Plate 2.3 Complex interaction between visual and linguistic structure, Melbourne Museum

Exhibition: *Heading*	**Clues To The Past**	
Sub-Heading	Fossils can tell us a lot about the way the world used to be	
Text Panel: *Level 1*	How are fossils formed?	*Genre:* *Explanation* *General statement to position reader*
Level 2	Fossils are formed when a living thing dies and its remains are preserved	*Core Explanation: how fossils are formed*
Level 3	This process may take millions of years	*Details: how fossils are formed*
Level 4	Remains are preserved when they are buried in sediment. This prevents the organism being destroyed by scavengers, bacteria or the weather	*Details: how fossils are formed*

Figure 2.1 Complex interaction between visual and linguistic structure, Melbourne Museum

This text is itself differentiated visually with three levels: the first level coincides with the 'general positioning statement' of the Explanation, and is in the form of a question: 'How are fossils formed?' This orientates the reader to the overall meanings to expect, and may in fact be enough information for a visitor to decide whether to read further or not. The second level, in smaller font, but still bold, provides the core of the Explanation: 'Fossils are formed when a living thing dies and its remains are preserved.' The third level, used for the third and fourth paragraphs of the text, give further details of this fundamental Explanation, relating to the time it takes (paragraph 3), and some of the means by which it takes place (*in sediment*, paragraph 4). Thus there is a complex interaction here between visual layout and linguistic organisation.

This example illustrates an important point about the use of multi-level headings: it is not simply a case of presenting sequential paragraphs in decreasing font size. It is important that the information at a particular level coincides with a particular function: here, the more distinctive fonts of Level 1 and 2 form the core of the Explanation: read together, they provide a coherent snapshot of the text as a whole. The information at Level 3, in paragraphs 3 and 4, is interesting and relevant to understanding the overall process, but can be skipped over without disrupting the core meanings of the text. Imagine a procedural text, with a number of steps explaining, say, how to imitate a fossil in stone, with each step being equally important to the successful completion of the Procedure, but the 'levels' diminishing with each step. In such a case, form and function would contradict each other, to the detriment of meanings in the text. The success or otherwise of multi-level text depends on the association of level with function: however large the font, if the function of the information it represents is inappropriate, the text will be unsuccessful.

A parallel notion of multiple levels could be usefully applied to texts presented via other media, such as audio guides, in either a CD-Rom or digital format. These audio guides are one of the great technologically derived innovations in the presentation of exhibition text, enabling audiences to skip selections and listen only to those items they choose. Art galleries, in particular, favour this as a way of mediating exhibitions, because extended commentary can be provided without artworks competing for visual attention with physical displays of texts. However, few audio guides make effective use of genre or of 'multi-level' text in the spoken format. That which is presented is typically an extensive art commentary; one which has a linear format, and which needs to be listened to from beginning to end, in order to understand the whole text. Of course, visitors can – and do – turn off at any time, but it is as if they are cutting off a conversation mid-way, and this can be extremely dissatisfying (Lamarche 1995). The texts used for audio guides should themselves be 'multi-levelled', with independent groupings of information ranging from the most essential and necessary for organisation, down to the most detailed. In this way, visitors will be able to quit the audio text at a point at which they have still derived some 'sense' from the presentation. The relevant sound bite must 'stand alone' (Serrell 1996: 177).

For the more conventional written texts, it is typically the case that aspects of design are used to reinforce the linguistic structure of the text: thus, as we have seen, headings are in the largest font, and so on. Special highlighting – a bold font, a change of font or colour, and so on – may be used to signal key points. These devices enable visitors to scan for the most important information, or to focus just on key points, and as McManus has demonstrated (1989a, 2000), visitors can take in an enormous amount of information without appearing to 'stop' and read the texts. Typically, that which is highlighted coincides with important organisational points at the *micro-level* of the text. The linguistic organisation of texts at the micro-level is discussed in the next section, and its intersection with aspects of visual presentation will then be revisited.

Micro-level organisation: the flow of information

The overall shape and structure of a text is a critical part of its organisational meanings, and clarity at the macro- and mid-levels is necessary to ensure cohesion and comprehensibility. However, that which is 'within' the text, its substance at the micro-level of clauses, has an equally important contribution to make to organisational meanings. At this level, the organisation of clauses and the flow of meanings between them can give a text a very particular orientation, influencing how the text is interpreted. In this way, organisation is a resource which makes a fundamental contribution to meaning. In addition, any problems at this level of organisation (as at any other level) can interfere with the basic meanings of the text, rendering it incomprehensible; thus effective and appropriate organisation is a necessary requirement of well-written texts.

Many clauses can be re-ordered and re-organised a little, so that they start or end with a different element. Consider the following clauses, which are fundamentally similar, but which have been re-ordered in some way.

> The fishing industry was given a boost by new technology in 1979.
> New technology gave the fishing industry a boost in 1979.
> A boost was given to the fishing industry by new technology in 1979.
> In 1979, new technology gave the fishing industry a boost.
> . . . and so on.

Each of these clauses is fundamentally the same in terms of their *representational* meanings, the basic representation of what is going on – what was happening to the fishing industry at a certain point in time. (Representational meanings in language are discussed further in Chapter 5.) Also, each of the clauses is similar in their *interactional* meanings, the basic stance taken up with the reader – they each present the information to the reader, in the form of a statement. (Interactional meanings in language are discussed further in Chapter 4.) The clauses are just different in their organisation. But as we have already seen, organisation is itself an important aspect of meaning, and where there is variation in word order, there is variation in meaning (Halliday 1985; Ferguson *et al.* 1995).

The significance of re-organising a clause is that it changes the orientation, or *point of departure* for a clause. The first three examples on this page each depart from different 'things' involved in the construction of the clause ('the fishing industry'; 'new technology'; 'a boost'); the fourth example departs from a point of time ('In 1979'). It may seem that some of these choices are more 'natural', more 'typical', than others, and that some are forced. This suggests that there are some default expectations as to how clauses will be organised. Yet none of the clauses shown on p. 36 is incorrect in any way. What makes one more appropriate, more effective, as a choice than another will depend on issues of context. In museums, as we will see, this depends on two levels of context. One is the context of the exhibit or exhibition, of which the text is a part, and the orientation or point of departure of the text needs to connect with that in some way. The other is the overall context of the text, and how the meanings flow from one clause to the next. We will see that this places certain demands on the organisation of clauses.

The organisation of a clause depends in the first instance on its point of departure, as just noted. This is called the *Theme* of the clause (Halliday 1994; Halliday and Matthiessen 2004). 'Theme' is a grammatical term, referring to what comes first in the clause. It is not used with the usual sense of 'theme', as in what a book, movie or story might be about in terms of overall content. It is simply that which is the departure point for the clause. Here again are the same clauses as before, with the Themes underlined:[11]

The fishing industry was given a boost by new technology in 1979.
New technology gave the fishing industry a boost in 1979.
A boost was given to the fishing industry by new technology in 1979.
In 1979, new technology gave the fishing industry a boost.

Choosing an appropriate Theme depends on two particular factors: for exhibitions, it depends on what the focus of the exhibition is, and for texts generally, it also depends on the sequence of Themes in the text as a whole.

In exhibition texts, there should be some symmetry between the Theme of the text, and the focus of the exhibit (accompanying object; diagram, illustration, etc.) particularly if this is a single object or image: 'Readers turn to labels expecting to discover *what* [it] is that they are looking at (and then to find out information about it). Unless this object or image is named in the Theme position of the label, the focus of the display can be lost.' (Ferguson *et al.* 1995: 17; the importance of this alignment between text and exhibition is also emphasised by Serrell 1996.) The text functions to support and illuminate the exhibit, thus visitors turn to the text expecting to find the focus of the exhibit as the point of departure for the text. In the following example, the exhibit on display is a common long-nosed bandicoot, however, the text begins with a different Theme, about the common brushtail possum:

Like the common brushtail possum, common bandicoots in general are extremely hardy and adaptable native animals.

Australian Museum;
cited in Ferguson *et al.* 1995: 17

Thus, there is no correspondence here between the focus of the display and the Theme of the text, and this '. . . is potentially confusing for readers, who are expecting to know *what* it is they are looking at.' (Ferguson *et al.* 1995: 17). There is nothing grammatically wrong with the construction of this clause, but in the context of a particular exhibition, it is textually inappropriate. It does not facilitate understanding for the visitor. Thus, the choice of what to use as the Theme or point of departure for the text must be guided by the broader contextual framework, in this case, the relation of the text to the exhibit it accompanies, and the overall exhibition of which it is a part.

Choosing an appropriate Theme is also dependent on the flow of meanings between clauses in the text as a whole. To understand this, it is necessary to explain the way in which the Theme as departure point for the message is counter-balanced by the point of arrival: the 'New' information which is added by the clause. 'New' is also a technical term, and its function is to move readers on from the starting point of the clause. It typically comes towards the end of the clause.[12] In revisiting the set of re-ordered clauses from above, we can see that each version of the clause not only has a distinctive departure point, but also a distinctive point of arrival:

> The fishing industry was given a boost in 1979 by new technology.
> New technology gave the fishing industry a boost in 1979.
> In 1979, new technology gave the fishing industry a boost.

It is the counter-balance between *Theme* and *New* which helps determine the flow of information between clauses. These two systems provide an organisation for the text, and facilitate the accumulation of meanings as a text unfolds. Each new clause adds (literally) 'New' information, as can be seen in the short text below about the 'Cat quilt'.

This short text, describing an object on display, a quilt about cats and bandicoots, takes the quilt as the Theme or point of departure, and builds up a body of information about the quilt. There is some development from 'quilt' to 'panels' in the second clause, however, the referential 'its' makes the link back to the quilt, and overall, the text flows smoothly with an unproblematic

---

Cat quilt

This quilt expresses a community's concern for the impact of domestic cats on native animals, in particular the endangered Eastern Barred Bandicoot.
Its panels illustrate the nocturnal relationship of the cats and bandicoots.
It is the work of 41 quilters from Hamilton, Victoria
and was first displayed during a 'Bandicoot Awareness Week' at the Hamilton Institute of Rural Learning in 1987.

Australian Museum

---

organisation. However, problems frequently do arise in the flow of a text, when the balance between Theme and New comes unstuck.

For texts to flow smoothly, without any sense of disruption, the information which is in Theme position of the clause needs to be 'Given' – that is, retrievable or understood, either from the context, or from the preceding text. When a reader begins reading a new clause, there should be no 'surprises'. If the information at the beginning of the clause is New, that is, not retrievable or understood, this will create a point of rupture in the text, and lead to a breakdown in its information flow. Consider the following example:

> <u>Modern gamelan gadon, or chamber grouping</u>, with instruments in the slendro tuning system, from Surakarta, Central Java. <u>In performance</u>, the group would include a female singer and a flute player. <u>The male musicians</u> would also sing. <u>Gamelan</u> have no conductor, being led by a drummer or rehab player. <u>Gadon ensembles</u> can accompany wayang kulit (shadow plays) or perform at private social functions such as weddings.
>
> Australian Museum

The first three clauses of this text each have a different point of departure. The text begins with the 'Modern gamelan gadon, or chamber grouping', then moves on to 'in performance', and then 'the male musicians', both of which are 'New' information. (Given that 'a female singer' has been introduced in the previous clause, it could be said that 'male' is Given in contrast with this, but the link is implicit, not explicit.) The text then goes on to 'Gamelan' and 'Gadon ensembles', which presumably do refer to the same item as in the first clause, and so are Given information, but because the term for the item is constantly varied, the text is still quite a challenge to follow. The individual clauses in this text are perfectly acceptable, but as a text, its meaning has broken down.

Sometimes, the ruptures are less obvious, but equally significant. They are less obvious, and so harder to explicitly identify, because there are implicit connections between items within the text; however, if connections are left implicit, then a breakdown in the flow of the text still occurs. Consider the following extract from a longer text:

> 'UV damages your skin'
> <u>UV rays</u> from the sun penetrate and injure the skin.
> <u>Developing a tan</u> is the skin's way of protecting itself from more sun injury.
>
> Australian Museum; cited in Ferguson *et al.* 1995: 18

In this text, the first Theme, 'UV rays', relates to the title of the text, 'UV damages your skin' and to the exhibition, which is about Ozone holes and UV. The negative effects of UV rays on skin are then introduced as New information (the rays 'penetrate and injure the skin'). The second Theme, 'developing a tan' is also New information: nothing in the context (of the exhibition) or in the text up to this point, has predicted that this will be discussed; it 'comes from nowhere'. The inclusion of New information in the Theme position, where

Given information should be used, creates a point of rupture in the text. Given that Australians reading this text would be quite familiar with the concept of a 'tan', and given that the preceding clause describes exactly what a tan is (that is, skin that has been penetrated and injured by the sun), it could be argued that the disruption to the text here is not so dramatic. And yet, some 'massaging' of the text, to get a more effective flow of information between Theme and New, produces a text which is much more smooth-flowing:

'UV damages your skin'
UV rays from the sun penetrate and injure the skin. The skin's way of protecting itself from more sun injury is by developing a tan.

In this version, the Theme of the second clause connects with the Given information about '*skin*' from the first clause, and the New information about '*developing a tan*' has been moved to the end of the clause.

As the relationship between Theme and New is so central to the flow of the text and its effectiveness in organisational terms, it is important to be able to check that texts have a smooth flow of information. There are a number of ways to ensure that this occurs.

The simplest way to ensure that an appropriate flow of information is maintained, is to make sure that the information in Theme position is retrievable: either from the context, as with the symmetrical focus of exhibit and text, or from preceding clauses. The Theme of a current clause can either repeat a preceding Theme, or pick up some information which has been presented as New, and take this as the next departure point. In the examples in Figure 2.2, *Themes* are underlined, and *New* is in italic.

In Figure 2.2, the same Theme (more or less) is kept in focus as the point of departure, and New information is added by each clause. (Note that in the last line, 'it' has been ellipsed. Ellipsis – or leaving something out – can in fact create a cohesive link; see Halliday and Hasan 1976; Martin and Rose 2003.) The second pattern of development is to 'pick up' something that has already been introduced as New information in a preceding clause, and use it as the Theme of a subsequent clause. This pattern is illustrated in Figure 2.3.

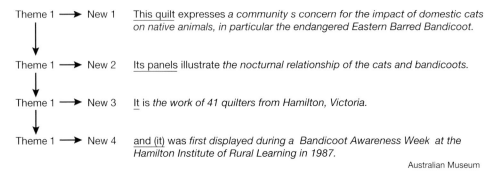

Figure 2.2 A linear form of thematic progression, with Theme repetition

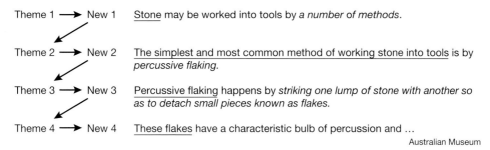

Figure 2.3 Developing the Theme via information presented in the preceding New

In Figure 2.3, the New information of each clause is picked up and developed as the Theme of the next. Another pattern arises where information introduced in the New is 'split' over subsequent Themes, as illustrated in Figure 2.4.

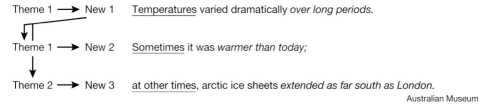

Figure 2.4 Split Theme developed from one New

Most texts make use of a range of these patterns. The pattern of constant Theme repetition is most appropriate for Report-style writing, or for short sections of text where one point is in focus for an extended period, but it can quickly become monotonous if there is no additional development. Similarly, if only the second pattern is used, the information will flow well but there may be a sense that the text never 'rests', as no one point is developed. Thus, a balance between the patterns of thematic development is more typical.

Knowledge about Theme and New is most useful when editing texts. In particular, it enables writers to identify probable points of breakdown, for instance, where New information has been placed in Theme position, and to adjust accordingly. In editing, writers need to check over their texts to ensure that Themes are retrievable, from preceding text, and – especially for the opening of the text – that they are symmetrical with the focus of the relevant exhibit. It is important to highlight that this advice is at odds with standard writing guidelines which advise writers to 'vary your sentence beginnings' – usually for the sake of interest. Yes, vary them by all means, but only if what you put in first position is (a) contextually appropriate and (b) Given information, that is, retrievable from immediate context or from immediately preceding text.

Of course, there are exceptions to every rule, and it is often the case, particularly in longer texts, where there is a need to shift a text on to a new point. This tends to coincide with an important stage in the text, for example, a new step in an Explanation. A common device here is to use a 'background' element to introduce New information effectively. Themes which are 'background' elements[13] are more marked than Themes which are typical nominal (noun) elements, and so they effectively 'draw attention' to themselves, making the New information included there appropriate, rather than disruptive. The following text, *'The fetus: from one cell to billions'* – already discussed in terms of genre – shows an effective use of background elements as Themes, to signal important shifts in the text. The relevant Themes for this discussion are underlined.

The fetus: from one cell to billions

The fertilised egg drifts into the uterus. <u>There</u> the egg attaches itself to the uterine lining, which provides nourishment.

The cells of the fertilised egg continue to divide. <u>Within about 2 weeks</u> it starts to look like an embryo. The embryo floats in a protective sack of amniotic fluid.

<u>At 8 weeks</u> the embryo has developed into a fetus. All the organs have formed and the heart is beating. Nutrients circulate from the mother's blood to the fetus from the placenta. The umbilical cord connects the placenta to the fetus.

<u>By 40 weeks</u>, the baby is about eight times bigger than it was at 12 weeks.

A baby is ready to be born.

Melbourne Museum

In this text, location (*'there'*) and in particular, time (*'within about two weeks'*, *'at eight weeks'*, *'by forty weeks'*) are foregrounded and brought into Theme position, coinciding with key steps in the Explanation of the development from a fertilised egg to a baby. These elements did not have to be thematised (clause four could have been *'It starts to look like an embryo within about two weeks'*), but by being thematised in this way, attention is drawn to these stages, and to the important role of time in the event being explained.

Thus it can be very useful for writers to have explicit knowledge about Theme and its development in a text. While this book is not a manual or guideline as such, it is appropriate here to give some explicit advice in this area (again, see Ferguson *et al.* 1995, for more details), particularly in relation to ways of adjusting a written text, in order to achieve appropriate thematic development. When editing, there may be a number of places in a text where the choice of Theme, or the balance of Theme and New, needs to be adjusted. It is usually the case that a text needs to be edited at least a little to improve the flow of information. This involves reordering information to achieve an appropriate balance between Theme and New. There are a number of simple ways of reordering information. The components of some clauses can simply be moved around, from front to back, or vice versa, as we have already seen:

Version 1: <u>In 1979</u>, new technology gave the fishing industry a boost.
Version 2: <u>New technology</u> gave the fishing industry a boost in 1979.

In examples such as these, it is literally the case that clause elements can be moved around, and this may be all that is needed to achieve an appropriate Theme choice. Other clauses may need a change of voice, from the active to the passive, or from the passive to the active, in order to achieve the appropriate information focus:

Version 1: <u>New technology</u> gave the fishing industry a boost in 1979.
Version 2: <u>The fishing industry</u> was given a boost by new technology in 1979.

Most 'Plain English' writing advice suggests avoiding the passive altogether, as it leads to an overly complex and scientific style of writing. However, the passive voice is absolutely central to a smooth flow of information, and while its overuse may indeed be stylistically inappropriate, its random removal from a text will have disastrous effects. The passive voice is necessary on some occasions simply to enable a particular element to be placed in Theme position, and this indeed is its function in English (Halliday 1994; Halliday and Matthiesen 2004; Ferguson *et al.* 1995).

Sometimes, a text needs to be changed in other ways in order to achieve a more effective Theme, by changing the choice of verb, for example, or the choice of nouns. Usually however, a way can be found to change the focus of the clause, according to what is most appropriate for a text at a particular point.

The details provided here about Theme, New and the flow of information are necessarily brief; it is not possible within the scope of this book to give all the linguistic details to explain all facets of these choices, their variations, and their complexities. The most important point to note is that the development of the text is neither fixed, nor unimportant. Organisation can easily break down at the micro-level of a text, and when it does, it is usually because of problems in the flow of information between Theme and New. By being alert to such potential problems, writers may be able to more readily identify points of breakdown in a text, and manipulate the relevant clauses (and subsequent clauses too, if necessary) to achieve a more effective flow. Choices at the micro-level of the organisational framework, in terms of choices of Theme and New, thus contribute in fundamental ways to the overall coherence and effectiveness of a text.

The contribution of Theme to organisation is important for another reason, and that is that the overall selection of Themes gives a text as a whole a certain point of departure, which can subtly influence the overall meanings of the text. As noted at the beginning of this chapter, otherwise similar texts can be organised in different ways, and give each distinctive meanings. Here, the question is no longer one of possible 'breakdown', it is not the case that one organisation 'works' and another does not, but rather, that they each represent a certain choice in terms of organisation, resulting in a different 'point of departure' for the text, and a different thematic focus. The organisational choices made in this way need to be evaluated against aims for the text as a whole and its role

Themes:	**Introduction**
The Kunwinjku	*The Kunwinjku* have always been the most prolific group of artists from the western Arnhem Land region. *Their artistic heritage* is rich and can be traced back through an unbroken sequence of changing rock art styles to 50,000 years ago, which is exactly the period archaeologists believe Aboriginal people first
The Researchers	arrived in the Australian continent. *The first researcher to document and publish on the variety and wealth of the region's rock art* was Sir Baldwin Spencer who visited Oenpelli in 1912. *Decades later* Charles Mountford and Catherine and Ronald Berndt conducted more intensive research on western Arnhem land art. *They* also assembled significant bark painting collections produced predominantly by Kunwinku artists who had moved to Oenpelli from their homelands further west. *The publications and exhibitions subsequently produced by these researchers* was instrumental in raising awareness of the beauty and significance of Aboriginal art for the first time.
	Australian Museum

within an exhibition. Thus, an understanding of Theme is important because it can be used to give a whole orientation to a text, and this is as much a part of meaning as any traditional notion of 'content'. This becomes particularly important in museum settings, where there also needs to be some alignment between the text and the exhibition (Ferguson *et al.* 1995; Serrell 1996). Consider the text shown above, and the subtle shift in Theme orientation between the early and later parts of the text.

Initially, this text takes as its departure point the Kunwinjku people and their art; however, Themes in the latter part of the text are oriented to the Western researchers who brought this art to the attention of outsiders. If the remainder of the exhibition also draws out these dual concerns, then such a duality is probably appropriate. If the intention is to focus on one or the other, however, this disparate development of Themes could be construed as misleading, by shifting the focus of the text. Thus the organisational choices made in this text need to be evaluated in relation to overall exhibition goals. Theme is thereby an important organisational resource for writers, contributing in a fundamental way to a sense of what the text – and the exhibition – is 'about'.

Integrating verbal and visual information at the micro-level

The intersection between visual and linguistic ways of signalling structure was noted previously, in relation to mid-level aspects of organisation. However, there are also interesting correlations at the micro-level. Highlighting (through a different font, a larger font, the use of underlining, colour and so on) is the main (typographic) resource to signal difference: that is, that which is highlighted deserves some special attention. Typically, that which is highlighted can relate to either the Theme or New in the text. When the grammatical Theme is highlighted, as in the following example, this foregrounds the topic focus for the visitor:

> **Stone** may be worked into tools by a number of methods. The **simplest and most common method** of working stone into tools is by percussive flaking. **Percussive flaking** happens by striking one lump of stone with another so as to detach small pieces known as flakes. These flakes have a characteristic bulb of percusssion and . . .

Such highlighting acts as an invitation to visitors to come and explore the topic under question – this is what the visitors will find out about, by reading the text. Alternatively, that which is highlighted can be the 'New', in the grammatical sense, the new information which the current text delivers. Once the topic has been established, and can be taken as 'given', the New acts as the *focus* of attention. Scanning for a sequence of 'New' points leads to an accumulation of meanings in the text.

> Cats are **one of many mammal species** introduced into Australia by humans. They now occur **throughout the continent**. There are about **3 000 000 domestic cats** in Australia and at least **6 000 000 feral cats.**

In Plate 2.4, the use of a very large font draws attention to 'arthropods' as the New information in the opening clause 'Eighty per cent of all animal species

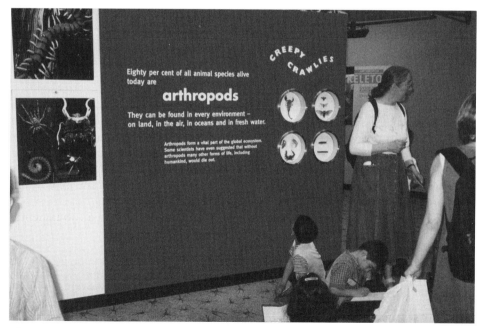

Plate 2.4 Typography supporting information structure, Natural History Museum, London

alive today are arthropods.' At the same time, 'arthropods' is made to stand out from the remainder of the text, by virtue of contrasting size, so it also functions like a heading, or Theme for the text. The non-conventional typography here effectively supports the information structure of the text in different ways – by acting as a kind of first-level heading, to draw visitors to the panel in the first instance, and by highlighting the New of the clause.

When there is a correlation between such visual highlighting, and the information structuring of the text, the overall meanings of the text are reinforced, and such devices can help visitors to scan for information, or to accumulate meanings as the text unfolds. However, if elements are highlighted at random, this might in fact interfere with processes of scanning and accumulating meanings, and make the text less, rather than more, accessible. It is interesting that contemporary layout and design often includes random variations of typographical effects: font types, sizes, colours, and so on. This variation typically cross-cuts any structural patterns of Theme and New, as illustrated in this example:

> The fertilised egg drifts into the *uterus*. There **THE** egg attaches itself to the uterine lining, which **provides** NOURISHMENT. The cells of the *fertilised* egg continue to *divide*. Within about 2 weeks IT starts to look like an embryo. The embryo **floats** in a *protective sack* of AMNIOTIC fluid.

This example is highly exaggerated, with the typography changing at random, and thereby having no particular correlation with information structuring within the text. Such layouts connote 'contemporaneity' for the text, and are visually appealing and interesting, generating a sense of dynamism in an otherwise visually static text. The dynamism comes from the intersection with and cross-cutting of the linguistic informational patterns: because the highlighting is necessarily an 'attention-focussing' resource, it does not just reinforce existing linguistic organisation, but adds its own layer of organisational meanings. It can be a productive resource, in that it may be a way to achieve highlighting of both Theme and New, or to enable consistent highlighting of a key word which is not necessarily the same as the grammatical Theme. (This is not the case in the example above, where elements are highlighted at random.) Also, as a stylistic resource, it may be favoured because of its contemporaneity, as noted. However, it may do little for the transfer of information, and thus, for the basic comprehension of the text. If ease of comprehension is the goal, more standard use of typographical layout may be more appropriate.[14]

Conclusions

The most important aspect of organising, as part of a framework for making meanings, is that it be understood not as a *post hoc* choice, something to be 'added on' when other matters, such as content, have been decided, but rather as an intrinsic meaning-making resource in its own right. Organisation is part of the meaning potential of language, and so also contributes to the meaning potential of exhibitions, as well as those made in the institution as a whole.

The organisational framework not only helps prioritise, foreground, and inter-relate other layers of meaning, but it can create 'additional' meanings of its own accord, independent of the subject matter. Thus, the 'same' subject matter can be construed and read entirely differently, depending on the organisational choices which have been made.

Organisation, then, is a meaning potential, a creative resource. The explanations in this chapter have concentrated on the *productive* side of this resource, how it is and may be used by professionals. The interpretative side of this resource, how it is or is not taken up by visitors, is also critical. It is not necessarily the case that a particular organisation will determine one reading for visitors. There is always the potential to resist, subvert, or reinvent a given organisation, by the visitors' own interaction with it. Thus, even the most clearly signalled Theme, at the level of language, may be bypassed by a visitor intent on something else.

Yet at the same time, it is undoubtedly the case that institutions must give serious attention to all aspects and levels of organisation. As well as having the potential to make meanings, the organisational framework has the potential to profoundly disrupt meaning making, if it is used carelessly or inconsistently. When an apparently 'well-written' text breaks down, for instance, visitors are likely to interpret this as their own problem, to lose interest, or to become frustrated with the visiting experience. Such breakdowns make institutions inaccessible, and frustrate other attempts to include diverse visitor groups, and to enhance visiting experiences.

The organisational framework, then, is something to be reflected on and considered at least two key points in the production process (whether that be the production of a text, a whole exhibition or even the whole institution). First, where possible, it needs to be considered at the level of design or conceptualisation, as an intrinsic part of the meaning-making process. What Themes will be foregrounded, as the departure point for other meanings (in a text, in an exhibition . . .)? What information will be accumulated as New in the unfolding of a text, of an exhibition? Second, organisation needs to be considered at the point of evaluation, and used to reflect on what has, or may have been, achieved. Are there any points where organisation breaks down? Where it is inconsistent? Contradictory? Where can organisation be improved?

Importantly, while the organisational framework is an intrinsic aspect of meaning in its own right, it necessarily works in conjunction with the other communication frameworks, those of interactional and representational meanings. Different kinds of organisation can enhance or inhibit the overall *interactional* meanings of a text, for example, as we have seen in terms of the generic structure of the text, which can implicate particular behavioural responses from visitors. Such connections will be explored further in Chapter 4. At the same time, organisation intersects with the overall *representational* meanings which can be made, for instance when a particular choice of Themes creates a particular 'angle' or focus for the subject matter, and these connections will be explored further in Chapter 5. The focus of this chapter has been

47

to demonstrate some of the ways in which organisational meanings can be seen to operate in museum texts, and some of the issues related to this framework which are of most concern to museums. The next chapter, Chapter 3, will focus on certain aspects of organisational meanings in more detail, looking at the ways in which organisational meanings can be seen to relate to issues of complexity and accessibility in text.

3

Focus

Making texts accessible: adjusting the level of complexity

Introduction

The organisational framework introduced in the preceding chapter is particularly important for cultural institutions, not least because it has significant implications for issues of *accessibility* in language. Texts can be organised in different ways to achieve different levels of accessibility, closely linked to different degrees of complexity, and of course the main challenge for contemporary cultural institutions is to produce texts which are informative and interesting, but which can be accessed and appreciated by a broad range of visitors. The issues introduced in the preceding chapter, such as the choice and sequencing of Themes, and smooth, appropriate introduction of New information, have a major impact on the accessibility of a text. Wherever there are breakdowns in the organisation of these resources, general comprehension – and therefore, accessibility – will be impeded. But accessibility relates to other factors as well, and this chapter focusses in detail on what it is in language which makes some texts more accessible, and others less so, identifying the main resources which contribute to these effects.

The chapter begins by discussing in detail the notion of 'complexity' in language, and relating this in particular to differences between written and spoken texts. Attention then shifts to the main linguistic resource which enables these differences, namely *nominalisation*, and a comparison is made with more general discussions of complexity, as in 'Plain English' advice, and some of the conventional approaches to and measures of complexity found in museum contexts. While the question, 'How complex should a text be?' may often be asked, it will be seen in this chapter that there is no 'right' answer: institutions, exhibitions and occasions will all make different demands on language. At the same time, however, there are some basic principles which enable complexity to be controlled as a resource, and which enable the extremes of complexity to be avoided.

Museum literature already widely discusses facets of this topic, under a number of related terms such as 'readability', 'accessibility', or 'intelligibility'. 'Readability' is used in two senses: it can refer either just to the visual presentation of the text (for example, whether the font size is large enough to be read comfortably), or to the 'comprehensibility' of the message. Baños (1995) makes a clear distinction between the two and refers to only the former sense as 'readability', and to the latter as 'intelligibility'. A favourable combination of these two produces 'accessibility', that is, whether the text is 'complete, concise and coherent'. I also favour the latter term, 'accessibility', with the corollary that it can only be defined contextually, and the necessary implication that there is, therefore, no one set standard (Ravelli 1996). In this chapter, I will not address issues of 'readability' in the sense of the physical presentation of the text. These are, indeed, crucial, but are already comprehensively addressed in museum literature (see for example Baños 1995; Ekarv 1999; Dean 1994, among others).[1] The focus here will be on the nature of language itself, and the resources within it which contribute to particular degrees of accessibility.

Written and spoken Modes of language

Whether or not a text is 'accessible' depends largely on how complex the text is, so to understand accessibility, it is first necessary to understand the nature of complexity in language. What, then, does 'complexity' mean? The most common way of beginning to understand complexity is to compare written and spoken language. It is a widely held belief that written language is generally more complex than spoken language, however, this is a gross over-simplification. In fact, written and spoken language are each complex, albeit in different ways, and understanding this is a key to being able to control levels of complexity (Halliday 1989, 2001, 2002b). Essential to this understanding is some background knowledge about the nature of written and spoken language: in what ways are they different, and in what ways the same?

Written and spoken language are of course two dimensions of the *one* language; they are not different languages. They are referred to as different *Modes* of language. But an important distinction needs to be made between the *Mode* of the language and the *medium* of its delivery. The medium is simply the channel of communication; the physical way in which communication takes place. Thus, if a person uses their voice to communicate, they are using a spoken medium. Or, if they are using ink on paper, then it is a written medium. However, as is well known, it is more than possible to 'talk like a book' or to 'write something spoken'. That is, the medium can be used in different ways, to achieve different effects. Just because an individual is using their voice to speak, it does not mean that they produce a 'conversation'. Or conversely, a written text does not have to 'read' like a heavy textbook. So, the medium is not a reliable indicator of the nature of the language at stake; the whole point for cultural institutions is that, a range of texts, all of the same medium, can still be very different in their 'written' or 'spoken' effects. There must therefore be some other way to understand the differences between written and spoken Modes.

The different Modes are distinguished in terms of two dimensions of the situational context in which language is produced. The first is the amount of *contact* and *feedback* arising between producer and receiver of the text (Martin 2001). Think of a range of texts, from a very casual conversation at one end, to a 'heavy' novel or academic textbook at the other. What contact and feedback are possible in these situations? With a casual conversation, there is visual contact between the speaker and hearer, and aural contact: each can see and hear the other. Thus, maximum feedback is possible, and speakers typically do adjust their conversation according to the feedback they get; backtracking, for example, when someone has missed a point, and so on. At the other extreme, a writer has neither visual nor aural contact with their reader, and there is either no or only minimal feedback. A reader could write to an author, if the author is still alive, with comments on a book, which might – perhaps – be incorporated in a future edition of the book, but basically there is little opportunity at this end of the Mode scale for feedback to have any impact on the text being produced. In between these two extremes, there are a range of other text types with different contact and feedback possibilities. On the telephone, for example, there is (usually) immediate aural feedback, but (until very recently) no visual feedback. Speakers adjust their language slightly to begin to accommodate this situational difference, for example, by describing and identifying things that the other speaker can't see. Or, with email, while there is no visual or aural contact, the speed of the exchange means that feedback can be almost immediate; and the tendency is for people to treat this as a more casual medium, although patently it is not (cf. Crystal 2001). Thus, Mode is a continuum of possibilities in terms of this dimension of contact and feedback, ranging from the 'maximum' possibilities of casual conversation at one end, to the 'minimum' possibilities of a 'heavy' book at the other as illustrated in Figure 3.1.

The second dimension of the situational context which differentiates texts along a continuum of Mode, is that of the *role* that language plays in the context of situation (Martin 2001), that is, the purpose or function of language in relation to other social processes. Again, this can be thought of as a continuum. At one extreme, the role of language can be seen to simply 'accompany' other things that are going on, as in playing a game of sport, where language is itself part of the action ('Throw it here!'). Language is part of the game, but at the same time, the game can carry on more or less independently of language, so language has only an ancillary role to play. At the other extreme, say in writing or reading a book, language does not just accompany the social process, it *is* the social process. Language may reflect on or re-construct some other social process (such as the history of a particular sport), but it is the process of reflecting which gives language its constitutive role in these instances. Again, between these two extremes, there are many other possibilities. Consider the type of language which accompanies different situations, such as providing a

MAXIMUM   *FEEDBACK*   MINIMUM

casual conversation   *telephone*   *email*   *academic treatise*

Figure 3.1 Continuum of feedback
Adapted from Martin 2001

Figure 3.2 Continuum of language roles
Adapted from Martin 2001

live commentary on a game of sport, versus writing a report on a game the following day for the newspaper, versus writing a history of a particular sport. In each of these situations, language plays a slightly different role, and thus this is another dimension of Mode variation as seen in Figure 3.2.[2]

Putting these two dimensions together – contact/feedback and the role of language – enables us to make sense of different Modes of language, independently of their medium. Thus, a politician's prepared speech, while delivered via a spoken medium, may have visual and aural contact, but may not allow for feedback, and it is likely to be slightly more reflective than active. Hence, the speech is not 'casual', like conversation. Or, a written text, which uses questions and commands to simulate conversational interaction, appears to incorporate some of the feedback dimension of more 'spoken' texts, and appears to be more active (even if both of these are illusory) and so the Mode of language is somewhat less 'written' than other, more heavy texts. Thus, because it is the nature of the language which varies, texts of the *same* medium can be quite different in their effect. This of course is the whole point for cultural institutions: as written texts can produce a range of effects, it is necessary to

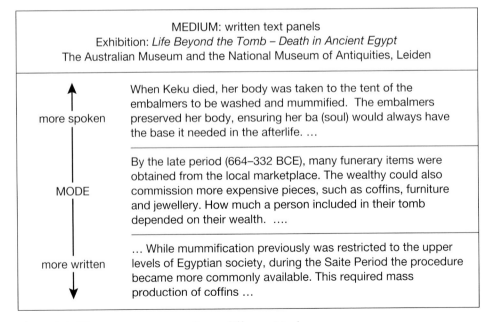

Figure 3.3 Three texts: same medium, different Mode

understand the variations more explicitly. Similarly, as spoken texts can also vary in the effects they produce, these too need to be understood in more detail. A text delivered in the spoken medium is not necessarily more accessible than a written medium text. Thus, some greater understanding of the differences between written and spoken Modes, and also the difference between Mode and medium, is required. The three texts in Figure 3.3, all presented in the written medium, are different in their Mode.

The texts come from the same exhibition, *'Life beyond the tomb: Death in Ancient Egypt'* (the Australian Museum and the National Museum of Antiquities, Leiden 2005), which explains some of Ancient Egypt's funerary practices. The more spoken of the texts is in the voice of an ancient Egyptian, called Namenkhamen, who tells the story of the death of his daughter, and the preparations for her funeral. This voice is used as a narrative to structure the main pathway through the exhibition, and the texts in this voice represent an individual, personal experience, oriented to personal, human involvement in action ('Keku died; the embalmers preserved her body . . .'). The more written of the texts represents an institutional, impersonal voice; concrete actions have been replaced by abstract and general concepts ('mummification; mass production') and by the relations between them ('This required . . .'). The middle text sits between these poles – it is still about 'people' ('the wealthy; a person') but these are now representative of a category, rather than an individual, and some actions are beginning to be represented in the passive voice ('were obtained'), which establishes a slightly less personal voice than in the more spoken text. Thus, while each of these texts is presented via the same medium, that of the written text panel, the language in them represents subtle but significant shifts in terms of Mode.

My primary interest in this chapter is to examine the issue of Mode in relation to texts of the same medium, that is, written labels. Many aspects of this discussion can also be applied to an analysis of Mode in relation to other media, such as audio guides, in terms of evaluating how 'written' or how 'spoken' the commentary actually is (often these are just fully scripted, written texts, read out loud; cf. Serrell 1996). However, one issue we will not address is the overall choice of media itself: whether to put a written label on the wall, for example, or to use an audio guide, or a docent-led tour. These are important choices, and very relevant to issues of meaning-making,[3] but most institutions will already have standard practices, influenced by issues of budget, audience and institutional preferences. Once the choice of medium has been made, however, there is still the potential for wide variation of accessibility within the one medium, and that is what this chapter seeks to address.

Complexity in language

Understanding the fundamental differences between written and spoken Modes is the first step in appreciating their different complexities. As mentioned, it is not in fact the case that one Mode is more complex than the other; they are each complex, in their own way. What, then, are the linguistic resources which lead to differences in complexity?

The fundamental nature of complexity varies between written and spoken language. The complexity of spoken language is distinguished by the fact that it is immediately tied to its situation, a form of action, with the opportunity for maximum feedback and contact. It is therefore by its nature dynamic, inter-active, and open-ended, and its complexity lies in the way turns are joined together. Listen to someone who is conversing for a while, or listen to your-self: as we chat, a long turn in conversation is distinguished by the fact that many clauses are joined together 'So I said . . . but then he said . . . so then we . . . but if it hadn't been . . . then we . . . but . . .well what I meant was . . .' and so on and so on. Clause is added to clause and they are strung together into one text. Halliday (1989) calls this the 'choreographic' complexity of language: spoken language is put together like an intricate dance; each step must be connected to another, to form a seamless whole.

In contrast, written language has little or no opportunity for contact or feed-back and it functions to reflect on action. Indeed, one of the main functions of written language is to communicate across time and geographical space, and thus to stand independently of any immediate context of situation. Ideally, written texts should function as independent packages, and one ought to be able to read a document without requiring access to the author for its inter-pretation (of course there are limits to the extent to which this is possible; eventually some distances, especially of time, prove too great). Written language is therefore by nature static, closed and more overtly organised; it works to package things up as effectively as possible. Thus in terms of the way clauses are joined together, written language is actually rather simple in this regard: while the individual clauses of a text are of course related to each other in various ways, they are presented as if they are discrete units. Punctuation is the main marker of this: capital letters and full stops show the boundaries of the units. Thus, in terms of explicit connections between clauses, written language tends to be rather simple.[4] The complexity of written language lies in the way it 'packs in' information within a clause. Halliday calls this the 'crystalline' complexity of language. Written language functions as a storage mechanism for information, and in order to be more efficient, content is squeezed in wherever possible. Similar content in spoken language is 'strung out' across the clauses. Compare the following examples[5]:

More spoken	More written
1 We need to preserve the environment 2 and, in order to do so, 3 we have to farm and produce things 4 in ways that we can sustain.	1 Environmental preservation depends on sustainable farming and production practices.

54

While these examples are not identical in their representational (that is, informational) content (the more spoken example has a 'we' that is not present in the more written example, for instance), they are reasonably similar in representational terms, that is, they capture similar kinds of information. It is not the case that one example contains 'more' information than the other; rather, that each example has its own way of presenting information. The more written example has squeezed the information in to the space of one clause; the more spoken example has spread this information out over several clauses. The greater number of clauses in the spoken example (related together as one larger unit of information) produces the choreographic nature of spoken language; technically this is referred to as 'grammatical intricacy'. It is possible to measure the degree of intricacy holding between clauses, and it tends to be high in spoken language, but relatively low in written language. In contrast, the fewer number of clauses in the written example, with the information being packed into this restricted 'space', produces the crystalline nature of written language. Technically, this is referred to as 'lexical density'; this too can be measured, and it tends be high in written language, but low in spoken (see Figure 3.4).

In museums, text writers are often interested in ways of measuring complexity in a text; this makes sense, as being able to give a specific calculation seems more 'objective' and 'scientific', than making assertions and generalisations about what's going on in language. And it is certainly the case that both lexical density and grammatical intricacy can be measured, in quite valid ways. However, I feel that to pursue such a path would be quite inappropriate in terms of the amount of time required to perfect these measurements.[6] What is relevant, interesting and achievable, is to ignore the exact measurements as such, and focus on the principles *behind* the measurements, as a key to understanding complexity. And here, the most important aspect of complexity for museums to deal with is that of lexical density.

Lexical density is a measure of the proportion of lexical items in a clause. Note that this is *not* a measure of the number of words in a clause or a text; rather, it is a measure of those words which carry *lexical* content (as opposed to grammatical content, as explained further on p. 56), and their proportion relative to one clause. This proportion reflects the extent to which lexical content has or has not been 'squeezed in' to a clause.

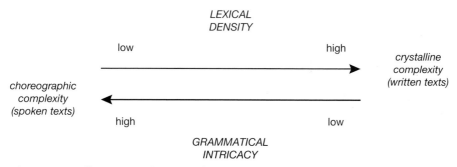

Figure 3.4 Different complexities of spoken and written language

A measure of lexical density relies on distinguishing lexical from grammatical items. Lexical items are those which carry 'content' in a traditional sense; words which could be reasonably defined in a dictionary. They are open class items, including nouns, verbs, adjectives and adverbs. For example:

Lexical items

nouns:	habitat, bird, embryo, egg . . .
verbs:	make, explore, see . . .
adjectives:	bold, beautiful, small . . .
adverbs:	slowly, completely . . .

Grammatical items are 'closed' class items; they are functional in nature, and tend to be the 'glue' of the language, including conjunctions, prepositions, determiners, articles, pronouns and so on. These are also crucial to the creation of meaning, but their meanings are not as concrete as those of lexical items.[7] For example:

Grammatical items

conjunctions:	because, and, so, however . . .
prepositions:	of, in, up, under . . .
determiners / articles:	a, the, these, this, those . . .
pronouns:	I, my, you, who . . .

Lexical density is measured by counting the number of lexical items which occur in a clause. The lexical items have been underlined in the clauses below:

Example	Lexical density	
Environmental preservation depends on sustainable farming and production practices.	Lexical items	7
	Clause	1
	Lexical density	**7**
We need to preserve the environment and in order to do so, we have to farm and produce things in ways that we can sustain.	Lexical items	8
	Clauses	3
	Lexical density	**2.6**

Remember that the measure is a proportional one, lexical items in relation to clauses; it is the *distribution* of lexical content that gives the impression of greater or lesser density. Typically, very 'spoken' texts have a low lexical density of about 2–3; more 'written' texts have a higher density. However, while this measure is available, I am not advocating that text writers in museums actually measure the lexical density of their texts (in fact, considerably more information needs to be given to enable this to happen, such as clarifying the boundaries of a clause, further information on differentiating lexical from grammatical items, and so on); nor am I saying that a certain level of lexical density (say, 3 as opposed to 7) is desirable, or will result in 'accessible' texts. Rather,

I am trying to illustrate general principles, that is, how the *perception* of (some aspects of) complexity is constructed in language, and some examples of more and less complex structures.

What the measure does reveal is that more written texts tend to have a higher lexical density. Squeezing in lexical content is an effective way to make efficient use of the available grammatical 'space'. A clause is an almost infinitely elastic package: information can be squeezed in and in without necessarily creating additional clauses. Compare the following examples:

Single clause	Lexical density
<u>Birds eat insects</u>.	3
All <u>common birds eat</u> a <u>wide variety</u> of <u>insects</u>.	6
All <u>common birds</u> on the <u>Australian continent eat</u> a <u>wide variety</u> of <u>nutritious insects</u> from many <u>sources</u>.	10

The ability to compact information into the space of just one clause is an important and effective functional feature of language. It enables written texts to be effective 'storage devices', preserving information in a reasonably economical way. However, this feature can be carried to an extreme, to a point at which the text becomes impenetrable, or what is commonly called, too 'wordy'. Much 'good writing' advice cautions the writer against 'wordiness' (Baños 1995; Ekarv 1999, to cite just two). In fact, the number of words is rarely the issue (although it is made to be); what is at stake is the *proportion* of lexical words per clause. Indeed, some advice, such as Richaudeau's injunction to use phrases of '8 to 20 words long' (cited in Baños 1995: 218) is not linguistically valid. Presumably in the right context, a clause such as 'Birds eat insects', would be unproblematic, and yet it is only 3 words long. And while a clause of 20 words is very likely to include a number of devices which are more, rather than less, complex, this is not necessarily the case, as revealed in the example above (p. 56) of 'We need to preserve the environment . . .', which has 25 words in total. This generalised advice can be a useful rule of thumb, because the lower and upper levels often coincide with a certain level of complexity, but this is a tendency only, and should not be applied as a blanket rule.

Rather than the number of words being the issue, a sense of 'wordiness' in texts is conveyed by the *nature* of the words which are chosen. Written language tends to emphasise *naming*, or things, as opposed to action (Halliday 1989, 2001, 2002b). Let's compare another set of 'more spoken' and 'more written' examples (see page 58).

There is a major shift between these examples in terms of the relationship between grammar (the structures chosen) and the role that these play in building up the meaning of the clause. In the first part of the spoken example, the verb is '*degrade*', and the meaning of this is what we expect of a verb, that of an

Example	Lexical density	
If <u>people degrade habitats</u> then the <u>resources</u> in <u>fisheries</u> will be <u>depleted</u>	Lexical items	6
	Clauses	2
	Lexical density	**3**
<u>habitat degradation leads</u> to <u>fishery resource depletion</u>	Lexical items	6
	Clause	1
	Lexical density	**6**

action, or event: something going on. The first noun, '*people*', represents something reasonably concrete (if general), and the second noun, '*habitats*', while less easy to define succinctly, also represents something reasonably concrete, an actual place, or type of place. So, the grammatical elements here do what we normally expect them to do: the verbs represent actions; the nouns represent things. That is:

people	degrade	habitats
meaning: thing	*meaning*: action	*meaning*: thing
grammar: noun	*grammar*: verb	*grammar*: noun

In the written example the situation is somewhat different. Look at '*degradation*': this is a noun in terms of the grammar, but what is its meaning? To understand the meaning of this, you would have to imagine some action taking place – people doing something to a place, perhaps. That is, 'behind' this noun, is the meaning of an event, an action. So the grammar is being used slightly unusually here. Similarly with 'depletion': this is a noun in terms of the grammar, but again has the meaning of an action 'behind' it. Conversely, the verb in this example, 'leads', doesn't convey very much in terms of what action exactly is going on; it does however show a causal link between the first noun and the second; these two things are inextricably related. So this is still a kind of an action, but of a less concrete type than the spoken example. Again, then, the grammar is being used in a slightly unusual way. That is:

habitat degradation	leads to	fishery resource depletion
meaning: action	*meaning*: relation	*meaning*: action
grammar: noun	*grammar*: verb	*grammar*: noun

There is evidently a major shift between the spoken and written examples. In the written example, the meanings of some 'actions' are represented by nouns, not verbs. How does such a shift in the grammar arise? Every clause, whether spoken or written, has a basic structure which centres on the verb, around which things are involved. In the spoken example, the basic structure is made up of concrete things, which are connected by concrete actions to other things. This is represented in Figure 3.5.

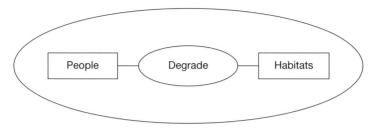

Figure 3.5 Spoken example: concrete things, concrete actions

In this spoken style, each action or event needs to be expressed by a single clause, and to build up a text, clauses needs to be linked to each other via explicit links, such as conjunctions. This is illustrated in Figure 3.6.

In contrast, the written example contains *abstract* things: elements which look and behave like nouns, but which carry the meaning of an action behind them. In effect, these abstract nouns, or *nominalisations*, package up the meaning of a whole clause into just one element of a clause: just one noun. Thus 'people degrade habitats' can become 'degradation', or more fully 'habitat degradation', which is still just one noun group. In turn, this nominalisation is related to another nominalisation, 'fishery resource depletion', by a simple relating verb

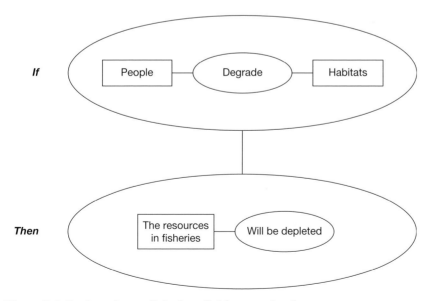

Figure 3.6 Spoken clauses linked explicitly to each other

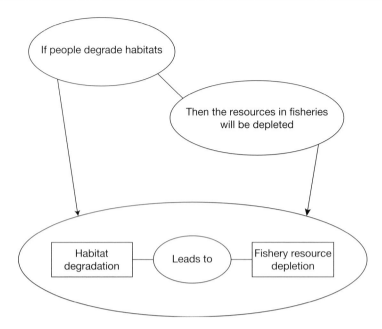

Figure 3.7 Nominalisation compacting the clause structure

group, 'leads to', again effectively packaging another clause into just one element. This condensation effect is illustrated in Figure 3.7.

Thus, the written example, through nominalisation, has more or less been able to package up the meaning of two clauses into just one clause. It is this process which gives rise to the impression of 'wordiness' in heavily written texts, and the higher lexical density: the lexical items have literally been 'packed in' to the clause.

Importantly, once an event is 'named' and expressed as a thing, the very rich resources of the English nominal group come into play. Nominal groups are an expansion around a noun. Nouns can be described, classified and modified, all within the boundaries of the nominal group, such that a lot of detail can be built up around a noun, while still only taking up the grammatical 'space' of one element of a clause. Consider the following (see also Eggins 2004: 96):

degradation
habitat degradation
habitat degradation of sensitive areas
extreme habitat degradation of sensitive areas
continued extreme habitat degradation of sensitive areas on the eastern seaboard
. . . and so on!!

Thus, the complexity of written language – its higher lexical density – comes from a tendency towards nominalisation, and the use of nominalisation and associated nominal group structures to 'pack' information into a clause.

More spoken texts connect concrete people and things with concrete actions; more written texts relate abstract 'things' to each other. This is why written language is often interpreted as being 'more complex' than spoken: in some respects, it is, condensing information in a way that makes clauses lexically dense.

Positive and negative effects of nominalisation

Nominalisation is, then, one of the key distinguishing features of written language, and certainly creates the effect of 'wordiness' in certain texts. It changes the lexical density and nature of the text, and thus puts a higher pressure on the amount of processing required to decode it; hence the need to read and re-read complex texts, and the sense sometimes that particular texts are simply impenetrable. Thus, a text overloaded with nominalisation is unlikely to be desirable in a museum context. However, nominalisation is still an important resource, and it has a number of different effects on other aspects of the language. These additional effects may be seen to be either positive or negative, depending on your position as a communicator.

First, one of the main functional contributions of nominalisation is in terms of its contribution to representational meanings. Nominalisation enables a technical view of a subject area to be established: every area of endeavour, whether it be strictly scientific or something more everyday, such as hairdressing, or gardening, has its own technicality. These are shorthand ways of naming important events or event sequences in a Field. Environmentalists in communication with other environmentalists, for example, wouldn't want to have to keep repeating a phrase such as 'you know when people degrade habitats . . .'. It's far more economical and efficient for them to say 'degradation'; once the process of 'degrading' has been nominalised in this way, it can then be expanded by, for instance, classifying it as 'habitat degradation'. Clearly this is highly functional and absolutely essential to developing the expertise in any Field. However, for an outsider to the Field, an apprentice or novice for instance, such technicality can be very negative. Technicality needs to be introduced and built up gradually.[8] If it is not, then the technicality functions to exclude, not to facilitate an efficient sharing of meanings. In fact this is what is derisively called *jargon*: someone else's unmediated technicality!

A second effect of nominalisation is that it changes the overall interactional meanings being expressed. In the examples on p. 58 about degradation, the 'people' of the spoken example have disappeared in the written one. In the written example, some person or persons is implied as being responsible for the 'degradation', but this is not explicitly expressed. As clauses move from a focus on concrete actions performed by actual people or concrete things, to abstract things related to abstract things, actual 'people' tend to disappear from the text. Again, this can be evaluated positively or negatively. It might be positive if, for some reason, a writer is trying to avoid explicitly mentioning an actual person; or negative if someone is seeking to identify responsibility. It is no accident that the metaphors for the most unpleasant 'actions' in our world are

61

nominalised, and avoid mentioning responsibility: 'collateral damage', 'ethnic cleansing', 'terrorism', etc.

Nominalisation also changes the overall organisational structure of a text. Because verbs are normally buried in the middle of a clause ('people degrade habitats'), it is very hard to make them thematic, in the sense described in Chapter 2. Thus, through nominalisation, the meanings associated with verbs can effectively be thematised: brought to the front of the clause and used as the point of departure ('habitat degradation leads to . . .'). Related to this, the overall argumentative structure of a text is also affected by nominalisation. In the more written texts, the explicit clausal connections present in the spoken text have disappeared, and the relationships between events are buried within the verbs ('leads to'). The connections are thus more implicit, and harder to interrogate. Again, positive or negative, depending on your standpoint.

Nominalisation is, therefore, a rich and complex resource, with multiple effects, both positive and negative, on the nature of texts. All this might be taken to suggest that written language is indeed the more complex Mode, however, it is just that I have emphasised this aspect of it here. If similar time was spent exploring grammatical intricacy, that too would soon reveal the complementary complexity of spoken language. Yet it remains the case that in cultural institutions, communication problems mostly arise with written texts, or with 'spoken' texts, such as audio guides, which have become too written in their Mode. It is therefore the need to understand the nature of written language which merits this emphasis.

Complexity in language and the myths of 'good writing'

Getting the balance right between the degree of spoken-ness and written-ness in a text is very important. Much of the writing on language in museum contexts is about, in one way or another, issues of complexity. However, within this literature, there are many myths about writing and about language which are recirculated as fact, and it is important to separate linguistic fact from fiction. Most of this writing advice could be said to fall under the more general umbrella of the Plain English movement, at least in terms of having a general preference for a style of writing that moves away from the extremes of heavy legalistic, academic, or scientific text, towards something that is more 'plain'. As noted at the beginning of this chapter, other terms referring to more or less the same objective are 'readable' and 'accessible' texts; 'considerate' text is also found (cf. Ambruster 1984). But it is important to reflect carefully on exactly what Plain (or readable, or accessible) English is or isn't. First, Plain English is not 'spoken' language. The texts people aim to produce when producing 'plain' texts are certainly less 'written', that is, further away from the extreme written end of the Mode scale; they are moving towards more spoken-like text, but they are certainly not 'spoken', if casual conversation is taken as the marker of the other extreme. The following fragment of conversation illustrates a more genuinely casual encounter:

Fran: . . . However, I mean what you said is, is maybe all very true David, but I mean, in the Public Service people are transferring from . . . areas
Brad: Ah I don't wanna be a bloody Public Servant
Fran: No no, but I'm just saying like; Like you're saying you know; you don't know anything about soil . . . but people are transferring from Fisheries to Education . . . now I can see no, no bearing . . .

Eggins and Slade 1997: 98

The text quoted above is certainly 'spoken' in style, but not the sort of text that museums would generally be aiming to reproduce! Thus, 'Plain' text is not the same as 'spoken' text. What, then, is Plain English?

Strictly speaking, Plain English is a movement begun in the US in the 1970s (Solomon 1996), with its genesis in the domains of insurance and legal documents. Today, 'plain' language is preferred in a range of situations, including business documentation for clients, media reporting, government information documents, workplace instructions and documentation, and of course, texts produced in cultural institutions for the general public.

The preference for Plain English reflects a shift in the onus of responsibility for the 'success' of a document from the reader, to the writer, and this coincides with broad-based changes in society to relations between employer and employee, and between provider (whether private or public) and client. First, there is now more explicit recognition, especially in countries like Australia, Britain and the US, that society is indeed heterogeneous, racially and ethnically multi-faceted, with various language groups and different degrees of expertise with English, and with broad-ranging levels of education (these have of course always been the facts in these countries, but they have not always been formally recognised). Thus there is an acknowledgment of diversity in the population, and an appreciation that all groups should have access to and equity in all facets of society.

At the same time, enormous changes have taken place in the workplace. Post-Fordist workplaces now have less rigid workplace practices; workers are likely to work in teams, engaging with peers and superiors, rather than being silent components of a rigid factory floor. The nature of the work undertaken is also likely to vary frequently for each worker; there is a need for flexibility and multi-skilling. All this places an increasing pressure on communication, especially written documentation, as does union and government promotion of improved workplace conditions, with a demand for standard operating procedures, instruction manuals, safety regulations and so on (Solomon 1996; Gee *et al.* 1996; Scheeres 1999; Iedema 2003). Again, such documentation is produced with recognition that the readers will be diverse in background and education.

It could be said that previously, the responsibility for understanding a written text was that of the reader. If the writer had included all relevant information, that was the limit of their responsibility, and it was up to the reader to do whatever work necessary to interpret the document. Thus if a document was impenetrable or confusing, the reader either needed to engage a lawyer or improve their level of education, or else suffer in silence. With the broad-based social changes just described, and with a more market-oriented economy, increasingly competitive in a globalised world, the onus is now on the writer to make their document maximally accessible. Hence, the great interest in Plain English, the success of which has led to huge improvements in a range of previously impenetrable documents.

The aims of Plain English, then, are well motivated, and there has been much success. And certainly within museum contexts, the vigorous pursuit of accessible, interesting texts is an important and relevant goal. However, there are a number of major problems with this movement and with the 'good writing' guidelines usually associated with it. The problems arise in terms of the vagueness of definitions put forward, the misinformation about language that is circulated, and inaccuracies in rules and measures that arise from this misinformation. I will examine here some of the writing guidelines found in museum contexts, critiquing them in terms of the linguistic fallacies they perpetuate. At the same time, I wish to stress that I have selected these guidelines precisely because they *have* offered some important and useful perspectives on language, not the least of which is simply drawing attention to it in the first place.

First, then, a major problem arises in the definition and understanding of the overall style being aimed for, so-called 'plain' English. As Solomon (1996) explains, Plain English is usually defined in terms of what it *isn't*, rather than what it *is*. A typical definition would be the following:

> Plain English is the opposite of gobbledegook and of confusing and incomprehensible language. Plain English is clear, straightforward expression, using only as many words as are necessary. It is language that avoids obscurity, inflated vocabulary and convoluted sentence structure.
>
> Eagleson 1990; cited in Solomon 1996

Compare this with definitions and explanations of an appropriate style in a museum context:

> information should be written in 'a lively, visually oriented style that captures the reader's interest' . . .
>
> Dean 1994: 113

> texts should not be 'too long and wordy'; 'too technical'; 'boring'
>
> Dean 1994: 117

> 'use a simple, but not simplistic, writing style in order to reach visitors'
>
> Baños 1995: 205

> 'keep the number of words in exhibition texts to a minimum'
>
> Baños 1995: 218

> text must be 'easy to read'
>
> Ekarv 1999: 201

text should favour 'the active form of the verb, the subject confronting the reader with the natural order of things'

Ekarv 1999: 202

and so on . . .

Such definitions and advice are intuitively appealing, as most people feel that they recognise 'gobbledygook' when they see it, or feel that they can distinguish a 'lively' text from a 'boring' one. And who would dispute the aim to make a text 'easy to read'? But when examined more closely, these definitions, and their related writing advice, contain a number of problems.

First, while we could not reasonably expect too much detail in a definition or a fragment of advice, note that little is actually defined (what is 'clear' and 'straightforward'? which vocabulary is 'inflated'? what kind of text is 'boring'?). Also, note that these definitions suggest that there is one kind of 'Plain English', one magic answer to communication problems. In fact, language is not monolithic in this way; it is contextually dependent, and a set of guidelines suitable for one occasion, might be completely inappropriate for another. In museums, the appropriate-ness of texts is dependent on so many factors – the purpose of the exhibition, institutional values, anticipated audience, place within the exhibition – and so on and so on – that any 'one' style will suit but a few occasions. Much greater flexibility and sensitivity is required in producing texts, than the holy grail of a 'plain' style would suggest. (It is interesting that in the case of design, no-one would seek out one layout and type of display for all exhibitions; while there may be common elements between exhibitions, they not only vary between each other but indeed are *expected* to vary.)

Consider instead an inherently more flexible definition of 'plain' English, as proposed by Solomon and Brown (1995):

> [Plain English is] the use of language and design features so that a document is appropriate to its purpose, the subject matter, the relationship between reader and writer, the document type, and the way the document is used.

This definition is much less intuitively appealing than the former type of definition; there is no identifiable evil ('gobbledygook'), and there are no simple rules to follow (such as 'avoid inflated vocabulary'). And yet, this definition is far more significant. Note the key word, 'appropriate': this suggests that texts may vary, according to those dimensions mentioned (purpose, subject matter, relationship, use . . .) and that there is no magical answer or simple definition as to what constitutes 'Plain' English. Any writing guidelines which advocate a monolithic style, or apparently simple solutions, must be treated with caution.

The writing guidelines based on the first style of definition tend to contain within them many misrepresentations of language. Most obvious here is the advice to 'avoid the passive voice', now enshrined as a matter of course in most grammar-checkers (which will identify the passive voice and advise writers to remove it). Certainly, an excess of the passive voice is associated with an impersonal and more scientific style of writing, one which is generally dispreferred in today's writing contexts. But as noted in Chapter 2, the passive voice is needed in English in order to enable the thematic focus of the clause to be manipulated. Indeed, this is its *raison-d'être* in the English language. Being able to switch between active and passive voice is one way to get the appropriate Theme in focus, and its random removal from a text will produce very odd effects in terms of information flow. Thus when guidelines give advice such as this, they reveal a profound misunderstanding of the nature of language.

Other fallacies, or misrepresentations, include the following:

- 'Use variety'. As we have seen in the discussion on Theme, variety arises when a text develops and expands a point, and moves on to include new information. Variety is interesting and is appropriate in most texts. But variety *for the sake of variety*, i.e. random changes in terms, can disrupt the information flow of a text and make it impossible to follow. Also, aspects of variety or consistency in the development of ideas need to take into account the demands of the genre at stake; for example a simple report, with one major topic focus, will demand less 'variety' in Theme position than other kinds of texts. Note that the advice to 'use variety' is somewhat inconsistent with the equally frequently given advice to 'be consistent'.
- 'Use active verbs'. As we have seen, a preponderence of the passive is likely to coincide with a dis-preferred style of writing, a more scientific, more 'written' one. But at the same time, the passive functions to enable an appropriate choice of Theme to be kept in focus, and so it can be appropriate to use on occasions.
- **'Keep sentences short' and 'avoid jargon'.** This advice, like much advice in the literature, is contradictory. As we have seen, 'jargon' is usually unexplained technicality. Certainly, there is no place for unexplained, unmediated technicality, but there is a place for technicality, indeed one of the main aims of exhibition text can be to introduce a general audience to some specialised terms and concepts. And technicality, through nominalisation, is precisely what enables condensation of structures in text: avoiding jargon/technicality altogether will inevitably lead to longer, not shorter, texts.
- **Sentences should be no more than 25 words and no less than 8 in length (or 21, or 18 or . . .).** As we have seen, while longer sentences do usually coincide with more complex, and hence less preferred structures, length per se is not the issue. Short sentences can be as impenetrable as long ones, and conversely, a long sentence might be perfectly accessible.

Thus, as appealing as such 'good writing' advice is, any such rules are inevitably limiting, and frequently contradictory. Many of these misconceptions also underlie important 'measures' (of complexity, readability) which are current in some museum contexts (Belcher 1991). The Fry method, for example, is a measure of readability deriving from educational contexts (Carter 1999). It is based on counting the total number of sentences and syllables in 100-word passages, with the average of the two plotted against a graph which relates the averages to an average 'reading age'. This method embodies at least two fundamental problems. First, as already stressed, a simple count of length will always be problematic in language. In this case, Fry equates fewer sentences with a lower reading age. The fewer sentences there are, the longer they must each be, so this contradicts other writing advice about 'shorter sentences'. In terms of number of syllables, it is the case that more complex, nominalised words are likely to have more syllables (Ravelli 1988), because nominalisations can (but do not always) contain various suffixes indicating aspects of the word's grammatical origin ('degradation' vs 'degrade', for example). So it is possible that fewer syllables will coincide with less nominalised, and hence more concrete, vocabulary. Again, however, this is a tendency only, and there is no necessary correlation between the two (for instance, 'infarction' and 'yesterday' both have three syllables; the number of syllables has nothing to do with their relative complexity). Similar problems are found in other reading measures, such as the Flesch Reading Ease test (reported in Serrell 1996), or the Fog Index (Gunning 1968). For good reasons, these kinds of tests should be viewed, at best, with caution (Campbell and Holland 1982; Carter 1999); and more probably rejected altogether (Coxall 1996; McManus 2000), because of their failure to take account of issues of meaning and comprehension.

Another more disturbing aspect of many language tests and 'measures' is the extent to which they perpetuate prejudices about language: the values of high versus popular culture, for example. Richaudeau's measures of memory retention (as reported by Baños 1995: 211) equate typical readers (slow, average, very fast) with cultural values (moderately cultured, fairly cultured, cultured) and typical publications (*Reader's Digest*, specialised magazines, scientific works). Presumably this means there could be no such thing as a quick read of the *Reader's Digest*, nor that anyone would pore over a scientific work and take time to digest it. The extent to which these measures appeal and perhaps even 'seem right' is simply a reflection of the extent to which they accord with our prejudices about language and about culture. Sometimes, practical implications of this kind of advice do seem to work: the Museum of London has had some success by envisaging texts as equating with certain well-known British newspapers: the *Sun* (a popular tabloid) versus the *Guardian* (a quality broadsheet) for example.[9] Yet I would suggest that success here is a result of a shared evaluation of these texts, and a result of the ability of the writers in question to vary their texts to suit different contexts. Thus, the guideline appears to work, but not because of any inherent value; rather because sensitive and successful writers are able to incorporate some contextual variability into their texts.

Rather than 'measuring' issues such as complexity, it is better to 'evaluate' the overall effectiveness of a text, by testing visitor comprehension. MacLulich (1994a; see also Ferguson *et al.* 1995; Ravelli 1996) develops one such evaluation procedure, testing visitors' comprehension against two versions of a text on the 'same' topic. While the changes between the two versions encompassed much more than just complexity (that is, it included representational, interactional and organisational meanings), the texts varied most significantly in those aspects of meaning which impinged on Mode and organisation: their relative complexity, flow of information, and overall cohesion. A sample of 114 visitors were shown a pair of texts: an 'old' version of a text (with significant organisational problems) and a 'new' version, following the principles outlined here, and in Ferguson *et al.* 1995. Overall, there was an improvement in comprehension of nearly 30 per cent, based on visitors' ability to select the diagram which best represented the scientific content of the text. Such evaluation, as reflected in the constant emphasis on formative and summative evaluation (Serrell 1996) is a much more worthy investment of time than any 'measure'.

If the available rules are so inaccurate, and available measures so problematic, what is the solution? In the absence of rules, one can only offer frameworks, as this book aims to do. However, a framework is not a lesser choice. The frameworks suggested here are the scaffold for knowledge about language (and communication more generally), and the intention is to give some understanding of the potential and issues at stake, and some knowledge to begin to have informed reflection on the issues. This book is not a linguistic textbook, and so cannot treat any of the areas in sufficient depth to give a full and necessary background. However, it does draw attention to the relevant issues, for example, that the source of most problems in complexity will be in terms of getting the Mode right, that is, a balance between a written and a spoken style, and that that balance will depend in a large part on the degree of nominalisation used, and the relative complexity of nominal group structures.

The degree of accessibility of a text simply cannot be measured with a fixed set of rules nor any magic (or scientific!) formula. It is simply not the case that a lexical density of, say, 7.5 is 'too high', or that a lexical density of '4' is accessible. What is 'accessible' is entirely contingent on a range of factors, some of which cannot be accounted for fully, such as the prior experience of the reader. However, it is possible to be well-informed about the features which contribute to perceived complexity in language, and about the sorts of text features and patterns which are likely to facilitate, or interfere with, a smooth flow of information in the text. It is also possible to be sensitive to the contextual variety of language, and to recognise that effective communicators have choices in terms of how a text is pitched, and that different kinds of texts may be appropriate for different occasions. Accessibility in cultural institutions is more likely to be achieved by writers who develop their skills in writing different kinds of texts, and by institutions which value and appreciate variety in language.

4

Interacting in and through language

Using language to relate, engage and evaluate

Introduction

Museums today are obviously preoccupied with how they interact with visitors and with their communities: from mission statements through to evaluation studies, the issues of relating to, interacting with, and meeting the needs of visitors and communities are paramount. The following extracts from the Annual Reports of a range of institutions illustrate just some of these concerns:

> During a challenging year, the Smithsonian Institution responded in new and creative ways to better serve the American people . . . In the coming year, we'll continue to offer all Americans, wherever they may live, an inspiring educational experience . . .
>
> Lawrence M. Small, Statement by the Secretary,
Annual Report, Smithsonian Institution, 2002

> We aim to engage, enthuse and educate, so that more people than ever before gain an appreciation of science and the world about them.
>
> Annual Report, 2002/2003, Natural History Museum, London

> Te Papa provides access to collections and shares knowledge through exhibitions, events and learning programmes. Te Papa attracts, informs, and engages New Zealanders and visitors to New Zealand.
>
> Te Papa Annual Report, 2002/2003,
Museum of New Zealand Te Papa Tongarewa

> . . . Our main challenge is to speak to the diversity of Museum visitors: young and old, well-educated and not, the hurried tourist and the devoted museum-goer. . . . By integrating its core themes of land, nation and people, the Museum is committed to sharing and communicating knowledge, engaging with its audiences and providing life-long learning experiences.
>
> Dawn Casey, Director, Annual Report of the
National Museum of Australia, 2002–2003

This interaction takes place at all levels, from the way in which an institution enables communities to participate in museum activities; to the type of exhibits that are on display; to the forms of the language used to communicate with visitors. In this chapter, the focus will be on how language enables interactional meanings[1] – on how it functions to create a relationship between interlocutors, with a primary emphasis on visitor relations, and a secondary emphasis on community relations.

It is important to point out that the sense of interaction as used here is inclusive of, but broader than, that which is usually meant by 'interactives' in museums. Interactive displays are devices which invite an explicit response from visitors, and this, of course, relates to the interactional framework. But the interactional framework is a part of *all* communication: as we will see, even texts which seem to be impersonal and distant, entirely 'neutral' by conventional standards, also manifest choices from within the interactional framework. Further, as well as referring to aspects of engagement between interlocutors, the interactional framework encompasses those aspects of communication where one speaker inserts their own stance and subjectivity into the communication, and again it will be seen that this occurs in all communication. Thus, as for Screven (1995), and Witcomb (2003), interaction here means more than a technical sense of interactivity. Screven's explanation of interactivity relates largely to the language of texts and ways in which they are displayed (in conventional labels, for instance, or flip-panels), and he identifies five levels of interaction, from the *conventional*, which still enables involvement, even if responses are largely passive; through to *covert* interaction, where questions and instructions simulate active engagement; through to *adaptive* interaction, where electronic resources enable responses to be adapted to individual needs. For Witcomb, interactivity is addressed in terms of exhibitions and museums as a whole, including but going beyond language, and she differentiates the conventional sense of *technical* interactivity, from that of *spatial* and *dialogic* interactivity, the latter enabling meanings to be genuinely negotiated, rather than passively transmitted.

Here, then, the interactional framework also goes beyond conventional and technical senses of interactivity, to encompass the ways in which interlocutors engage with each other in the communication process. Museums, through their communicative practices, take up a 'speaking role', and enable roles to be taken up by others, both visitors, and relevant communities. They also construct a certain style of communication, and project a particular stance towards issues of (representational) content. There is an enormous potential, through language, for constructing, negotiating and adjusting these dimensions of meaning. This potential can be thought of as a vast semantic 'space' – and choices here are a matter of positioning oneself within this space. There is no real right or wrong as such, as all choices create some kind of meaningful text. But the overall interactional choices in a text need to be evaluated against the norms and expectations for the relevant context, and this needs to be situated in social, historical and cultural terms, and in relation to a particular point of view (for example, an institution's and a visitor's perspectives on appropriate roles may not be aligned).

An important part of the interactional picture is thus understanding the role of the visitor. Many existing visitor studies focus on identifying who the visitor 'is', in terms of a target audience (for example, Belcher 1991: 178ff.; Dean 1994: 20ff.). However, my interest here is to identify who the visitor 'can be', in terms of the *role* they are able to take up, as motivated by the text: how is the visitor positioned and addressed by the text? The target audience focus is important but is a complementary perspective to that adopted here. I do, however, acknowledge that the emphasis here on texts and their interactional meanings does not fully account for the individual as a social being. Falk and Dierking (2000), for instance, place the visitor and their role in meaning-making at the forefront of their enquiry into the nature and role of learning in museums, and warn against paying too much attention to exhibition 'intentions', to the exclusion of other factors. At the same time, however, they emphasise that an effective model of learning must also account for the sociocultural context in which an individual's learning takes place; as they say, 'In a very real sense, the world in which each of us lives is socio-culturally constructed.' (p. 39). And an important part of this sociocultural context is the *textual* side: texts are social products, created and understood *through processes of interaction*. It is important then, to examine this side of texts more closely: how do texts enable interaction? what sorts of interaction are possible via and through texts? and how do these potentially impact on an individual and their meaning-making experiences? This enquiry does not replace a concern with the individual and their learning processes, but complements it, enabling closer examination of one area of input into an individual's experiences. The chapter will begin by outlining some of the major interactional shifts in museum communication practices, and then focus on some of the ways in which roles, styles and stances are created through language, as a means of enabling and shaping interaction.

Interaction in context

In historical terms, there have been some fundamental shifts in museums' concerns with visitor and community relations, from one where the visitor was virtually ignored, and stakeholder communities relevant only as subjects, to one where both are now central. In particular, there has been a dramatic shift in the conceptualisation of the visitor, and this has virtually defined recent and wide-ranging changes in museum practices. Visitors are now identified as the 'lifeblood' of a museum (Belcher 1991: 171) and even 'the only reason for museums to exist' (Dean 1994: 19), and the relatively new emphasis on the visitor is central to the reconceptualisation of the museum itself as a communication tool. Even more importantly, the re-envisaged relations between museums and visitors characterise the communication agenda of the *post-museum* (Hooper-Greenhill 2000), where dynamic and responsive relations with visitors are enacted, and multiple interpretations of texts are provided for. This contrasts with the authoritative relations of the modernist museum, which conceptualised visitors as an undifferentiated, mass audience, and as the recipients of a transmission notion of pedagogy.

71

Clearly, language has an enormous role to play in redefining these relations; it is only necessary to listen to two people talking together, to appreciate that language quickly reveals many aspects of their relationship (Hooper-Greenhill 1994: 122). To understand how this works, we need to ask what sort of variation there is in the interactional dimension. The interactional dimension can be described in terms of a range of variables, which capture aspects of the overall 'persona' (O'Toole 1994) created through interactional choices. Most of these descriptions represent continua, that is, scales of possibilities, with recognisable extremes at either end, and many variations in-between. That is, the choices are not a matter of 'either/or', but of 'more' or 'less' (Martin 1992). Figure 4.1 represents a small selection of these general types of descriptions, characterised in relation to the modernist and the post-museum (Hooper-Greenhill 2000; Witcomb 2003).

The characterisation of these differences as 'old' and 'new' is a necessarily simplistic encapsulation of potentially diverse variations in museum practice, and Belcher (1991) demonstrates that these different approaches have tended to ebb and flow with time. The point is to highlight these differences as being indicative of major trends, and to examine some of the ways in which such differences are constructed, via communicative resources such as language. As trends, rather than absolutes, the differences captured in Figure 4.1 highlight some of the major shifts in interactional meanings in 'old' versus 'new' museological approaches to communication. Instead of playing the role of the authoritative expert, 'giving' information to the novice visitor, museums today are more likely to play a role in partnership with visitors, inviting them to explore information and ideas, and enabling them to participate in the formation of knowledge. Instead of the overall tone of texts and of exhibitions being very learned, serious and formal, there is scope for texts to take up different styles, including relatively informal and personal approaches ('What do *you* think about . . .?'). Associated with this, the overall positioning or stance taken up in relation to the information conveyed is no longer just the neutral, objective stance of formal, scientific texts, but may include texts which include emotional appeals, subjective perspectives on the information, and even approaches which question and challenge the very information conveyed. Much has changed in the overall meanings which can be conveyed, in terms of who or what the museum is, and how it relates to its visitors. We will now consider how the roles, style and stance of communication can be enabled by choices in language.

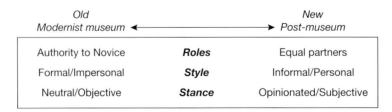

Figure 4.1 'Old' and 'New' interactional approaches

Changing roles

As indicated in Figure 4.1, one of the most obvious dimensions of the inter-actional framework is that of the *roles* which institutions and visitors can and do take up. But how is it that language can create and change such roles and relations? Or put the other way, how are relations between people, that are somehow 'in the context', realised in and expressed by the communication process? Consider the following texts:

> **Javanese Gamelan**
> Modern gamelan gadon, or chamber grouping, with instruments in the slendro tuning system, from Surakarta, Central Java. In performance, the group would include a female singer and a flute player. The male musicians would also sing. Gamelans have no conductor, being led by a drummer or rebab player. Gadon ensembles can accompany wayang kulit (shadow plays) or perform at private social functions such as weddings.
>
> Australian Museum

> **Exploring the Mind and Body**
> How have the anatomists knife, the x-ray machine and the microscope changed the way we live and the way we view ourselves?
> Follow the quest of the explorers of the body and mind and discover the human landscape.
>
> Melbourne Museum

> **Tasmanian Aboriginal Centre 1997**
> We do not choose to be enshrined in a glass case, with our story told by an alien institution which has appointed itself an ambassador for our culture.
>
> Melbourne Museum

Does one of these texts engage you more than another? Do you feel more aligned with one rather than another? Does it sound as if different types of people are speaking? Or perhaps, as if 'no one' is speaking at all? Just through the language that is used, texts convey and construct a certain kind of interaction with their readers. Here, the text 'Javanese Gamelan' presents a conventional, authoritative presentation of knowledge; its content may be of immense interest to a visitor, but the (compliant) visitor is positioned to 'receive' this knowledge – to store it up and think it over. In contrast, the introductory text panel, 'Exploring the Mind and Body', uses questions and commands to involve visitors in an active, mindful exploration of the Gallery of which it is a part, 'discovering' knowledge for themselves. The third text is in the voice not of the institution, but of one of the communities represented therein; it also takes up an authoritative, and challenging, position, in fact distancing itself from conven-tional institutional voices, and thereby enabling visitors to reconceptualise the role of the institution in relation to such communities.

The choices made in these texts reflect and construct different relations between the interlocutors, that is, they reflect and construct the *Tenor* of the context of

73

the situation. The Tenor depends on two key variables: the relative power of the interactants, and the degree of social distance or contact between them (Kress and van Leeuwen 1996; Martin 1992; both based on original work by Poynton 1989). In terms of power, interactants are always positioned relative to each other: either there is no difference, in which case there is equality, and solidarity, or there is a difference, in which case one party to the interaction has more power than the other – higher status, greater authority, more autonomy. On the other hand, social distance refers to how close or distant the interactants are; whether the social contact is frequent or occasional, and whether the social contact encourages intimacy, or distance. Clearly, the dimensions of power and social distance frequently overlap: greater power tends to go with greater social distance. An institution which positions itself authoritatively and which limits the visitors' opportunities to interact will necessarily also imply a greater social distance between themselves and their visitors. In this way, power and social distance together begin to define the overall roles which are and can be played by institutions and visitors.[2]

The issues of power and social distance have particular manifestations in language. The major impact of power can be seen on the behavioural potential of interactants in the communication situation, and in particular, the degree of *reciprocity* in behaviour (Poynton 1989; Kress and van Leeuwen 1996). In museums, it is traditionally the institution which controls both the choice of exhibition and the manner of its display: institutions select, display and interpret. Thus, it is the institution which defines what counts as 'knowledge' or as 'information' or as a 'relevant experience'. Museums define the relevant behavioural potential for visitors, who are given the right to receive and share in this knowledge, but not to co-construct it. Visitors are thereby positioned to take up the roles defined for them by the institution, and the careful control of these processes has been clearly identified with the regulatory and pedagogic potential of these institutions (Bennett 1995). As part of these processes, it is important to note the 'fundamental lack of reciprocity' inherent in written forms of communication: 'you cannot talk back to the writer' (Kress and van Leeuwen 1996: 147). While there can be a close and 'conversational' relation between visitors and museum communicators, as visitors search to 'make meaning' from their experiences, museums nevertheless exert considerable authority over these interactions, 'through the agency of the label texts' (McManus 2000: 99–100). This agency is invoked through the roles which interlocutors adopt in communication.

How is it, then, that roles are actually conveyed in language? In fact, of all the possible roles which can be taken up in communication, they can all be connected to just four primary roles (Halliday 1994; Halliday and Matthiessen 2004). The primary roles are illustrated in Table 4.1, and depend on whether one is 'giving' something to the other interactant, or 'demanding' something of them, and whether one is dealing with 'information' (linguistic matters), or with 'goods and services' (behavioural matters).

To give information means that one speaker or writer 'hands it over' to the other – we make statements, in written or spoken form. Most of this book is

Table 4.1 Basic speech roles

Speech roles	Giving	Demanding
Information	*Statement* Lava solidifies quickly.	*Question* What is the Universe made of?
Goods and services	*Offer* Would you like to take this home?	*Command* Touch the screen

Adapted from Halliday and Matthiessen 2004; Eggins 2004

in this form. By doing this, we take up a role in the communication. At the same time, we create a role for others: the appropriate response to a statement is to *acknowledge* it ('Lava solidifies quickly.' 'Ok; yeah; that's interesting'). Thus the speaker/writer takes up a fundamentally authoritative role, and is in control of the communication. On the other hand, when we ask questions, the roles shift. While the speaker/writer is still in control, as it is they who ask the question, the other interactant is now invited, and expected, to respond in a much more active way ('What is the Universe made of?' 'I don't know really; atoms?'). So the other interactant is now explicitly included in the co-construction of the communication. Similarly with 'goods and services' – that is, exchanges about material, not just linguistic, matters.[3] When these are given, there is a role for the other interactant, but it is more or less just to accept ('Would you like to take this home?' 'Yes please!'); when goods and services are demanded, the other interactant is expected to explicitly respond through their actions ('Touch the screen.' 'Sure; ok!')

Thus the roles that 'demand' enable more explicit responses on the part of the other interactant in the communication. They enable greater reciprocity and decrease the power differences between the interactants, because the other party to the communication is invited to respond. At the same time, the roles which are concerned with material, rather than linguistic matters, enable more physical responses. This is why questions and commands are so favoured as ways of engaging attention in otherwise static museum texts – because they invite more explicit or more physical responses, and represent a more explicit degree of interaction.

Because of their impact on roles and relations, questions and commands are typically identified as being a feature of 'good' writing practice in museum contexts, and they certainly have a number of important features. Questions and commands relate to a number of interactional goals for labels, for instance, in that they 'focus attention to particular ideas or features of exhibit content' and 'encourage active attention to exhibit content (Screven 1995: 102–103; see also Ferguson *et al.* 1995). Further, questions can add to the intrinsic incentives for reading, as they contribute to 'mindfulness' on the part of visitors, and provide a context for understanding (Screven 1995: 101, 111; Hirschi and Screven 1996).

Interactive devices such as questions and commands are not, however, inherently 'good'. Commands can be responded to negatively (McManus 2000), and throwing in a question here and there is not necessarily always appropriate, is it? Also, as questions predict answers, those predictions need to be followed through – that is, answers must be provided (Screven 1995). Indeed, because questions do predict answers, they can be effectively used as a structuring device in text, predicting forthcoming information and text structure (Ferguson *et al.* 1995), and in this regard, they complement other organisational features of text, as discussed in Chapter 2. This draws attention to the special nature of questions in museum texts: in the majority of cases, the expected response is provided not by the *visitor*, but by the subsequent *text*. It is the visitor's 'absence' of response which is supposed to provide the motivation for reading further (Museum: 'What is the Universe made of?' Visitor: 'Well, I've got no idea actually!') It is the potential for a response from the visitor which makes such a device more engaging, but the actual response needs to be provided elsewhere, in order for the communicative 'exchange' to be complete. In addition, while questions are a way of inviting a more overtly interactive relationship, because the visitor is invited to respond, questions are also a means of controlling that relationship: it is the person posing the question who decides what the question will be about, and hence, how attention will be focussed.

In order to be successful, questions must be relevant to the needs and interests of visitors, must be based on formative evaluation, and must interact effectively with exhibit content (Screven 1995). They need to be used sensitively, in relation to a number of other contextualised variables. In Plate 4.1, a question is used to engage visitor's attention, 'Now what does Prehistory mean to you?' and to provide a scaffold for the remainder of the exhibition, which aims to show that a knowledge of prehistory is relevant in a number of different ways to contemporary life. However, the general nature of this question (potentially applicable to any subject matter – 'What do volcanoes/fashion/dinosaurs mean to you?') and the likelihood that the majority of visitors would not, in fact, have any great knowledge of Prehistory, means that this is a potentially empty prompt, and could even evoke a negative response ('it doesn't mean anything to me, actually'). Thus, questions are not on their own a 'magic solution' to facilitating interaction, and this exhibit has in fact since been replaced. In the same way, there is nothing inherently 'bad' about statements; the text above from the Tasmanian Aboriginal Centre ('We do not choose to be enshrined in a glass case . . .', p. 73) shows a text using statements precisely to validate the authority of its speaker – an authority which has not in the past been overtly recognised in many museum exhibitions.

Another interesting feature of the roles enacted through language is that they can be realised both directly and indirectly. Statements, questions, offers and commands are typically realised in language by particular grammatical forms, as illustrated in Table 4.2.

Table 4.2 indicates that there are typical correlations between speech functions (semantic roles) and grammatical forms; that is, a statement is usually realised by a declarative, and so on. However, the speech functions and grammatical

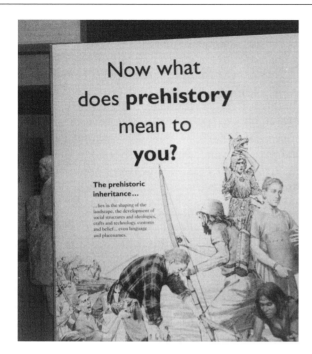

Plate 4.1
Using a Question in an
exhibition, Museum of London
(exhibit since replaced)

Table 4.2 Typical correlation between speech function and grammatical form

Typical correlations		
Speech function: semantic role	*Grammatical form*	*Example*
Statement	declarative	This is an antelope.
Question	interrogative	Is this an antelope?
Offer	modulated interrogative	Would you like to see an antelope?
Command	imperative	Don't touch the antelope!

forms do not have to correlate in this way, and interesting effects arise in the interactional framework when they do not. This is most interesting for the speech function of the command: there are many ways to get interactants to respond to our demands, other than by giving them a direct imperative. Consider the following options:

Don't touch the antelope! (imperative)
This antelope exhibit is very fragile. (declarative)
Do you think you could keep your hands off the antelope? (interrogative)

In the context of the museum, each of these grammatical forms would (or should!) be interpreted as the speech function of command. After all, the appropriate response to the interrogative 'Do you think you could keep your hands

77

off the antelope?' is not to answer the Question ('Yes, I think I could') but to actually not touch the antelope. These instances operate on two levels, and can be read in two ways: the 'literal' level of the grammar, and the 'metaphorical' level of the speech function (hence, the 'naughty' child who responds to the literal form of the interrogative, ignoring the semantic force of the command). They are indirect ways of realising the same speech function, and modify the roles and relations taken up by the interactants. The imperative form is the most direct way of realising a command, and is a direct inscription of power: one interactant tells the other what to do, and there is only one appropriate response. Declaratives and interrogatives are less direct ways of realising the speech function of command, and in effect are a way of disguising or backgrounding the power of the speaker/writer.

It is important to reflect on both direct and indirect realisations of the command, and consider whether the resulting interactional meanings are appropriate (cf. Baños 1995: 207). Let's consider two examples of indirect realisations of commands, and evaluate them, returning in the first instance to a text already seen in Chapter 2:

Genre: Procedure	**Are you a responsible cat owner?**	
typical text features	————————————————	*Actual text features*
	Do you know . . .	
commands: *imperative voice* 'desex your cat'	*Desexed cats that aren't allowed to roam live longer and are cheaper to keep.* They don't need treatment by a vet for injuries from fights or road accidents.	*statements:* *declarative voice*
'don't let them roam'	*Keeping cats at home improves relations with the neighbours.* They won't be complaining of cats trespassing on their land, scent marking, fighting and killing 'their' wildlife.	
	(and so on: text continues for 3 more paragraphs)	
	Australian Museum	

While this text is clearly trying to influence the behaviour of visitors, by encouraging visitors to be responsible cat owners, it does so by using the less direct, declarative form 'Desexed cats . . . live longer', rather than a direct imperative such as 'Desex your cat'. The indirect command creates a slight distancing effect: instead of the institution directly telling the visitor what to do, the institution 'steps back' a little, and tones their directive role down, enabling a more reciprocal role between institution and visitor to be created. The next text, 'Bones at work', also uses indirect commands, but in this case, it is less successful:

Bones at work

Different kinds of joints enable skeletons to move in many ways. As you and the human skeleton work out on the exercise bikes, you may discover which joints in your own skeleton are involved in this form of exercise.

Australian Museum

This text is positioned next to a display of two bikes, one being ridden by a skeleton, and one available for the visitor to ride. The bikes move in parallel, so the visitor can see how their bike moves in relation to the skeleton's. One of the functions of this text is to tell the reader that they can get on the bike: they are allowed to! invited to! Yet, the text is all in the declarative form ('As you and the human skeleton work out on the exercise bikes . . .'), and this indirect expression makes it slightly harder to recognise the actual function of the text. In a context where 'don't touch' is still a common feature, visitors may need to be told explicitly what they can and can't do.

Interactional choices are relevant not just at the micro-level of sentences, however, but also at the macro-level of the whole text. At the macro-level, whole texts are able to assume and construct particular social relationships, with the overall *genre* of the text constructing particular roles for both the museum and visitors (White 1994). A text with the genre of *Directive*, for instance, takes up the speech role of command, and positions visitors to respond to this command. *Exposition* and *Discussions*, on the other hand, involve persuasive argument, and position visitors to agree with a particular point of view. Of these, the Exposition is more authoritative, setting forth the author's opinion of one side of an argument, and the Discussion is more inclusive, inviting readers to share in the process of canvassing two sides of a debate. It is also possible to use these classifications in relation to a whole exhibition and the overall 'message' it constructs for visitors (White 1994). Is the major theme running through the exhibition one which aims to change behaviour, or one which canvasses information? Is the persuasion very overt, or more covert? Through the overall choice of genre for an exhibition and the texts within it, museums construct an overarching set of roles for themselves and their visitors. Consider again the entry panel (shown on p. 80) from the exhibition 'Ecologic – creating a sustainable future' at the Powerhouse Museum, Sydney, already introduced in Chapter 2.

This entry panel sets up a number of arguments (statements about the state of the environment) to build up to a persuasive thesis 'It's time to think differently and become more efficient . . .'. It is structured as an Exposition, persuading visitors through arguments. Covertly, however, this also functions as a Directive, with the ultimate aim being for visitors to change their behaviour (and not just 'acknowledge' this information as being important). Within the exhibition, a number of exhibits do just present information for contemplation (for instance, a display which explains how human activities are

---

Ecologic – creating a sustainable future

Sustainability is about the future of life on earth. It's about meeting our own needs in a way that leaves enough resources for future generations.

The environment supports us. We can't have a viable society or economy without a healthy environment.

Right now we are using up natural resources faster and faster. We are reducing the diversity of living things, and we are polluting the earth with toxins. Human population is increasing and so is the amount each of us consumes. We use energy, water and materials to make almost everything.

It's time to think differently and become more efficient about the way we use our resources. It's time to be creative and imagine our future. This exhibition shows that anything is possible . . .

Powerhouse Museum

---

changing natural flows of carbon and water in the environment), but many of the exhibits are explicitly Directive in function, suggesting that behaviour be changed in a general way (for example, that we should support sustainable systems, or use less resources, to enable more equitable wealth distribution) or in very specific ways (for example, that we should turn off switches, to use less energy). In contrast, the exhibition 'Cyberworlds: computers and connections' in the same museum, has no explicitly Directive or Expository function; its aim is to examine the interface between computers and people, and 'look at progress and where it might lead'. As a text, the exhibition is more like a Report or an Explanation – presenting information for perusal and explaining how things work. It does comment on the social significance of computers, but other than positioning the museum as an authoritative analyst of this domain, and positioning the visitor as an interested recipient of this information, it does not construct any particularly persuasive role. Thus, exhibitions vary in terms of the overall interactional roles taken up in relation to visitors, and through the range of exhibitions available within a given institution, an institution's, and its visitors', overall behaviour potential is defined through these kinds of interactional resources.

The interactional roles discussed here have focussed on relations between institutions and visitors, but there is, or can be, an additional dimension to these role relations, where there is specific inclusion of a particular stakeholder community. The relations here are more complex, and include both the ways in which the institution relates to the community, and the ways in which the community is positioned to relate to the visitor. Interactional roles, then, encompass more than just the institution and its visitors, and potentially complex relations can hold between museums and their respective communities. The complexity of these relations means that simple models of power, where the museum is positioned as the 'authority', are no longer appropriate, and we need more complex accounts of their nature and impact (Witcomb 2003).

In terms of community relations, one of the main challenges for contemporary institutions in recent years has been the appropriate acknowledgment and inclusion of Indigenous communities (see for example, Griffin 1996; Specht and MacLulich 2000; Sandell 2002; Peers and Brown 2003). In a number of instances, this concern has driven the agenda of particular exhibitions[4] and also the agenda of whole institutions, such as the Museum of the American Indian, or the Museum of New Zealand Te Papa Tongarewa, where its website declares:

> Te Papa's relationships with communities throughout New Zealand, including iwi (tribal groups) and other Maori organisations are critical to our overall success in telling the nation's stories . . . as well as to our development as a bi-cultural organisation. . . . Te Papa develops and maintains a broad range of relationships with iwi and Maori organisations, involving diverse levels of activity from both iwi and the Museum.[5]

In such cases, an understanding of relevant interactional roles needs to be expanded, to include an understanding of institutional, visitor, and community relations. This is part of the greater reflexivity demonstrated by institutions generally in the latter part of the twentieth century (MacDonald 1998). This greater reflexivity and inclusion stretches the conventional genres used for display and exhibitions, as can be seen at the Melbourne Museum, where the *Bunjilaka* Gallery '. . . is the Aboriginal Centre; its exhibitions tell stories about Indigenous people, land and law across Australia'.[6] As noted in Chapter 2, this gallery includes both conventional, institutional voices, and the actual, personal voices of Indigenous Australians, as complementary ways of interpreting the exhibition contents. For reasons of cultural sensitivity, it is not possible to reproduce the personal voices here, but their juxtaposition with conventional, institutional voices expands the interactional potential of the exhibition. Actual Indigenous knowledge is valued in this way, enabling representatives of the culture to speak for themselves, and not just be spoken about. The different interactional potentials also position visitors to engage in multiple ways with the exhibition content, thereby potentially disrupting and displacing complacent views both of Indigenous cultural knowledge and of institutional roles in relation to that knowledge. What is particularly effective about this strategy is not just that a personal voice is allowed to speak, but that that voice is positioned with and treated with authority within the exhibition. In the past, personal voices might have been used to add interest to an exhibition, but their role and content would be deemed to be less authoritative than content deriving from dominant institutional paradigms, such as scientific or historical ones. Yet the inclusion of personal voices in *Bunjilaka* is an acknowledgment that there are other ways of knowing, other than the Western scientific one, and that such views not only merit inclusion, but absolutely *must* be included.

In the context of this strategy, it becomes relevant to include a section which is literally 'voices' – videos and tape recordings of Indigenous community members, telling their stories and experiences. It also becomes relevant to challenge and critique the conventional genres of display, by, for instance, juxtaposing the nineteenth-century views of a pioneering Australian scientist,

Sir Baldwin Spencer, with those of Irrapmwe, a leader of the central Arrente people of Alice Springs from around the same time. Also, a set of filing cases are set up as if to showcase objects, but are labelled 'Restricted material', and upon opening, are revealed to be empty, with the label explaining that the contents have been returned to their owners. Such practices simultaneously critique the conventional interactional positions taken up by institutions (as the ones with the authority to possess such objects, for instance), and reflect the new interactional roles being taken up, working with the stakeholder community, and enabling visitors to engage with diverse views. Thus, the overall shift in interactional roles, in terms of the inclusion of stakeholder communities, has a concomitant impact on the genres which are deemed appropriate for conveying these new interactional relations.[7] In such ways, an exhibition like this attains a level of dialogic interactivity, and meanings are negotiated, rather than given (Witcomb 2003).

In the past, and still sometimes today, a common role for institutions to take up in relation to Indigenous knowledge and culture has been to speak 'for' the culture in question. Purser (2000) in fact castigates the Berlin-Dahlem ethnographic museum for retaining a 1970s exhibition of Indigenous Australians, which presents an outdated, social Darwinist view, whereby Indigenous Australians are represented as being 'more primitive' than other Pacific cultures. The interactional role taken up by the institution – a paternalistic, colonialist one, speaking *for* the subjects, is no longer acceptable, especially where 'those cultures exist and have at least some chance to represent themselves' (Purser 2000: 169).

Changing styles

The roles that interactants can take up are only one part of the interactional picture. The interaction which arises through communication is also affected by other factors, including the overall *style* of communication – whether formal or informal, friendly or unfriendly. The term 'style' needs to be used with some caution; in fact, any change in any aspect of communication could be said to have an impact on style, so in that sense, it is a loose term which does not carry much meaning. Here, however, I am using it in a relatively narrow way, to capture the impact of a specific set of interactional resources.

Style here refers to that continuum where communication ranges from the formal and impersonal at one end, to the informal and personal at the other. There are three key points on this continuum: the language of formal occasions, or the 'public style'; the language of everyday social interaction, or 'social style', and the language of intimates, or the 'personal style' (Kress and van Leeuwen 1996; see also Eggins 2004; Macken-Horarik 2004), each reflecting different degrees of contact between the interactants.[8]

The extremes of these styles would be exemplified by heavy, 'written' texts at one end, and chatty, 'conversational' texts at the other. Not surprisingly, the full range of this continuum is rarely found in written museum texts. Written texts in museums tend to exemplify a range somewhere between the heavy, written end, and something mid-way on the continuum: texts which are more conversational in some aspects of their style, but far from informal conversation as such. There are two reasons for this. The first is that, by presenting texts in a written form, the demands of the written Mode are so strong, that these impact on the interactional style; that is, we expect the more formal style that is normally associated with written texts. The second reason is that, as noted by Baños (1995), texts which are too familiar can be 'irritating'. Closing the distance between institution and visitor too much can create discomfort, in the same way that a stranger who behaves as if they are a close, familiar friend, can create discomfort. The ingenuine nature of such a position is all too evident to most visitors, who – as they step through the doors of the great Gothic edifices or modern architectural masterpieces of showcase institutions – are not unaware that they are stepping into sites which are specialised, elite and powerful. Such places should strive to be friendly, but do not have to be a friend. The more typical range of variation found in museum texts can be seen in these examples:

MORE FORMAL, LESS PERSONAL	LESS FORMAL, MORE PERSONAL
Hardware	**Spot Australia's Hot Spots**
Hardware is the name given to the physical components of electronic computers, such as screens, disc drives and electrical circuitry. 　The computer in its modern form was developed during and after the Second World War (1939–1945). Pre-war calculating technologies suited business and scientific requirements, but they did not satisfy the demands of the military for versatile and faster information processing. 　This was achieved by designing electrical circuitry that was the basis of a new type of machine – the electronic stored-program computer. Melbourne Museum	This map shows you where, and when, eastern Australia's main 'hot spot' volcanoes were active. 　As Australia moves northwards with continental drift, over stationary 'hot spots', you can see that volcanoes burst into life where weaknesses in the crust passed the hot zone. 　These particular hot spots possibly formed beneath the floor of the Coral Sea 65 million years ago. Australian Museum

Here, the more formal text, while quite impersonal, is by no means as 'heavily' written as texts can be (it avoids the extremes of nominalisation, dense nominal groups and so on that were discussed in Chapter 3). The more informal text creates a slightly closer interactional relationship with the visitor, including the visitor in the text as 'you', and so engaging their personal attention. And yet, the text is clearly not that of a personal, individual 'voice', but remains an institutional one, and so some degree of distance and formality remains between visitor and institution.[9]

These potential differences in style are created by a number of linguistic features, including some of the resources which have already been introduced in this and preceding chapters. First, the characteristic features of heavy, written texts, such as nominalisation and complex nominal groups (as discussed in Chapter 3), are associated with impersonal, formal styles, as they create lexical terms which tend to be more technical and less accessible. These create a greater distance between writer and reader, and so increase the formality. At the same time, such resources effectively remove human agency from a text, and so literally make the text less personal. Second, the interactive speech roles discussed in the preceding section, such as the use of questions and commands, tend to be perceived as less, rather than more, formal, as the greater reciprocity of roles implied by those devices coincides with greater equality, which is generally associated with less formal contexts. In addition to these resources, there are a number of other features which have an effect on interactional style, including the *grammatical voice*, type of *address*, and overall *lexical choice*.

The predominant *grammatical voice*[10] which is used has a significant impact on the style of a text. In Chapter 3, I explained that the primary function of grammatical voice – switching between the active and the passive voice – is textual; a change in voice is one way to adjust the Theme – the point of departure – of the clause. But a change in voice has other effects too. When a clause is presented in active voice, this tends to foreground human actors (where they are present); thus the text appears to be more personal, and so more informal, just because 'people' are a part of the text. When the passive voice is used, the potential arises for human agency to be backgrounded, and even omitted altogether, as illustrated in the following example.

Active voice	Early humans of archaic Homo Sapiens scavenged for food along the Thames valley. Museum of London	*Human Agent (early humans) is foregrounded.*
Passive voice (with Agent)	The Thames valley was scavenged for food by early humans of archaic Homo Sapiens.	*Human Agent backgrounded.*
Passive voice (without Agent)	The Thames valley was scavenged for food.	*Human Agent omitted.*

(And as we have noted, nominalisation achieves the same effect, as in *Scavenging occurred along the Thames valley.*)

For any one clause, the choice between active or passive voice will not necessarily have a major impact on style. But over a whole text, the predominance of one versus the other will have a major impact. A text which is predominantly in the passive voice will seem to be very impersonal, literally because there are no 'people' in it. This is why Plain English style guides advocate avoiding the passive voice altogether, because of its potential impact on the style of the text, and because in many writing contexts today, the more informal, more personal style of text is preferred. Certainly a predominance of the passive voice maximises the authority of the writer, and maximises the distance between the interactants, and this is unlikely to be an appropriate goal for any contemporary institution. However, as noted in Chapter 3, the functional purpose of the passive voice is to facilitate appropriate organisational development in a text, and so it is not necessary to avoid it altogether, nor is it appropriate to remove it randomly from a text. But it does have an impact on style.

Along with the grammatical voice of the text, another resource which impacts on style is the overall *address*, particularly in terms of the ways in which *personal pronouns* are used. In museum texts, the institution addresses groups of people; it is generally not possible to identify individuals by name ('Louise, please touch the screen') and so the resources of personal pronouns are drawn upon as the major way of achieving the appearance of individual address. A personal pronoun such as 'you' implies an immediate and close relationship, and addresses visitors as if they are individuals. Referring to them by a general term or name (such as 'visitor' or 'school children') implies a less direct, and less personal relationship (because the address is in terms of a category, which is a formal, institutional device). There are a range of ways of referring to people which reflect different degrees of distance or closeness between interactants. Similarly, there are a range of ways of referring to oneself, which reflect different relations, including the option to have an 'impersonal' voice and no reference to oneself at all! The combined address of oneself and of others constructs a particular balance of intimacy. Again, while one instance may be important, it is usually the overall predominance of a particular choice in a text which has the greatest impact on style.

Referring to self and other:	
Most personal	*We* will show *you* the secrets of the shroud.
↕	*The museum* will show *you* the secrets of the shroud.
Least personal	The secrets of the shroud are shown here.

Thus in the following text, the combined resources of referring to the visitor as 'you', and the museum as 'we' (along with the visitor), with the active verb, 'take' enable this text to engage with the visitor's own reflections on and interest in the subject matter, and reflect one of the most common resources for making a text more personal in its style, and less formal.

Mineral environments
Minerals form in widely differing environments. Various combinations of temperature, pressure and chemical elements result in about three thousand

minerals which make our planet. We now take you through some of their environments, from those that are familiar, such as caves, salt lakes and volcanoes, to some beyond your experience, deep within the earth.

Australian Museum

It is relevant to note that, because pronouns such as 'we' and 'you' refer to something (that is, they 'stand for' nouns), there can occasionally be problems in identifying what these pronouns refer to. Generally it will be presumed that 'you' is the reader, and 'we' is either the institution (as above), or the institution and visitor, as a general representation of people, as below:

Evolution is a fact

We are a result of thousands of millions of years of evolutionary change. Evolution is the process that transformed simple cells into all life forms known today. The evolutionary process is continuing. To understand how it works we must examine the nature of life itself. What things make our bodies the way they are?

Australian Museum

Sometimes, however, 'we' and 'our' can have a dangerously exclusive implication. For instance, a text which identifies a particular cultural or geographical group as the main subject, and then refers to this group with 'we', 'us', or 'our', may include some visitors in self-identification with that group, but exclude others. This can be done purposefully, with effect, as in the text 'Tasmanian Aboriginal Centre', from the Bunjilaka Gallery, Melbourne Museum, quoted earlier in this chapter ('We do not choose to be enshrined in a glass case . . .'), where the whole intention is to identify one group in contrast to others. But such effects can sometimes be unintentional, and inappropriate.

In addition to the overall grammatical voice and pattern of pronouns used, another resource which impacts on style is the overall *lexical choice*, that is, the nature of the words which are used. While there is no such thing as true synonymy between lexical items (because they all carry their own implications and associations – compare *dog, puppy, mutt, canine, hound* . . .) it is nevertheless the case that words which are generally synonymous can often be seen to vary in style, with formal and informal equivalents of more or less the same term. Again, much 'good writing' advice advocates the use of 'terms which your readers are familiar with' (see, for example, Dean 1994; Screven 1995; Bitgood 1989). This is because familiar terms suggest inclusion, rather than exclusion. Yet as with other issues of accessibility discussed in Chapter 3, it is not possible to simplistically prescribe which terms will be familiar to visitors, and which will not, largely because visitors themselves are so varied in their background knowledge and experience. However, it is possible to generalise that the more nominalised, technical terms are likely to be less familiar. It is also possible to say that sometimes, terms which are *too* familiar can be a problem: because they will be familiar *to a particular group only*. Resources which suggest familiarity and involvement are always group-specific: for instance, slang terms, abbreviations, in-group terms, will appeal to some but exclude others. Those who intimately share the same context are able to effectively use context-dependent terms defined within a local frame of reference; this is the language of 'social solidarity' (Macken-Horarik 2004). It is an effective way to invite identification, but can be inappropriate if the audience for the communication is a diverse one.

And yet, as is always the case with language, a fabulously elastic resource, the exceptions prove the rule. In the Bunjilaka Gallery at the Melbourne Museum, unfamiliar terms are foregrounded and prioritised, precisely as a way of destabilising conventional (that is, culturally dominant) visitor and institutional relations to the subject matter, Indigenous culture and society in Australia. The following simple text demonstrates this point:

> Ngalyipi palka (bark sandals)
> These ngalyipi palka were worn when crossing scorching sand dunes. They are made of fibre from the bark of a Crotalaria species called ngalyipi, a tough desert shrub.
>
> Melbourne Museum

In this text, the unfamiliar (at least, to non-Indigenous audiences), Indigenous term is given priority, using it as (grammatical) Theme for the title of the object label and for the opening clause of the text. The potential exclusivity of the Indigenous term is mediated by providing a more familiar equivalent in brackets; the Indigenous term is then used without additional mediation in the remainder of the label. By using the unfamiliar term as Theme, in the same way that any 'standard' (that is, non-Indigenous) term would be used, and by mediating the usage in the first instance, the label effectively shows that this term *should* be a familiar one, or at least, one that visitors can become familiar, and comfortable, with. In terms of style, the text is relatively formal, using the passive voice (*were worn*) and suppressing the Human Agency (who made the sandals?) While these resources make the text less personal, they also give the object the same authority conventionally accorded to other objects in other exhibitions. Here, then, it has been productive to ignore both the advice to use 'only those terms your readers are familiar with' and the advice to 'avoid the passive voice'. And while the text is not representative of 'new' institutional voices, in that it is not particularly informal, and presents as quite authoritative in its role, it is 'new' in that it uses language creatively, to reflect institutional goals in terms of constructing an appropriate interactional relationship with visitors, and demonstrating an appropriate interactional relationship with one of its stakeholder communities.

Changing stance

In the interactional framework, an important part of meaning is inserting 'oneself' into the communication process – in terms of foregrounding opinions and perspectives on the content or subject matter of the communication. This is a way of taking up a stance in relation to the communication, and the relevant continuum here is that between texts which appear to be 'objective', and those which appear to be 'subjective'.

The distinction between objectivity and subjectivity is an extremely important one in Western culture, especially in domains such as science, journalism and academia. 'Objectivity' is generally taken to mean being free of bias; being neutral, factual, unemotional, reasonable . . . 'Subjectivity' is the opposite: personal, emotive, biased, unreliable . . . It is a very strongly held belief in Western culture that language can be objective (witness, for example, the constant references in the press to 'unbiased', 'factual' reporting in journalism, and the furore when the 'opposite' is identified). And yet, as '. . . part of a larger academic questioning about our assumptions in every major discipline' (Serrell 1996: 11), it is now recognised that there is simply no such thing as actual objectivity. All communication involves selection, interpretation, a point of view: meaning can only be made in relation to other possible meanings, and so it is always relative. So how is it that such a strongly held belief about objectivity has taken sway?

At issue is the *apparent* objectivity of texts. While no text is, or ever can be, actually 'objective', many are dressed up as if they are. There are conventionalised ways of making meaning which have become accepted as the 'objective' way of speaking. Martin (1989) traces this back to a split in Western culture between reason and emotion: texts which are neutral, that is, which do not explicitly foreground emotion and subjectivity, are considered to be 'reasonable'; texts which are explicitly emotive, are considered to be less reliable. Thus, by drawing on conventionalised ways of hiding subjectivity, a text can be presented and accepted as if it is objective. Compare the 'objectivity' of the following texts:

'OBJECTIVE'	'SUBJECTIVE'
Hardware	**Stilled Lives** by Janet Laurence
Hardware is the name given to the physical components of electronic computers, such as screens, disc drives and electrical circuitry. Melbourne Museum	. . . I wanted to create a cosmos, a panoramic work of great diversity. Drawing connections across cultural and natural objects, I am referencing the past while transforming it into a contemporary present. Melbourne Museum

The subjectivity of the second text above, on the right, is very clear: it is a personal, individual voice, speaking about their own desires and actions. The first text, on the left, is more objective in its stance. If, however, there is no such thing as a truly 'objective' text, what is it that makes the first text (a) appear to be objective and (b) actually subjective? The text appears to be objective because it adopts an impersonal, institutional voice: it has the authority of 'everyone' concurring with the content. In addition, the content is presented as an uncontested fact ('hardware is the name given . . .'). These are devices, then, for making the text *appear* to be objective. Implicitly, however, the text is still subjective for a number of reasons. In the first instance, the content is selective: to choose to write about this, rather than another topic, represents a meaningful choice. The very selection of this topic as subject matter constructs and gives value to that topic; those who have made the selection are invoking their subjectivity in this way. At the same time, the text appears to be objective because it represents a point of view with which most people would concur: of course, this is obvious, how could there be any other way of talking about this subject matter? With such a neutral subject matter as electronic hardware, it is hard to see how this text could be said to be subjective – the subject matter does seem 'obvious' and 'natural'. But imagine an alternative perspective, a parallel universe, where the 'facts' here would be quite contentious, and where an alternative version of the text might read something like: 'Electronic hardware is a burden on the environment.' An alternative version reveals the subjectivity of the otherwise uncontentious original. With more obviously contentious topics, where alternative points of view are more evident (such as those involving a contentious scientific advancement, or different versions of an historical event), it is easier to interrogate the apparent objectivity of the text. In the end, however, the only objectivity that there is is just that, 'apparent'. All texts are subjective, either explicitly or implicitly so. Thus, what is generally accepted as 'objective' texts are those where the subjectivity has been hidden, or where the point of view presented is not disagreed with, and so is not noticed as being 'a point of view'.

A range of resources enable a text to take on an *implicitly* subjective, or 'objective' stance, some of which we have already encountered. Instead of using personal pronouns, an institutional voice is assumed, using third-person reference, the passive voice, and nominalisation, as ways of removing human agency from the text. Two additional types of resources contribute importantly to the explicit or implicit subjectivity of the text: the first of these is *modality*, a range of resources for presenting information as 'factual' or as 'negotiable'. The second of these is *Appraisal*, a range of resources for including evaluation and attitude in a text. I will deal with each of these in turn.

Modality: a resource for softening and negotiating claims

Modality is a resource for introducing the negotiability of facts. Statements like 'lava solidifies quickly' or 'lava does not solidify quickly' are different statements of fact (one positive, one negative). But they are both represented as facts. They can be rejected outright ('That's not true') but otherwise do not allow for any negotiation. Museums are often in the difficult position of trying to convey factual information, and yet recognise that many 'facts' are open to negotiation. Statements such as 'Lava may solidify quickly' or 'Lava should solidify quickly' or 'Sometimes lava solidifies quickly' all introduce a speaker angle in relation to the facts. Traditionally this has been explained as a lack of 'certainty', that the speaker is not sure of the facts. More recently, however, this speaker intrusion has been re-explained as a form of negotiation: the speaker is positioning themselves in the semantic space, allowing for the 'fact' in question to be negotiated or disputed (White 2003; Martin and Rose 2003). It's useful to think of modality as a way of 'softening' or 'modifying' claims. Modality can apply to all of the speech functions introduced earlier in this chapter. When it applies to statements or questions, it conveys meanings of *usuality* or *probability*: *it might fracture*. When it applies to commands or offers, it conveys meanings of *obligation* or *inclination*: *you should desex your cat*. Both types of modality can occur with different values or degrees of strength: from high, to median, to low. Thus, *the rocks might/may be 1000 years old*; *You may/should/must stop that*![11]

Modality is expressed by a variety of linguistic resources, including modal verbs (*can, may, should, will, must, might . . .*), modal Adjuncts (*perhaps, possibly, probably . . .*), and other expressions which carry the same values, such as expressions of time (*sometimes . . .*) or belief (*I believe, it is believed that . . .*). Some expressions of modality foreground the subjectivity at stake, as when the source of the modality is explicitly identified: '*American Indians believed that . . .*'. Other expressions of modality are more implicit, and make the stance seem more objective, as when the 'institutional' voice speaks: '*It is believed that . . .*'. The following examples illustrate a few of these resources in play.

Inserting modality into a text		Modal value
Modal verb: obligation	For too long we have measured the country's wellbeing by its economic growth, which is just a measure of money exchanged. There are other measures which *should* be added, which recognise the value of our environmental and social wellbeing. Powerhouse Museum	*Median*
Modal adjunct: probability	The minerals of the Consols Mine were different to the Broken Hill ore body. They were rich in silver and were *probably* part of a younger geological process. Australian Museum	*High*
Modal metaphors[12] *Modal verb: probability*	The converging black and white stripes on the thorax and the two black 'eye spots' *are thought* to imitate a zebra mouse, a rodent of similar size that exists in the same habitat. *It is thought* that this mimicry *may* offer the beetle some protection from predators. Natural History Museum, London	*Low*
Interrogatives (explicit interaction); modal auxiliary	*A market centre?* The large, defended site at Uphall Camp *may* have acted as a local market centre in the 2nd-1st centuries B.C. Excavations have revealed circular houses, granaries and traces of ironworking. *Are other, similar sites awaiting discovery?* Museum of London	*Low*

Text examples without modality are presented as factual, and non-negotiable. It's interesting that this is how the potentially contentious topic of Evolution is introduced at the Australian Museum, Sydney:

> Evolution is a fact!

Modality is a resource then for the speaker to take up a stance in relation to the subject matter, indicating the negotiability or otherwise of facts, and potentially modifying claims. A related resource for modifying claims comes from the way in which *sources* are acknowledged. An absence of sources (as in, '*Hardware is the name given to . . .*') emphasises the 'factuality' of the Statement. Once a source is acknowledged, the writer distances themselves from the claim; this is a resource typically used by journalists to deal with difficult claims (*The Minister claimed that . . .*).[13] Interestingly in museum texts, it is most often seen in relation to the description of belief systems for particular cultures, as in:

> **Thunder Eggs and Agates**
> American Indians believed such rocks came from thunderbolts hurled from the sky by gods.
>
> Australian Museum

This attribution creates a kind of distancing effect from the actual claim in question: the writers acknowledge the belief, but do not share it. As long as such a device is applied equally to all cultures and their beliefs, it is not necessarily problematic. It only becomes problematic if the knowledge and beliefs of one cultural group are presented as factual, in contrast to the knowledge and belief of others.

Interestingly, to return to the Bunjilaka Gallery from the Melbourne Museum, cultural knowledge is presented not as beliefs at all, but as facts:

> **Mapping Country**
> Aboriginal people have detailed knowledge of the land, which is necessary for physical and spiritual well-being. This knowledge is expressed through art.
>
> Melbourne Museum

The institutional voice here, presenting Aboriginal people as 'having' and 'expressing' knowledge, gives a much stronger, factual presence than a statement such as 'Aboriginal people believe that the knowledge of the land is necessary for physical and spiritual well-being'. In this latter form, there is room to be 'distant' from the claims being made. The more factual representation is a careful way of acknowledging the significance of the claims being made; the non-negotiability of the facts here is a way of validating the cultural knowledge being represented.

Appraisal: a resource for incorporating opinion

One of the most obvious ways to incorporate opinion, evaluation, or attitude in a text, and so reveal explicit subjectivity, is to use the resources of *Appraisal*, that is, attitudinal lexis and related resources which carry some explicit attitude (White 2003; Martin and Rose 2003; see also Coxall 1991). Appraisal tends to be used to encode a point of view in one of three different ways: in terms of Affect, or emotional reactions (*the pioneers were happy; children might be frightened by this*);[14] in terms of Judgements of people and their behaviour (*it was a corrupt government; he was a skilful leader*); and in terms of Appreciation of the aesthetic qualities of objects or things (*it's an extraordinary building*). All of these may be either positive or negative in value, and such lexical items reveal the speaker's stance towards the subject matter.

It might be anticipated that some subject matter is more likely to be appraised than others, such as more personal topics, where explicit subjectivity could be anticipated. But surprisingly, Appraisal is often found in relation to less personal topics, as in the following:

Secondary Minerals
Weathering has corroded the top of the primary ore body forming an *unusually* deep gosson. *Spectacular* Secondary Minerals grow within its network of cavities.

Australian Museum

Here, both the adjunct, *unusually*, and the appraisal item, *spectacular*, reveal the writer's evaluative stance towards the subject matter. Similarly:

Biodiversity
Biodiversity is the *rich* variety of life on earth. This exhibition *celebrates* and explores Australia's *precious* and *unique* biodiversity.

Australian Museum

Here, both Appreciation (*rich, precious, unique*) and Affect (*celebrate*) are used in this entry-level text to validate the significance of the subject matter, and to try and position visitors to share this opinion.

Interestingly, it is possible for Appraisal to be *evoked*, that is suggested, rather than explicitly *inscribed* through a particular lexical item. That is, a statement which seems 'purely' factual can be open to being read in a particular way. This is most likely to occur when a segment of text is coloured by another Appraisal value (Martin and Rose 2003). Such a pattern is illustrated in one of the examples we have seen before:

We do not choose to be enshrined in a glass case, with our story told by an alien institution which has appointed itself an ambassador for our culture.

Tasmanian Aboriginal Centre 1997,
Melbourne Museum

Here, the explicit Judgement value inscribed in 'alien' adds additional colouring to the phrase 'has appointed itself an ambassador for our culture'. That is, the latter phrase also evokes a negative Judgement. This example also highlights the fact that the values attributed via Appraisal are very much dependent both on the context of other choices in the same text, and on the reading position of the reader. 'Ambassador', for example, would normally be a term invoking positive Judgement: it is usually a respected position in society. Here, however, its value is coloured by the preceding choice of 'alien', and the compliant reader is expected to share the negative values loaded on to 'ambassador'. Appraisal values must therefore be judged in context.

It is interesting to see how Appraisal is used in an art context, where explicit evaluations might be expected. Consider the following examples from an exhibition on the sculptures of Louise Bourgeois, a New York-based sculptor.[15] The examples are reproduced without their original context, but each comments on some aspect of the artworks in question.

> the prominent eyes search for truth . . .
> the glass in its transparency hides nothing . . .
> (this work). . . is a metaphor . . . for the fragility of the quest for knowledge, for
>   certainty . . .
> (Nature Study) asserts simultaneously the power of the mother . . . and the sexual
>   potency of her mate . . .

In these examples, there are some explicit inscriptions of Appraisal, such as 'prominent' and 'transparency' (which are both examples of Appreciation). More interesting, however, are the implicit values, which can be attributed to the examples as a whole. Each example, at least in my reading of them, evokes Judgement values. The art works are attributed with positive evaluations of socially significant human behaviour: to have great tenacity or resolve, to be truthful, to be very capable. In this way, the art is given social significance within the broader culture. The art is, after all, just an assemblage of objects and shapes: but as art, it has so much more value. To say so directly, however, would sound almost silly in this context: 'This is a very important artwork because . . .' The more implicit Judgements give an air of apparent objectivity to the texts, while encoding an actually subjective point of view.

Conclusions

Interactional meanings in museum texts encompass a number of different aspects: interaction can be interpreted in terms of the roles that are created for and may be taken up by institution, by visitors, and also by other groups implicated in museum interactions; in terms of the overall style of communication, and in terms of the overall stance presented towards the information or knowledge being conveyed. These resources, while addressed separately here, work together, to create a framework within which institutions position themselves and others, evoke attitudes and construct personas. Such interactional meanings are conveyed by a variety of linguistic resources, and tend to represent continua or gradations of meaning, rather than clear-cut categories. The relation of museums to their audiences is one of the key defining features of the 'new' museology, and thus, some understanding of this framework is central to understanding and evaluating how these relations can be played out. The potential stance which is taken up in relation to knowledge is no longer exclusively an 'objective' one, but includes more explicitly subjective voices. Indeed, critical reflection must reveal that 'objectivity' can only ever be a myth. The predominant style has shifted away from one which is associated with heavily written, technical texts, that is, an impersonal and formal one, to one which is more personal and informal, albeit not a conversation as such. Overall, roles for visitors and institutions have shifted to include more reciprocal relations, where visitors are invited and enabled to engage more actively in communication processes. However, it must be remembered that actual power still lies with the institution,[16] and there is thus an obligation to treat this power with respect and understanding.

The interactional framework is one aspect of meaning-making in museum texts. As with each of the communication frameworks proposed in this book, it operates in conjunction with the others, and interactional effects can be seen as a result of choices in other frameworks. For example, a text which is organised in such a way as to be a highly written, highly complex text necessarily has a different interactional impact on visitors than one which is organised to be more like a spoken text. Similarly, and as we will see in the next chapter, a text which is constructed to represent a particular view of history interacts with visitors by positioning them to accept that point of view. Thus, the frameworks are intertwined; I have focussed on the interactional one here in some isolation, in order to draw attention to its main variables, and the main resources for achieving interactional meanings in museum texts.

As with all the frameworks of meaning, it is important to note that any interpretation or acceptance of the choices made in the construction of a text depends on the reading position which is adopted by the visitor: meanings can be accepted, rejected, or used tactically (Cranny-Francis 1992). This is especially true of the interactional framework. Choices made to construct a text as intimate and engaging do not automatically mean that the text will be received in that way. This is because, in context, the same interactional features can be interpreted differently by the interacting participants: one may not share the type of interactional values set up by the other. What is at stake here is the deployment of resources to create certain meanings, whether or not all accept that choice.

5

Representing the world through language

Using language to portray, interpret and construct

Introduction

In their public role, the communication responsibilities of museums are very diverse, and include their role to collect, research, curate, organise and exhibit objects (Coxall 1991; Pearce 1991; MacDonald 1998).[1] An intrinsic part of this communicative process is the museums' role to *interpret* these collections: to explain what it is the objects are meant to 'say' – why they have been chosen, what they reveal, what they relate to. Objects are 'always contextualised by words' (Hooper-Greenhill 1994: 115); they *do not* speak for themselves. Museum texts have a fundamental role to play in creating a picture of the world for the museum to present, and create rich representations of what is going on:

CATERPILLARS SPIN SILK FROM
GLANDS NEAR THE MOUTH

The environment supports us.   CRYSTALLINE SILICA –
                                              QUARTZ – HAS MANY
                                              REMARKABLE PROPERTIES.

Pintupi people needed few objects for
survival in the desert.

*Arrangements of belts and pulleys like
this are known as 'line shafting'.*

Every text, as well as creating interactional relations, and as well as being organised in a particular way, also creates a representation of some aspect of the world: it is *about* something (caterpillars, Pintupi people, belts and pulleys . . .) and gives particular information about that something. These representational meanings constitute the third core framework to be addressed in this book. This aspect of meaning is closest to the traditional sense of 'content', and enables us to 'represent patterns of experience' (Halliday 1994: 106). Here we are concerned with how events are portrayed – what are the activities which are construed as taking place, and what is represented as being involved in those activities – and the implications of such choices. Representational issues will be considered here from two points of view. The first relates to questions of technicality and accuracy in representation: for institutions which are concerned with mediating a large amount of technical content, it is important that this is done successfully. The second relates to options and alternatives in representation: every story can be told in many different ways, and different representations will construct different pictures of such issues as agency, responsibility and ideology. We will see that representation is a process of active construction of meanings, rather than passive transmission of 'truth'. 'Things' may exist, but we see them 'according to what is said about them' (Hooper-Greenhill 1994: 116). Choices in the representational framework both reflect, and actively construct, the Field in the context of situation, that is, the subject matter being communicated.

Representing technical concepts

In many museum texts, an important communicative role is to use, explain and mediate technical terms and concepts, and this needs to be done in a way which accurately reflects and presents the relevant knowledge base. This is one part of the representational picture. However, it is necessary to explain here what I mean by 'accuracy'. One of the major points to be made in this chapter will be that there is no 'truth' which must be represented by texts; there is just a picture, or point of view, which is actively constructed through choices in language. Given this, 'accuracy' would seem to be a redundant concept. However, 'accuracy' as used here is *according to a given ideological perspective*, such as, a contemporary Western scientific paradigm. In the context of a particular paradigm, certain representations will be deemed to be 'accurate', and others not so. In the context of another paradigm, that which is 'accurate' will be quite different. Thus, accuracy must be judged in the context of the discursive frame of which it is a part. Generally in this chapter, when referring to 'accurate' representations of technical concepts, I will mean in relation to a standard Western scientific paradigm, as this is one of the issues of concern for museum text writers.

As one of the major goals in mediating technical concepts is also to explain them, that is, provide sufficient detail for specialist concepts to be understood by non-specialists, this goal is often seen to be in conflict with another goal for museum texts, that of accessibility. Because 'accuracy' is often presumed to be equated with extensive, technical knowledge, it is also presumed to be equated with dense, impenetrable texts. For some, this might even appear to be a virtue: the more dense and impenetrable, the more 'significant' the knowledge contained therein. 'Accessible' texts are therefore presumed to be – if not inaccurate – then at least less detailed; these are presumed to be texts which have been 'dumbed down', where the knowledge represented has been so distilled, as to no longer be of interest. Yet the apparent conflict between these goals is a false one: dense texts, full of technical details, are not necessarily more accurate; and accessible texts are not necessarily less effective in conveying detailed, accurate concepts. Indeed, as discussed in Chapter 3, MacLulich's (1994) evaluation study has demonstrated that a text which has been carefully constructed to be clear and accessible may be *more* effective in conveying the relevant technical knowledge, than a text which has a dense presentation of the scientific concepts. In MacLulich's study, visitors were asked to reconstruct the taxonomic relations from a text which attempted to explain the role of '*cartilage*' and '*bone*' in differentiating fish species. The original version of the text presented confusing relationships between the main categories, and the representational relations and thematic structures were clarified in a text revision. Based on this revision, there was an improvement of more than 30 per cent in visitors' ability to successfully reconstruct the appropriate taxonomy from the text. The more accessible text was in fact more effective in conveying the desired scientific concepts.

Indeed, many museum writers today do recognise that heavily technical texts are usually quite impenetrable: 'The use of jargon or technical terminology is generally an impediment to effective reading' (Dean 1994: 117). Writers are therefore encouraged to use language that is 'more familiar' to visitors. While I would generally agree with these points, an important corollary needs to be made: technicality is *an absolute necessity* in many museum texts. In many exhibitions, one of the major goals may be to explain particular aspects of a scientific world view; to do so without some technicality would be to distort that view. Generally, technicality should be *mediated*; that is, the technicality should be explained, not presumed. It is only when technicality is not explained, that it takes on the pejorative connotations of 'jargon'. Jargon is just the use of technicality in a way which excludes (think particularly, of computer boffins and their use of jargon!). As noted in Chapter 3, technicality itself is an important quality of museum texts. The text about 'Ngalyipi palka' (bark sandals), introduced in the preceding chapter, demonstrates that unfamiliar terms can even be used effectively to disrupt complacent world views. As such, the advice to avoid technicality in favour of more 'familiar' terms is oversimplified. Technicality is an important representational resource and needs to be understood more fully.

Technicality in the first instance mainly means use of technical terms and definitions of technical concepts. Ferguson *et al.* (1995) explain some of the more effective ways to introduce and define technical terms. Definitions can be set up in a number of ways, as illustrated in Table 5.1 overleaf.

In addition to these resources, there are a number of synonyms for the structures using 'is' or 'are' to define terms, such as 'means', 'refers to', 'indicates', 'represents', and so on (Eggins 2004). For instance:

> The species name, citrea, <u>refers to</u> the lemon color of the bird.
>
> Smithsonian, National Zoological Park

Definitions usually occur as part of a longer description, with other details of the object in question, and these additional details may serve various purposes, such as establishing the significance of the object. In the text at the bottom of p. 98, the engine in question is first described in terms of its popularity and efficiency, with the key defining information (that they 'have three cylinders and pistons') occurring in the second paragraph.

Table 5.1 Some basic ways to give definitions

Resource	Example	Notes
Use 'is' or 'are'	Goliath beetles **are** giant scarabs. Natural History Museum, London *Mucuna argyrophylla* **are** from the family Leguminosae (pea family). Natural History Museum, London The striking Black-throated Blue Warbler **is** one of the most common breeding songbirds in the . . . northeastern United States. Smithsonian, National Zoological Park	*Fixes the identity by setting up a relationship of synonymy*
Use 'is called' or 'is known as'	. . . This change **is called** *metamorphism*. Natural History Museum, London Arrangements of belts and pulleys like this **are known as** line shafting. Powerhouse Museum	*Provides a name for the element being defined*
Use juxtaposition	Habits: Feeds mostly on small plankton called copepods in the subantartic. Displays **tail fluking (tail raised out of the water), spyhopping (head raised out of the water)** and flipper waving. South Australian Museum	*Associates technical name and common name by proximity. Either can be placed first. Can be used to remind visitors of previously defined terms*

Adapted from Ferguson *et al.* 1995: 40–42

Triple expansion engine model

Triple expansion engines were the most popular and efficient steam engines of the late 1800s.

initial descriptive statement (establishes significance of object)

They were commonly used in ships until the 1950s. These engines have three cylinders and pistons. The steam passes in sequence from the smallest cylinder to the largest, driving each in turn.

Powerhouse Museum

additional descriptive details and defining information

Many definitions are more complex and require more elaborated explanations, as in this text below:

Marshall Engine

This engine was built in England by Marshall, Sons and Co. Ltd . . . *The engine is a cross-compound engine,* which means it has two cylinders laid side by side.	*initial definition*
The steam works first in the small, high-pressure cylinder and is then passed to the larger, low pressure cylinder. . .	*definition unpacked in a series of steps*

Powerhouse Museum

In this text, the engine in question is first identified as a particular type of engine; this in itself needs explanation however, as the term 'cross-compound engine' is a kind of nominalisation which gathers together a number of sequenced steps in the one name. These steps are 'unpacked' in the subsequent text, so that the term and what it signifies becomes clearer for the visitor.

Definitions and explanations apply to more than strictly 'technical' things; they also apply to abstract concepts, and generalised processes, as illustrated in these two examples.

Ecologic: creating a sustainable future

Sustainability is about the future of life on earth. It's about meeting our own needs in a way that leaves enough resources for future generations.	*double explanation of 'sustainability'*

Powerhouse Museum

Surfers

Surfing is a look, an ideology, a spiritual quest, an adrenalin rush, a cult of cool, a burst of rage, even a religion . . .	*descriptive explanations of 'surfing'*

Powerhouse Museum

Not all ways of defining technical terms are successful however, and some methods should be avoided (Ferguson *et al.* 1995). In particular, the use of '*or*' to juxtapose technical and common names can be very confusing: does it suggest synonymy, or does it suggest alternatives? The examples given in Ferguson *et al.* (1995: 42) highlight the problem very clearly:

Most Australians have skin that can't produce enough pigment or melanin to protect them from our strong sunlight.

Here, the use of '*or*' is intended to convey synonymy between the terms, but could easily be taken to indicate alternatives, that is, that the skin can produce two types of things, which is inaccurate. Better punctuation, with the use of commas, would mitigate this, but not entirely solve the problem. Contrast this with the following example:

Gamelans have no conductor, being led by a drummer or rebab player.

99

Here, the use of 'or' is intended to convey alternatives: gamelans can in fact be led by two different kinds of musicians. However 'rebab' could easily be mistaken as a synonym for 'drummer', leading to an inaccurate reading of the definition. This example could be made clearer with a more explicit clause structure, such as '. . . by a drummer or by a rebab player'.

Synonymy can also be created through juxtaposition of a nominal (noun) group with another nominal group, or with a whole clause; this is a common strategy in everyday language (as in, *The President, Mr George W. Bush*). However, because the relationship is an implicit one, by association only, it requires the reader to make the link themselves, and so can sometimes be slightly problematic. This potential problem is compounded if the juxtaposed element is brought to the front of the clause, and made dependent, as in the following examples:

> *A family business established in Italy in 1918,* <u>Fendi</u> has a reputation for high quality leathergoods and innovative fur designs.

> *Important for survival,* <u>silk</u> provides support and protection for these insects.

In both these examples, the information would be clearer if relations were spelt out explicitly: 'Fendi is a family business established in Italy in 1918, and it has . . .'; 'Silk is important for survival, and it provides . . .'

Similarly, the structure of nominal groups is often used as a way of 'squeezing in' defining details, again leading to some potentially complex structures. As noted in Chapter 3, the nominal group is an elastic and pliable resource, and as such is a creative resource for writers. It should be exploited to effect, but writers should be aware that increased complexity can be a problem. The nominal group: 'The triple expansion reciprocating marine steam engine' is one nominal group which could benefit from some unpacking! Less obviously, but equally importantly, is the following example:

> The umbrella-like swift was used to unwind wool. It was clamped to a table edge and turned as the yarn was rolled neatly into a ball.

Here, 'umbrella-like' is used to define 'swift'; this means that, on the one hand, a somewhat complex nominal group has resulted, and on the other hand, the 'defining' information is more or less 'buried' in the descriptive detail of the nominal group. If this explanation is important, it should be spelt out more explicitly, for example:

> The swift looks like an umbrella/has an umbrella-like structure . . .

One of the main problems in using definitions is balancing the conflicting goals of defining terms appropriately, and not overloading the exhibition with information. It is important to recognise which terms may indeed be 'specialised', and need explanation (often, specialists themselves are so familiar with their area of specialisation, that they have forgotten what it is like to stand outside it), and to recognise that many terms may need to be *re*-explained, as the exhibition unfolds, because visitors may not approach the exhibition in a strictly linear sequence. The direction from which a visitor approaches an exhibit, and the presumptions made about what they have read on the way, can be very important in determining the comprehensibility of the text. In the exhibition containing the swift (from the Australian National Maritime Museum, Sydney), there are in fact two texts related to the same display, but they are each approached from different directions and don't make much sense without the other. The texts in question are as follows:

Text A: Whalebone swift	Text B: Using a swift
Making this intricate and ingenious swift required the skill of an experienced scrimshander. Over 60 pieces of polished whalebone were used in this example.	The umbrella-like swift was used to unwind wool. It was clamped to a table edge and turned as the yarn was rolled neatly into a ball.

The swift in question is displayed in a circular cabinet. This cabinet stands to the right of a walkway which runs in between two related, but separate exhibitions as shown in Figure 5.1 in a schematic form. From this direction, Text A is the first text to be seen, and Text B is hidden further around to the right of the cabinet. The cabinet can also be approached from the left, if the visitor has followed a display arranged along the right-hand wall. From this direction, Text B is the first text to be seen, and Text A is hidden around to the left.

The order in which the texts is approached is important; only Text B gives defining information; Text A describes the swift as 'intricate and ingenious', but doesn't say what it is or does. In fact, when I first saw this exhibit, I approached it from the walkway, and found Text A a bit perplexing, so I moved on. Only later, revisiting this part of the museum, did I see that the exhibit was explained by another text, and so I was able to make more sense of it. Also, if approaching Text B from the wall cabinet, visitors would not necessarily expect to look for an additional text around the side to the left, and so this might be missed. So from either direction, the display is problematic, and the effect of the combined technical and descriptive information is lost. This display needs to be rethought to maximise its effect. Clearly, issues of design and the nature of the language used are intimately related, which is why the communicative frameworks need to be extended beyond language, as is suggested in Chapter 6.

Part of the solution for such display problems might be in terms of repeating important definitions at key points, either through a repetition of full examples, or through juxtaposition of common versus technical terms (as previously explained above). However, this in itself raises an additional problem, namely that of leading to information overload. Technicality is something which should

101

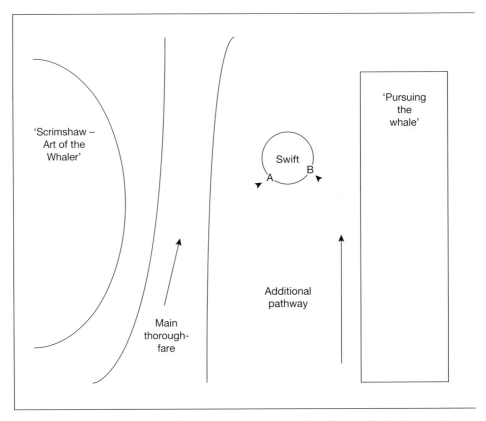

Figure 5.1 Schematic layout of 'swift' display, Australian National Maritime Museum (not to scale)

ideally be built up cumulatively – over a text or an exhibition. In fact one of the functions of technical terms in language is to act as a kind of short-hand, for longer sequences of explanations, so that the short-hand term can be used to move the text forward to other concepts (Unsworth 1997). So if individual texts and texts across a whole exhibition constantly go 'back to basics', this can interfere with the accumulation of meaning. Constant repetition of definitions may have the advantage of allowing visitors to access the texts in any order, thus not setting up any reliance on visiting in a set sequence. However, without allowing for some accumulation of meanings across the texts, the constant repetition can also be very tiring. As illustrated in the discussion of the *'swift'* example (p. 101), exhibition layout is typically not linear, and even linearly organised exhibitions can be approached randomly, so the path of access cannot be fully predicted. This means that some repetition is absolutely essential. How, then, to balance these competing pressures?

As always, there are no simplistic answers here, but there are a number of different strategies which can be deployed. One strategy is to identify the technical terms which are most important and useful in the exhibition, and to clearly explain these. These terms can thus become familiar technical terms for visitors. All other potentially technical terms are replaced with common equivalents (Hooper-Greenhill 1994: 126). In this way, the quantity of definitions is limited by limiting the number of technical terms; these particular ones can therefore afford to be repeated. Another strategy is to take advantage of more complex visual layouts of exhibition texts to separate out technical information, for example by dividing the text into two sections: the main section can contain the exhibition text, with relevant technical terms highlighted in bold (but not further explained within the text) and to the side, there are definitions of these highlighted technical terms. The placement of these explanations to the side, clearly related to but separated from the main text, enables visitors to access or ignore this information as they wish. Such a strategy is used consistently in the Queensland Museum's exhibition, 'Endangered Species', as exemplified here:

GREATER BILBY *Macrotis lagotis*
ENDANGERED (Qld) VULNERABLE (Federal)

Range The extent of the area in which an animal can be found.	PROBLEM: The Greater Bilby was once found as far east as Surat in Queensland. Its **Range** has contracted alarmingly and today a total of around 600–700 animals live in far south-western Queensland near Birdsville. Recent reports suggest that it may still survive near Cunnamulla.
	Queensland Museum

The remainder of this text highlights a number of other technical terms, such as 'habitat' and 'translocate', which are also defined to the side of the text. In this way, the technical definitions can be both easily accessed by those who are interested, and ignored by those who are not. Such a strategy effectively provides an additional 'level' of information, to be accessed as needed, and this can be an effective solution to the competing pressures of the need to define technical terms, without creating information overload (cf. the discussion of multi-level texts in Chapter 2). Practitioners in the field would be aware of many similar strategies for counter-balancing these pressures. What is important to remember, is that part of the representational picture being built up in an exhibition may be specialist in nature; as it is the responsibility of museums to mediate this specialist knowledge for the general public, ways need to be found to do this effectively, while maintaining interest in and accessibility of the information being presented.

Building up more complex representations: taxonomies

Successful explanation of technical concepts is only partially dependent on the technical terms as such. An additional part of the picture is the way technical terms and definitions build up to form more complex, holistic representations (Martin 1993). As Ferguson *et al.* (1995: 43) note:

> Scientific knowledge itself is much more than a set of technical terms. It is a way of classifying and ordering the world, of understanding how things, and classes of things, relate to each other. As such, taxonomies are an important feature of science and scientific writing.

While this quote would seem to suggest that taxonomies are relevant only to strictly 'scientific' subject matter, the issue of complex representations applies to any content area, and to all aspects of collecting and displaying 'objects'. There are intrinsic relationships between practices of collection and display on the one hand, and webs of interpretative relations on the other (Pearce 1991; MacDonald 1998). Pearce notes (1991: 137) that: 'Even the accession of a single object is perceived as part of a set, either in relationship to others of its kind or in relation to the other elements in the life history of the original owner or collector.' The process of classifying objects: '. . . transforms a "natural" piece into a humanly defined object, which is to say an artefact . . .' (p. 152). The practices of collection, interpretation and display have always been inter-related with concurrent notions of science, with, for instance, 'a particular kind of taxonomic knowledge' developing in the seventeenth century, and a flourishing of museums and exhibitions in the nineteenth century, as a '. . . key means of appreciating and "colonizing" reality' (MacDonald 1998: 6ff.). Bennett (1995: 96) notes that the development of a 'historicised' approach to knowledge was a necessary institutional condition for the development of new disciplines such as geology, biology, and art history, among others, and that a shift to more 'visible' and populist forms of classification was a key feature of the museological shift to mass education (Bennett 1998b). Thus, while literally scientific taxonomies are a key feature of the modernist museum's agenda (Witcomb 2003), a more generalised sense of intepretative relations is relevant to all museological practice.

It is important to emphasise here that, when considering museum texts, the taxonomic relationships at stake *are those constructed in and by the text*, not any 'real world' relations as such (Martin and Rose 2003).[2] This is exactly the point of Pearce's and MacDonald's observations: that it is museum *practices*, textual and otherwise, which construct what we consider to be 'science' or 'knowledge'. There are two key strategies in language for building taxonomic relations (Ferguson *et al.* 1995; Martin and Rose 2003). The first strategy is that of superordination, where one element is said to be a type or a kind of another element; this gives a relationship of a *class* to its members, or *subclasses*. These taxonomic relations are usually signalled by forms of the verb 'to be', as in:

VERTEBRATES <u>are</u> animals which have a backbone.
MAMMALS <u>are</u> vertebrates which have:
   – fur or hair;
   – milk-producing glands
   – three bones in the middle ear.

Australian Museum; cited in Ferguson et al. 1995: 44

Thus in the previous example, the major class is that of *'animals'*, of which vertebrates are a sub-class, and mammals a sub-class of vertebrates.

In addition, taxonomies can be signalled through composition relations, where one element is said to possess, or be a part of, another. These taxonomic relations are usually signalled by forms of the verb *'to have'*. Revisiting the above example:

VERTEBRATES are animals which <u>have</u> a backbone.
MAMMALS are vertebrates which <u>have</u>:
  – fur or hair;
  – milk-producing glands
  – three bones in the middle ear.

Further, taxonomic relations can be formed through repetition (where the repetition of one element enables it to be tracked through a text); synonymy, and relations of contrast (including antonymy, as well as cycles or scales of elements, such as hot–warm–tepid–cold) (Martin and Rose 2003). All of these strategies can create relations between elements within a text, building up an overall picture of the Field at stake: 'To inventory, classify and organize is to give meaning to the world' (Jacobi and Poli 1995: 68). Importantly in museum texts, however, synonymy needs to be used with extreme caution, as apparently 'obvious' synonyms may not be evident to all readers. As noted in Chapter 2, the use of synonymous items in Theme position can make it very difficult to keep track of information, and as noted in this chapter, the connection of synonyms with the preposition *'or'* can make it difficult to determine whether the terms are indeed synonyms, or whether they are alternatives.

Most important of all for museum text writers is that the taxonomic relations are clear and unambiguous. Ideally, visitors should be able to construct their own mental summary or 'picture' of the relationships at stake. The text, 'Endangered Species', illustrated overleaf in Figure 5.2, provides an effective picture of the taxonomic relations at stake.

While this text is quite clear, a hyper-Theme (cf. Chapter 2) at the end of the second paragraph, after 'conserve them', would have made the last set of relationships unambiguously clear, namely: 'Threatened species may be either *endangered*, *vulnerable* or *rare*.' Sometimes, basic taxonomic elements may be so 'obvious' to curators that they are left out, and yet, they can supply important links and relations for visitors (Falk and Dierking 1992: 75ff.).

One reason the 'Endangered Species' text is so clear, is that it carefully concentrates only on a few central ideas. The accessibility of a text (cf. Chapter 3) can be compromised if too many taxonomic relations are introduced into the one text. Consider the following example:

Mephisto
Although Britain and France developed several types of light, medium and heavy tanks during the World War I, the Germans produced only one: the A7V. The

prototype was completed and demonstrated in April 1917, but because of production delays the first operational A7V (Chassis Number 501) was not rolled out of the Daimler plant at Berlin-Marienfelde until October 1917. Only 20 A7Vs were built by the Germans, the rest of their tank force was made up of captured Allied vehicles.

Queensland Museum

In this brief text, a number of taxonomies, or parts of taxonomies, are introduced. On the one hand, there are the participants in the war: *Britain, France* and the *Germans* (and later, 'the Allies'). Then, there are the tanks: Britain and France produced several types (*light, medium, heavy*); the Germans produced only one (*A7V*). There were *operational* A7Vs, and – by implication – *non-operational* ones; they each had special numbers (such as *501*); they had *Chassis* (and by implications, *other parts*!). There is the particular plant which produced the A7V (*Daimler*) in the location *Berlin-Marienfelde* (were there other plants in this location? other locations for plants?). Finally, the structure of the last

Endangered Species	(Some) Key points	Taxonomic Relations
Queensland has many different types of native plants and animals. Each is known as a species.	Species = a type of plant or animal	Species = plant/animal
Some of our species have disappeared forever – they have become *extinct*, meaning they have not been located in the wild during the last 50 years. Others are *threatened* – they are in danger of becoming extinct if no effort is made to conserve them.	Species = *extinct or threatened*	extinct threatened endangered vulnerable rare
An *endangered* species is one in immediate danger of becoming extinct in the wild if the threats continue.	Three types of threatened species: – *endangered*	
A *vulnerable* species is one that will soon become endangered if threats to its survival continue.	– *vulnerable*	
A *rare* species is one that occurs in small numbers but is not at present endangered or vulnerable, but is at risk. <div style="text-align: right">Queensland Museum</div>	– *rare*	

Figure 5.2 Taxonomic relations in a text

clause could be taken to suggest that some AV7s were built by non-Germans ('Only 20 A7Vs were built by the Germans'), though the end of this clause suggests a different meaning (namely: *The Germans had only 20 A7Vs in their tank force; the rest of their force . . .*). In a short space of text, this is an enormous amount of information to make sense of. The text needs to be rewritten to clarify the most important elements and the relationships between them.[3]

As already noted, one of the most important things to understand about taxonomic relations, is that they do not derive 'from' any real world phenomena as such, but are our own constructions and representations of such phenomena. The text 'Mapping country', introduced in Chapter 4, shows a sensitive way of bringing together two different world-views of the one phenomenon:

Mapping country
Aboriginal people have detailed knowledge of the land, which is necessary for physical and spiritual well-being. This knowledge is expressed through art.
 – Designs mostly represent the journeys of ancestral beings. Specific symbols represent particular landscape features they created. Some symbols even represent the ancestral beings themselves.
 – In this way, designs are condensed versions of elaborate stories associated with both everyday and religious life.
 – Knowledge is the key that allows the symbols to be read, like a map.

Bunjilaka Gallery, Melbourne Museum.
(Text accompanies a map contrasting
Pintupi and Western views of country)

This text explains the central role of cultural knowledge in interpreting the stories told through the use of symbols and designs in Aboriginal art, particularly as it relates to Aboriginal use of and views of the land. Through the combined definitions of designs, symbols and knowledge, the visitor can understand some of the cultural significance of these phenomena for Aboriginal people. Importantly, however, it is the *role* of designs and symbols in relation to defining 'knowledge' which is explained, not the 'actual' knowledge itself (as this is privileged information, and is the domain of particular community members only). At the same time, these phenomena are given – through the processes of defining and taxonomising – cultural significance within a Western view as well, because these phenomena are treated in the same way that 'Western' phenomena would be. That is, the text builds a taxonomy of technical concepts: through composition ('Aboriginal people have detailed knowledge of the land . . .'), explanations ('Designs . . . represent journeys; symbols represent . . . landscape features (or) ancestral beings . . .') and definitions ('Designs are . . . elaborate stories; knowledge is the key . . .'). It would have been helpful in this text to spell out the taxonomic relations between 'art', 'designs' and 'symbols' (for example, *art is made up of designs and symbols*; or *art is made up of designs; designs are made up of symbols*, etc.), but otherwise, the text effectively gives a technical explanation of 'knowledge', in a way which is culturally sensitive to Indigenous views of knowledge, and in a way which accords with conventional Western ways of explaining complex concepts. In this way, two different world-views are brought closer together through the representational choices made in this text.

Overall: building a representational picture of the world

The accuracy and clarity of technical information is only one, fairly small, part of the representational framework. Of arguably greater importance is the overall representational picture being constructed, that is, '. . . how our experience of "reality", material and symbolic, is construed in discourse' (Martin and Rose 2003: 66). Whatever the 'reality' which exists, it needs to be communicated via language (or other symbolic means). Thus, that which is communicated is not a passive transmission of 'reality', but an active construction of it. It is an ongoing general belief about language that it somehow represents the 'truth', that language is simply a conduit for channelling pre-existing meanings, and that content is simply 'there' to be conveyed (Reddy 1979). And yet the opposite is the case: because communicating always involves making choices,[4] there are a myriad ways to represent any one 'reality' or content area, and the nature of the representation itself will reflect back on the 'reality', and actively construe it, that is, bring it into life. All levels and aspects of text reflect this case: from the selection of the name of an object . . . to the role of a whole clause construction . . . to the overall patterns flowing through a text . . . to the assemblage of individual texts into a larger communicative whole, such as an exhibition.

If language mediates and constructs reality, how is this done? While there are many resources which contribute to this, the fundamental resources are found in the way a basic clause is structured. Every clause through its structure creates some representation of reality, and it is most easy to understand this by using examples which contrast in meaning; this reveals the 'constructedness' of the representation at stake, and the way in which linguistic resources are marshalled as part of an active construction of meanings. Every clause represents some kind of 'event' going on: it may be a doing, a happening, the event may simply be a state of 'being', but something is going on. The fundamental elements of a clause, as far as representational meaning is concerned, centre around the *Process*: this is the nature of the action taking place, and is realised by a *verb*. The Process may be quite a concrete sense of action, it may reflect emotional happenings or aspects of cognition, and it may represent states of 'being'. Following are some clauses with Processes highlighted.

> Caterpillars <u>spin</u> silk.
> The environment <u>supports</u> us.
> <u>Do</u> you <u>like</u> spiders?
> Arrangements of belts and pulleys like this <u>are known as</u> 'line shafting'.
> Crystalline silica <u>has</u> many remarkable properties.
> Cells <u>are</u> tiny individual units.

In addition, every Process is brought into being by some kind of *Participant* – a thing or element which is involved in the Process, either being responsible for the Process taking place, or being affected by it in some way. Participants are usually realised by nouns or nominal (noun) groups, and there may be one or more than one Participant in a clause, as highlighted again here:

> Caterpillars spin silk.
> The environment supports us.
> Do you like spiders?
> Arrangements of belts and pulleys like this are known as 'line shafting'.
> Crystalline silica has many remarkable properties.
> Cells are tiny individual units.

Together, the Process and Participant construct the basic structure of the clause. Another element, the *Circumstance* can provide additional information about where, when, why or how an event took place, as highlighted in the following example. This is an optional element in a clause, in that not every clause needs to include circumstantial information, but when it is included, it adds crucial details to the overall picture. There may be no, one or more than one Circumstance/s in a clause.

> Caterpillars spin silk from glands near the mouth.
> Every offspring receives a combination of DNA from both parents.
> People walked across / from the Continent / nearly half a million years ago.

What is most interesting for museum texts about the fundamental structure of the clause, as constructed by the Process and Participant/s involved in the Process, is the way in which issues of Agency and Responsibility are conveyed. Who caused the Process to happen? Did it happen by itself? Was anyone or anything affected by the Process? As well as representing different kinds of actions (more concrete, cognitive, states of being, etc), Processes can be grouped into two different types dependent on the way in which responsibility is constructed in the clause, in terms of whether the Process is brought about 'from within', or 'from without' (Halliday 1994: 162). Where the Process is brought about 'from without', there is a sense of someone or something 'causing' the Process to happen, and thus creating a definite sense of responsibility for the action.[5] With these examples, it is then interesting to see what *roles* are ascribed to Participants: were they the Participant responsible for causing the action to happen? is this mentioned explicitly, or merely implied (for example, with the passive voice)? Were there other Participants affected *by* the action? Where the Process is brought about 'from within', the action seems to happen 'by itself'; there is a Participant which is part of the action, but not a cause of it as such. The examples on p. 110 highlight this difference.

In such ways, interesting – and potentially controversial – patterns of meaning can be established in a text, in terms of the nature of the action which took place, and the roles which Participants are ascribed in relation to those actions. Consider also the texts A, B, C and D that follow, and the way different views are created of Indigenous history in Australia.

Event 'A': two Participants	Europeans *invaded* Australia.	Responsible Participant foregrounded (active voice)
	Australia *was invaded* by Europeans.	Responsible Participant backgrounded (passive voice)
	Australia *was invaded*.	Responsible Participant omitted, but still implied (passive voice)
Event 'B': one Participant (*in Australia* is a Circumstance)	Europeans *arrived* in Australia.	No 'responsible' Participant; the event 'just happens'

A When Europeans arrived, the way of life of the Warlpiri people was changed.
The best land was taken over by Europeans for cattle and sheep and the
Aborigines had only the desert land to live in.
In 1928, a severe drought forced Warlpiri people from the desert. Some tried to
get food and water on the better land and fights broke out. A large group of
Warlpiri people were killed by Europeans. The Warlpiri refer to this as the Killing
time.

Australian Museum; cited by Ferguson et al. 1995: 7

B Driven back to the most barren lands or crammed into slums on the outskirts of
cities, the Aborigines were subjected to a terrifying policy of 'assimilation' which
involved kidnapping children to make them better 'integrated' into European
society. At the end of the 1960s the nomadic Aborigines were herded by force
into communities.

Le Monde[6]

C Pintupi people needed few objects for survival in the desert, relying instead on
their extensive knowledge of the country, its food and waters. These objects all
had a specific purpose and were being used at the time of the first contact with
Europeans in the 1950s.

Melbourne Museum

D We do not choose to be enshrined in a glass case, with our story told by an alien
institution which has appointed itself an ambassador for our culture.

From the Tasmanian Aboriginal Centre 1997,
exhibited at the Melbourne Museum

Each of these extracts represents a different view of Indigenous history in
Australia. Text A, from a now-dismantled exhibition *Aboriginal Australia,
1985*, was reasonably progressive for its time: it acknowledges the violence
perpetrated against Aborigines, and seems to offer a sympathetic point of view.
However, there are some interesting representational patterns in this text. While

'Europeans' are foregrounded thematically ('when Europeans arrived'; cf. Chapter 2), their actions are presented as either 'just happening' (they 'arrived'), or are 'softened' by being presented in the passive voice ('the best land was taken over by Europeans'; 'a large group of Warlpiri people were killed by Europeans'). The Warlpiri people are constructed as being acted upon by other people and things ('a severe drought forced Warlpiri people from the desert'; 'a large group of Warlpiri people were killed by Europeans') or else as participating in actions which are not very effective ('Some tried to get food and water'). A number of actions are presented as 'just happening' ('fights broke out'; 'the Aborigines had only the desert land'). Thus while the violence against Aborigines is acknowledged in this text, the extent of the Europeans' responsibility for this is slightly diffused, and a picture is built up whereby Aborigines are powerless (Ferguson *et al.* 1995; compare also with a similar text discussed in Purser 2000).

Text B also backgrounds the grammatical responsibility – there is no mention in this extract of who is responsible for the actions at stake, although this is clearly implied. The power of Text B comes from its uncompromising choice of Processes: 'driven back'; 'crammed'; 'subjected to'; 'kidnapping'; 'herded'. These are all Processes which imply two active Participants, and it is clear here who is 'the doer' and who is 'the done to'. Other lexical choices add to the overall picture here: 'barren lands'; 'slums'; 'a terrifying policy' – all choices carrying negative Appraisal (cf. Chapter 4).

In contrast, in Text C, Aborigines are presented as being in active control of their world: 'Pintupi people needed few objects'...; 'relying instead on their extensive knowledge of the country . . .'. This active view is enhanced by the discussion of the objects, which 'had a specific purpose' and 'were being used . . .'. The issue of arrival/invasion is defused by the representation 'the time of first contact'.

In Text D, the use of the first person voice, 'we', and a negative process, 'do not choose', creates an even more active representation of Indigenous cultures. In this brief extract, the 'activity', or power, of the 'alien institution' is negated; the alien institution can no longer tell 'our story' or 'appoint itself ambassador' for the Indigenous culture.

Even in very brief extracts, then, it is evident that vastly different pictures of the 'same' subject matter can be created. Such representational meanings have their greatest impact when considered across a whole text, for it is in a sequence of clauses that the most interesting patterns are found: overall, what types of actions are there? what Participants are involved? what roles do they take up in relation to the actions and the other Participants? It is the accumulation of meanings which carries weight. Of course, representational meanings are also conveyed not just by grammatical structures as such, but simply by *words*, that is, lexical items. Every lexical item carries with it many associations, and will contribute to the overall ideologies and attitudes conveyed in a text. To *kidnap*, for example, carries with it connotations of criminal activity, whereas another verb, such as *take*, does not. Those who live in a *ghetto* will be judged to be different from those living in *lodgings* (Coxall 1991). The choice of words can have a powerful impact on a text, and this needs to be considered as part of the representational picture, for 'a way of saying is also a way of seeing' (Coxall 1999: 215).

Overall, then, representational meanings are constructed through the lexical and grammatical choices made in individual clauses; the accumulation of meanings across clauses in a text builds up a particular view of the subject matter at stake. Where this subject matter involves ongoing contestation in everyday lives, the various possibilities are bound to be controversial, for representational meanings are as interesting for what is *not* included, as for what *is* included. Wherever there is uncertainty over the representational meanings in a text, writers only need to imagine what they *could* have written, in order to understand the significance of what they *have* written. It is the ability to recognise the omissions and alternatives, which enables the recognition of the constructedness of meanings (Coxall 1991). This is true for all the frameworks, but is particularly pertinent for the representational framework. One of the most well-known controversies in museum practice is that of the controversial *Enola Gay* exhibition at the Smithsonian in 1995 (Wallace 1995; Luke 2002), which related to the use of the *Enola Gay* to drop an atomic bomb on Japan in the Second World War. Controversy over the exhibition arose largely because there were two key stakeholders with vastly different experiences of the subject matter: the victims of the atomic bombing of Japan in the Second World War, and those who fought in the war, with the exhibition timed to coincide with the 50 year celebration of the end of the war (Serrell 1996: 6). 'Balancing' such opposing views is a near-impossible task (Gieryn 1998), and reveals the power of the representational framework when it intersects with contested histories. In Australia, the new National Museum in Canberra has attracted considerable controversy for its representation of Indigenous history, precisely because the Museum has foregrounded a view of Indigenous history which has been conventionally suppressed. For some stakeholders, this is a radical position to take, and so they can therefore accuse the Museum of being 'political' or 'biased'. Of course, apparently 'conventional' texts and approaches are equally biased, but have tended to be received in contexts which have not questioned the points of view presented therein. Such domains, where ideologies have been or are in conflict, foreground the constructedness of meanings, because they highlight the fact that choices have been made in the representation of the subject matter: 'The public imag(in)ing of the past is a contested area' (Hooper-Greenhill 2000: 8). Certain constructions make sense within a given discursive frame, resonating and interconnecting with a complex set of related choices, all combining to create a dominant framework of understanding. When that framework is not universally shared, the disparities, elisions, and contradictions of the different approaches become transparently clear.

However, it is not just 'obviously' controversial issues which are interesting in terms of the representational framework. Every clause and every text constructs representational meanings; even apparently mundane choices contribute to an overall picture, and are interesting for the choices that have (and have not) been made. Consider the many exhibitions taking place around the world on the 'same' topic – such as Dinosaurs, or Whales, or Evolution, or Steam Engines. While all the exhibitions on the 'same' topic might overlap to some degree in their content, none will be identical. Not only will there be some difference in the 'facts' which are conveyed, the overall picture of what Dinosaurs (or Whales or . . .) 'are' will be different. The following snapshots from a range of exhibitions on dinosaurs give some indication of this potential variety:

Triceratops Horridus

This skeleton measures 17 feet from nose to tip of tail. It is the world's first Triceratops skeleton ever mounted.

It is a composite exhibit mount consisting of bones from seven individuals.

This specimen was put on exhibit in the Smithsonian's Arts & Industries Building in 1905. Triceratops was an herbivorous or plant-eating dinosaur that lived during the Cretaceous Period of geologic time, over 65 million years ago. Its large horns were probably used for defense and sexual display. It was one of the last surviving dinosaurs of the Age of the Reptiles.

National Museum of Natural History, USA

Velociraptor

Taxonomy: Saurischia, Theropoda, Maniraptora, Dromaeosauridae, *Velociraptor*
Type species: *mongoliensis*
First described by: Osborn (1924)
Period: *Upper Cretaceous*
Time span: 84–80 mya
Length: up to 1.8 m
Diet: carnivorous
Found in: *Mongolia*

Natural History Museum, London

Mission Infossible

An evil empire, led by Professor Needle, is creating counterfeit fossils to confuse palaeontologists, museums and the public. Discover how Dr. Briggs and his team of palaeontological experts dismantle this fossil factory and bring the evil-doers to justice. In this 30-minute theatrical production filled with mystery, suspense and action, you will learn about fossils and their scientific value.

Royal Tyrell Museum/Alberta Community Development, Canada

More than dinosaurs: the evolution of life

How did life begin? How have changes to the earth affected the history of life? What other living things besides dinosaurs have become extinct? *More than Dinosaurs: evolution of life* explores these questions and more. The exhibition shows how evolution and extinctions have shaped the history of life on earth.

Australian Museum

113

These texts come from a range of exhibitions, as well as a range of places within exhibitions. 'Triceratops Horridus' and 'Velociraptor' both pertain to specific exhibits, but the former is a descriptive text, the latter an object label. 'Mission Infossible' is an introduction to a theatrical production about dinosaurs and palaeontology, while 'More than Dinosaurs' is the introductory panel to a whole exhibition. While no single text can be taken to be representative of any one exhibition, this small sample nevertheless gives an indication of the range of ways in which the 'same' subject matter can be treated. Representationally, they are all quite different.[7] 'Triceratops' focusses on three core areas: describing the skeleton on display ('This skeleton measures . . .'; 'It is the world's first . . .'), classifying Triceratops in scientific terms and describing its features and behaviour ('Triceratops was . . .'; 'Its large horns were probably used . . .') as well as drawing attention to the nature of the display itself ('It is a composite exhibit . . .'; 'This specimen was put on exhibit . . .'). 'Velociraptor' provides (at least in this extract) only 'scientific' information; its grammatically truncated form is familiar from traditional practices of taxonomic object labelling; the information given classifies in strictly scientific terms: 'Saurischia'; 'mongoliensis'; 'Upper Cretaceous', and with definite, if not precise, details: '84–80 mya'; 'up to 1.8m'. In stark contrast, 'Mission Infossible', from its playful title on, provides an imaginative, as opposed to a scientific, view of dinosaurs, using this to engage audiences in a world not of scientific facts and labels, but of 'goodies' and 'baddies' ('An evil empire is creating . . .'; 'Dr Briggs and his team bring the evil empire to justice . . .'). Of course, this device is used as a lure, with the intention that 'you will learn about fossils and their scientific value'. The lure in 'More than dinosaurs' is a set of questions designed to pique visitors' interest; importantly, these questions are not just about dinosaurs, but about questions of life, evolution, and the role extinction, including that of dinosaurs, has played in 'the history of life on earth'. Thus while this exhibition may include a range of 'facts' about dinosaurs, the introductory text makes it clear that these facts will be related to larger issues, 'life', 'changes to the earth', 'other living things besides dinosaurs'. In all of these examples, it is the combination of particular Participants ('life', 'an evil empire', 'Saurischia', 'an herbivorous or plant-eating dinosaur') and particular Processes ('begin', 'affected', 'creating', 'dismantle', 'measures', 'is') as well as absence of Processes in 'Velociraptor', which creates these 'pictures'. There is no given set of factual 'truths' about dinosaurs which must be conveyed; nor is it the case that there is one enormous 'pool' of information and that any one text/exhibition is just a selection from it (and hence following that logic, that each of these texts just represents different parts of the same 'pool'). Rather, the picture that is constructed, the 'facts' (or fantasy) that are conveyed, are made manifest by linguistic choices, and these choices actively construct a picture of what the subject matter 'is'.

Even within *one* exhibition, the 'same' subject matter might be approached in a number of different ways. An exhibition on sharks, for instance, might cover their scientific classification, their role in ecology, their mythical status in popular culture, even their economic role (White 1994). The different perspectives which emerge clearly need to be related to the overall objectives of the exhibition. As part of this, there are important correlations between a given perspective on a subject area, and the genre of the texts chosen to interpret the exhibition. As introduced in Chapter 2, the genre of the text guides its overall purpose, and in Chapter 4, the relationship between genre and interactional relations was discussed. In terms of the representational framework, certain genres tend to privilege certain representational constructions. For instance, if the purpose of the text is to classify and describe, the Processes of 'being' are likely to predominate (as in 'Triceratops <u>was</u> a plant-eating dinosaur'); if the purpose of the text is to tell a story, then more action-oriented Processes are likely to predominate (as in 'Dr Briggs and his team <u>dismantle</u> the fossil factory'), and so on. However, the relationship goes both ways, that is, the selection of the representational choices (Process, Participant and Circumstance) will contribute to the overall genre of the text. For instance, if there are a lot of action-oriented Processes, the text will be more likely to function as a narrative, and if there are a lot of 'being' processes, the text will be more likely to function like a classification or description. Thus, the genre influences the representational meanings, and the representational meanings contribute to the genre. Not all genres are equally appropriate to meet a certain objective, however. Narratives might be fun and engaging, and hence useful for that reason, but they are not necessarily effective in conveying complex scientific information: some types of text '. . . can introduce simplistic effects that may impoverish the scientific discourse' (Decrosse and Natali 1995: 168; see also Serrell 1996; Martin 1993). It would be interesting to explore the relationship between genre and representational choices further, for instance by surveying the dominant generic choices in exhibitions, and their co-patterning with representational meanings. The dominant generic choices in the design of exhibitions are explored further in Chapter 6.

In many cases, as noted at the beginning of this chapter, there is widespread agreement as to what constitutes an appropriate representation of a particular subject area. This does not mean that alternatives are not possible, but that from the point of view of a given paradigm or ideological framework, alternatives are deemed to be inappropriate. For example, from the point of view of contemporary science, there are some 'facts' about evolution and nature, which are thought to be indisputable. It is not uncommon to see, especially in popular science books for instance, such expressions as the following[8]:

> Not all dinosaurs were huge and lumbering. Some were built for speed.
> The body of Diplodocus was designed to bear enormous weight.
> Insects evolved a system of branching tubes known as tracheae.

The particular Processes in these clauses, and the role the Participants play in them, create a view of evolution and nature which is at odds with contemporary scientific thinking. The passive constructions 'were built' and 'was designed' suggest that an external Agent was responsible for 'creating' dinosaurs in a particular way. The last example suggests that Insects were somehow consciously involved in making decisions about their development. None of these representations accord with actual scientific thinking on these topics. More appropriate representations need to avoid such implications, using other Processes, and creating different Participant roles, to achieve a different effect. For instance:

> Not all dinosaurs were huge and lumbering. Some were lithe and fast.
> The body of Diplodocus was able to bear enormous weight.
> A system of branching tubes known as tracheae evolved in insects.[9]

An interesting view of the Earth and its potential 'agency' can be seen in the following text:

> After its formation around 4,560 million years ago, *the Earth soon developed* seas, an atmosphere, and the first stirrings of life. Over time climate and sea level have fluctuated widely, but *the Earth has continued to support* a huge diversity of life, despite five mass extinctions.
>
> Natural History Museum, London

The image of the Earth 'developing' seas, atmosphere and life suggests that the Earth was responsible for these events, and may not be appropriate, from a scientific point of view. Interestingly, a slight re-structure of the clause, as in 'Seas, atmosphere and . . . life soon developed on Earth' does not have the same implications (though again there are additional implications for Theme development). Whether this view of the Earth's responsibility is appropriate or not is open to discussion; the original construction perhaps accords with contemporary ecological views of the inter-relatedness of life, and the fact (or opinion!) that the Earth is not a static, inactive resource, but an active participant in the processes of life. Again the issue is not one of correctness, but of appropriateness from a given point of view, and of sensitivity to the potential implications of particular structures.

Representational meanings need to be carefully reviewed to ensure that inappropriate messages are not conveyed. Where there is a dominant scientific paradigm, this can provide a kind of benchmark, against which the representational meanings of texts can be compared. Where scientific information is in dispute, or where the information is by nature more open to contestation and difference (where cultural knowledge is concerned, for instance), the only 'benchmark' can be explicit and open discussion about what messages are appropriate, and why. Many writing guidelines allow for varied opinion in the preparation of an exhibition, especially in the 'brainstorming' stage of developing initial concepts. But from there, texts are seen to emerge 'unproblematically', when it is the case that, even with an agreed agenda, texts can contain and produce various messages, some of them implicit. It is not a case of searching for a 'correct' representation, as that does not exist. Nor is it a case of attempting to write a text that accounts for all points of view, as that is not possible, and would no doubt produce something incomprehensible (Coxall 1991). Rather, it is a case of seeking to be aware of the significance of representational meanings, and of the way the choices in individual clauses, and patterns across whole texts, build up a picture of the subject matter at hand. It is also a case of being aware that one view of the world never accounts for all perspectives.

Given that any general subject matter can be represented in a myriad of ways, an evident challenge for museum writers is deciding *what* to write in the first place. It is not the role of this book to address this matter in detail, but the initial decisions about the scope and focus of representational meanings in a text need to be made in relation to institutional goals, exhibition objectives, the particular exhibit in question, current curatorial knowledge of the subject, and visitors' expectations and likely starting points. The latter, in particular, needs to be explicitly addressed through formative evaluation, so that texts and their representational meanings will be relevant to their audience. Visitors may be seeking information which is different from what curators might think is important (Falk and Dierking 1992: 76ff), and it is therefore important to evaluate 'where the visitor is at' and compare it with 'where you want them to be' (Screven 1995: 110).

Conclusions

Representational meanings encompass both micro-level issues, to do with effective definitions of technical terms, as well as macro-level issues, to do with the whole representational picture constructed through choices in language. As emphasised throughout this chapter, there is no pre-determined way to convey a particular subject matter: the subject matter is constructed *through* the representational choices. This does not mean that there is no 'reality' out there, just that reality always has to be mediated, if it is to be communicated, and that that process of mediation itself contributes to the meanings being conveyed. It is therefore important for museum communicators to be aware of the representational meanings conveyed through museum texts. Sometimes it is hard to distance oneself from a text, but by envisaging alternative representations, imagining other ways of writing, and by considering the omissions, as well as the inclusions, it should be possible to provide sufficient distance to see the constructedness of the text at hand.

In the representational framework, issues of ideology are clearly foregrounded, though they do in fact permeate all the communication frameworks. For instance, to construct or take up a particular role in a relationship reflects an ideology about interaction, and about one's role in interaction; and to organise a text in a particular way reflects an ideology about the prioritisation of meanings, and about the accessibility of texts. But representational meanings are the ones most likely to be open to contestation, and to connect with material disputes, and with different experiences of history. For instance, in the majority of Western countries, there is ongoing contestation over cultural and resource issues where Indigenous and Immigrant communities are concerned. Thus, any presentation in these areas will advantage some stakeholders, and not others. Similarly, any historical 'story' with more than one stakeholder (i.e., every instance of history!) can be told in ways which privilege some views over others, and which can therefore re-open, and re-inscribe, old wounds. Thus, attention must be paid to meanings conveyed through the representational framework. Not to produce a neutral view, an unbiased text, because that is not possible, but to ensure that the representational meanings are aligned with museum and community objectives, and are sensitive to various stakeholders.

Most importantly, from the perspective of the representational framework, it is necessary to remember that objects *do not* speak for themselves: those who say and believe they do, are simply hearing their own pre-existing frameworks speaking back to them. The so-called speaking objects are merely confirming and reaffirming an existing framework. From the point of view of the visitor, who may choose to experience objects in that way, there is nothing wrong with that per se: what is more satisfying then to see an object, and feel some connection with it? Or to feel that one can relate that object to other things? But the danger is, for museums to present such objects as if they don't need mediation, as if everyone will bring to those objects the perspective that the museum communicators feel is 'obvious'. This is self-delusion, and is the surest way possible for a museum to retain an 'exclusive' status (Hooper-Greenhill 1994: 20). By attending to representational meanings, at multiple levels, and considering the potential which is opened up by this framework, museums have the opportunity to ensure their relevance to particular communities, and to effectively scaffold the learning opportunities they provide for visitors.

6

Extending the frameworks

Understanding exhibitions and museums as texts

Introduction: an expanded notion of 'text'

In discussing museum texts in terms of their language, and the ways in which the organisational, interactional, and representational frameworks can illuminate the meaning-making resources of these texts, it has been impossible not to draw connections between the written texts and the immediate situational setting to which these texts relate. Texts in museums are necessarily connected with the exhibits, exhibitions and institutions of which they are a part. In the preceding chapters, we have seen some of the ways in which the language of museum texts *actively constructs* meanings across each of the communication frameworks, and thus how language contributes to the overall meanings made in museums. The meanings at stake need to be interpreted in context, and the immediate context is that of museums themselves as a kind of 'text': a space which makes meanings, and which can be 'read'. As texts, museums are a powerful, communicative resource; all their constitutive practices – the written and verbal texts that take place there, the choice of exhibits and method of their display, the activities that are made available to visitors, and more – make meaning, in multiple ways (cf. Coxall 1991; MacDonald 1998). Language is one, important part of these meaning-making processes, but to more fully understand the significance of language and its contribution to meaning-making, it is necessary to broaden the perspective, and to explore an expanded notion of 'text', that is, of the museum itself as a kind of text.

An interesting example of an exhibition, or rather, an exhibition entry, functioning as a 'text' can be seen in the Natural History Museum, London. The reorganisation of the Geology Gallery (renamed Earth Galleries) saw the installation of an escalator, whisking visitors up from the entry level to the top, third, floor of the building. As the escalator moves up, visitors pass through the interior of a giant, revolving globe, 11 metres in diameter, symbolising the earth as a geological structure. Once at the top, visitors then wend their way around and down the various floors, until they reach the bottom again (although there are a number of ways to proceed, and not all exhibitions need to be traversed).

This is a highly symbolic entry, and has an impact on all three of the core frameworks: that is, the organisational, interactional and representational.

Plate 6.1
Entrance to the Earth Galleries,
Natural History Museum, London

Organisationally, the primary function of the entry is to control, or at least initiate, the pathway of the visit. The escalator is approached by an avenue lined with classical bronzed figures, symbolising gallery themes, such as the Earth's past, present and future (Bloomfield 2002). By whisking visitors from the entry up to the top floor, a sense of excitement and anticipation is created: what will be found at the top? The size and startling novelty of the central Earth draw attention to the content of the galleries, and mark it as a space which *must* be visited. The various exhibitions are given relevance and made cohesive by the literal centrality of the globe, which functions to symbolically connect all the related spaces. Interactionally, the strong degree of control on this pathway (there is only one way to go: up) asserts the power of the institution, as does the size of the globe, but at the same time, the visitor is invited to participate, through traversing the escalator. The excitement and anticipation generate a positive expectation for the experiences to come. Representationally, the framing of the Earth on either side by vast monochromatic walls, and the use of low light levels (Bloomfield 2002), create the effect of the Earth being suspended, and mark the Earth and the journey 'through' it as a moment of symbolic wonder, constructing the earth as something to be marvelled at, and hence worthy of further exploration.

The success of this renovation is attested by the fact that the previously least-popular gallery in the Museum – the dry, dull, geology gallery – soon became its second-most popular gallery, surpassed only by the eternally appealing

Dinosaurs. The entry functions to make the whole Earth Galleries a cohesive, inviting and interesting text: it functions as 'a metaphor for the journey of discovery for visitors to the galleries beyond' (Bloomfield 2002: 392). The one 'experience' – of traversing the escalator – makes meanings in multiple ways, and some of the ways in which these meanings have been constructed will be explored in more detail in this chapter.

In this chapter, I will extend the communicative frameworks that have been proposed to 'museums as text'. This will necessarily be exploratory and suggestive only, as it would be near-impossible to provide a comprehensive account of this in the limited space available here,[1] but the frameworks which have been introduced and applied in relation to language will be extended in order to cast light on some of the ways in which meanings are actively constructed in other 'types' of text. While many of the communicative effects of this broader sense of text 'remain mysterious' (Hooper-Greenhill 2000: 4), they are nevertheless still cultural artefacts and open to (some) systematic interpretation.

'Museums as texts' encompasses a number of different levels, or different perspectives on this notion. It can mean the way in which a whole institution makes meaning – from the sense of authority it constructs, to the way it validates an approach to knowledge, to the way in which it functions as a unified whole. These meanings are made through semiotic resources which are realised both *physically* – through the design and layout of the building, for instance – and *discursively* – through policies which dictate appropriate institutional goals, for instance. At the same time, 'museums as texts' might refer just to the level of exhibitions: the ways in which one exhibition can facilitate particular forms of visitor interaction, can prioritise some meanings in the exhibition rather than others, and can construct a picture of what the subject matter 'is'.[2] The texts which arise at the levels of exhibition and institution are *multi-modal* texts, that is, texts which make their meanings by drawing on a variety of semiotic resources. As noted, these are both physical and discursive, and include the resources of language. These relations are illustrated schematically in Figure 6.1.

In considering exhibitions and institutions as multi-modal, meaning-making texts, I will be adapting previous work which has attempted a similar exploration (Kress and van Leeuwen 1996; O'Toole 1994; O'Toole and Butt 2003; Pang 2001, 2004; Ravelli 2000; Stenglin 2001, 2004a, 2004b; van Leeuwen 1998; White 1994).[3] As noted, however, the discussion undertaken here remains exploratory and suggestive; the main purpose is to indicate the *potential* of this approach, and to show that an extension of the communicative frameworks beyond language, to broader notions of 'text', can be a productive one. This approach aligns with Falk and Dierking's (2000) attention to the physical context of the learning environment, with the additional emphasis that even an apparently 'physical' phenomenon (such as a building) is itself a socio-cultural construct.

Importantly, the descriptions and analyses presented in this chapter are based not just on general interpretations which can only be substantiated by intuition, but on *explicit* features of these texts which are seen to realise certain features,

121

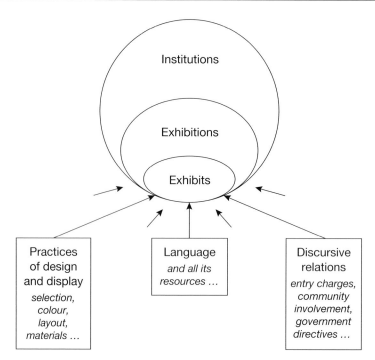

Figure 6.1 Language as one meaning-making resource in museums

within a given socio-cultural context. That is, the reading and interpretation of these texts is based on an analysis of actual semiotic resources – such as the use of placement, the size of an object, the use of lighting – to create particular effects. While the reading of these texts is still contextualised, and open to alternative interpretations, it is nevertheless the case that there must be some explicit relation between context, meanings, and the resources being used. It is not enough to simply look at one of these broader 'texts' and to declare a certain interpretation; that interpretation must be grounded in some explicit analysis.

This chapter addresses two levels of this expanded notion of 'text'. To begin, it addresses the first key level of text in museums: that of the exhibition. The chapter then addresses the second key level, that of the institution itself. Each level will be discussed in relation to each of the organisational, interpersonal and representational frameworks, although selectively so. The examples used are illustrative and are intended to be indicative of the potential of this approach.

Importantly, there is a rank-based relationship between the different levels (Halliday 2002a). This means that the units are hierarchically organised in relation to each other: the smaller units (such as exhibitions) build up meaning in relation to the larger unit (such as the institution). At the same time, the larger units are made up of meanings at the lower level. Thus the relationship is two-way: exhibitions impact on institutional-level meanings, and insitutional-level meanings impact on exhibitions. However, for the sake of clarity, the levels will be introduced and dealt with separately.

Reading spaces: exhibitions

In contemporary cultural institutions, one of the most significant communicative texts is that of the exhibition. It is the predominant form of pedagogy within museums, and defines the museum experience for many visitors, producing and communicating knowledge (Spencer 1999; Kaplan 1995; Hooper-Greenhill 2000). An exhibition, created through an organisation of exhibits and spaces, a selection and construction of content, and a construal of role relations, is a meaningful text: it is a space that visitors move through, and a space which they 'read'. It is a 'three-dimensional composition' (Belcher 1991: 41). It is here that institutions invest their greatest interpretive energy, and where, arguably, they have their greatest communicative impact. Exhibitions make meaning across and through the three communicative frameworks: content is selected and constructed, a stance is created towards this content and towards the visitor's potential behaviour, and potentially disparate elements are shaped into a larger, cohesive whole.

. . . as organisation

While all of the communication frameworks contribute to the meanings of this kind of complex, multi-modal text, the organisational framework is perhaps the most obvious place to start in terms of 'reading' an exhibition. The very process of moving through an exhibition is one which contributes important meanings to the exhibition as a whole, and indeed it is the 'organized walking' which takes place in museums which has been identified by Bennett as one of the defining characteristics of museological practice (Bennett 1995, 1998a). The relative placement of displays and pathways between them might function to draw visitors towards an object, or encourage some sequential reading of different displays, or allow for more open relations between them. These are not just formal devices, but create meanings about what is important, what story is being told, and the visitors' roles within that space.

Many of the fundamental elements of organisation are well documented in museum literature; organisation is the 'art and science of arranging the visual, spatial, and material environment into a composition that visitors move through' (Dean 1994: 32), and can have a significant impact on visitor behaviour (Falk 1993). One of its major functions is to facilitate the creation of 'text' – to integrate disparate elements into a whole, meaningful unit. In museums, and especially in exhibitions, one of the major resources for achieving this is through the direction and control of visitor pathways.[4] Basic visitor pathways have been well mapped out in existing museum literature, especially in terms of their practical implications (Falk and Dierking 1992) and there are a relatively limited number of formal patterns available that can operate as circulation paths, such as the arterial, comb, chain, star (or fan) and block patterns (Royal Ontario Museum 1999: 186–197, citing Lehmbruck 1974; Belcher 1991). However, there is a related aspect to consider with navigation and pathways, and that is the extent to which a pathway is directed or regulated, and the

123

extent to which it is open or random. In their description of pathway types, the Royal Ontario Museum alludes to this, for example, with the arterial path, 'the main path is continuous and no options exist for the visitor' (p. 186), but the block pattern is 'relatively unconstrained' (p. 187). These features can be described more systematically, in terms of the degrees of freedom allowed the visitor, described either as *suggested*, *unstructured* and *directed* approaches to traffic flow (Dean 1994: 53–54), or in terms of a *constant, variable*, or *stopped* flow rate (Pang 2001, 2004).[5] Thus there is a range from the 'freedom of choice' allowed in the suggested approach, to the 'minimal opportunities' of the directed approach. That is, is the visitor given one choice of pathway, which must necessarily be followed if they wish to traverse a space, or are there multiple choices, among which the visitor can choose?[6] In this way, the direction and control of pathways creates both organisational and interactional meanings – shaping the exhibition space as a text, and positioning the visitor's behaviour within that space.

It is interesting to reflect on how pathways are 'made'. How are they constructed, and recognised? Most important is the creation (or absence) of a *vector*. Some linear alignment between components of a space, or between spaces, realises a connection between them (Kress and van Leeuwen 1996). This can be as simple and obvious as a corridor; an evident vector which must be followed, or as subtle as the use of lighting, or a repetition of colours, to indicate a preferred pathway. Any device which draws attention to the connection between spaces, can function as a vector, including the use of colour contrast, or sequencing of objects. Plate 6.2 illustrates the use of colour to create a strong vector through the exhibition. The absence of obvious vectors leaves visitors to make their own connections, thus, a collection of objects arranged randomly within a gallery will leave the visitor to wander between them at will. Vectors can be structurally highlighted with the use of clear signage: 'This way to . . .', but signage on its own does not necessarily create a vector, it merely highlights an existing one.

Pathways can also be created or reinforced with the use of *framing* practices, and framing contributes important organisational meanings to the exhibition as text. Framing defines the degree of conceptual difference or similarity between components of a 'text'. Strong framing highlights difference, suggesting separation; weak framing blurs the boundaries between otherwise separate spaces, and so suggests some connection between them, an overlap or seamlessness of ideas (Kress and van Leeuwen 1996: 214).[7] Framing can be expressed in or realised by a number of different devices. Physical devices, such as walls, doorways and framed archways can be used to signal the separation of spaces. A shift in design practices – a change in colour, for example, in display types, in the use of lighting – can be used to signal change between spaces, and so signal strong framing. Alternatively, continuity in these elements can indicate weak framing, that two otherwise separate spaces should be seen to somehow relate to each other. Such a continuity can be seen in Plate 6.2, which shows small displays to the right of the pathway, indicated as belonging together in relation to a larger whole, through the repetition of design practices.

Plate 6.2 Strong vector creating a pathway through the exhibition: continuity of design on the right unifying the separate elements, Cité des Sciences et de l'Industrie, Paris

Thus a number of different resources combine to create pathways and organise the flow of movement through an exhibition. Importantly, however, the different pathway options are not merely curiosities of form, which affect features such as how the traffic moves through the space; the pathways themselves are socio-cultural constructs, that is, ways of making meaning, and they bring particular *information values* to the organisation of the space (Kress and van Leeuwen 1996). The construction of a pathway depends on the relative placement of objects and other spaces (such as doorways or corridors) within an exhibition, and it is this which makes meaning. When the placement is organised with clear vectors and definite sequencing, there is a sense of one part of the exhibition being visited 'first', and others 'after'. That which is first functions as 'point of departure' for the exhibition: it sets up the 'Theme' of the exhibition (in the sense established in Chapter 2), and functions as 'Given' or 'understood' information (Kress and van Leeuwen 1996). That which follows functions as the 'New' information, or the point of arrival. Placement is ideologically laden; it is not a question of whether any component actually is or is not known to the visitor, but rather, it is a question of how the information is presented, that is, *as if* it has that value: '. . . readers have to read it within that structure, even if that valuation may then be rejected by a particular reader' (Kress and van Leeuwen 1996: 187).

At the Singapore History Museum, the exhibition 'From Colony to Nation' uses a strongly directed, linear circulation path. As described by Pang (2001,

2004), the placement of exhibits along this path is used to construct a 'story' in which the earlier, communist phase of Singapore's history is represented as a 'colony in chaos', whereas the current, communitarian phase of Singapore's history is represented as 'a unified nation', celebrating its diversity, economic growth, and national strength. 'Given', then, is the threat and instability of one possible regime; this is the point of departure for the exhibition; 'New' is the stability and security of the current regime: this is its point of arrival, and the message which should be read by the compliant visitor is clear. Such a message is not a 'fact' which is simply conveyed by the exhibition, but a version of history which is *constructed by* the exhibition, through semiotic resources such as the placement of exhibits in relation to each other. In this way, the shaping of the space also contributes to representational meanings: to a sense of a particular 'content' to be attributed to the elements of the exhibition and to the exhibition as a whole.[8]

It is also important to appreciate that an organisational option such as relative placement is a *way of making meaning*: it is one of the resources which actively construes content, and thus helps construct what an exhibition 'is', what it is 'about', and what values it conveys. The organisation of the exhibition does not derive from anything inherent in the 'facts' which are being conveyed, as might sometimes be suggested: 'The degree to which subdivision should be directive or random is constrained by the extent to which the story is sequential' (Royal Ontario Museum 1999: 181). A perspective such as this is a fallacy. While it may seem 'natural' to see some stories as being sequential, this is just a product of culture, history and ideology constraining possible points of view. As with language, it is the *process of constructing the story* which makes it appear to be sequential – or otherwise.

Of course, there are pathways and forms of placement other than the sequential ones, and these give rise to different information values. The other form of placement most often exploited in exhibitions is that of centralised placement, where a 'Centre/Margin' structure operates. Here, the Centre functions as a nucleus, and the items placed at the Margins are equal in value to each other, but (literally) marginal in value compared to the Centre.[9] Similarly, ordered and reasonably symmetrical placement of objects, without a particular 'Centre' as such, gives the objects the 'same' information value, making them equal in status.

In the exhibition, The Dead Sea Scrolls (Art Gallery of New South Wales, July–October 2000), centralised placement was used to underscore the significance of the core objects, the Scrolls themselves. The Scrolls, literally central to the exhibition, were displayed in enclosed stands around the circumference of a relatively small, central circle, with explanatory texts and related, but less significant objects, arranged around the margins of the gallery space. The objects themselves therefore functioned as the lynch-pin of the whole exhibition, and the additional components of the exhibition, while interesting, were marked as being in some ways peripheral. Thus, centralised placement was used to give these objects significance. At the same time, however, the Scrolls were contextualised in relation to broader themes of archaeology and history, and a complementary form of placement along the horizontal axis was used for the remainder of the exhibition. The exhibition as a whole had a 'prefix' of a long entrance gallery, giving contextual information to the exhibit, and a 'suffix' of an additional gallery with related archaeological explanations, each functioning to underscore the centrality of the main exhibits. The 'prefix' provided background to the Scrolls, and thereby functioned as 'Given' in relation to the Scrolls as 'New'. In turn, the Scrolls then functioned as the 'Given', against which the additional archaeological gallery could be interpreted, as 'New'. In this way, linear placement also contributed to the significance of the objects, working together with the complementary centralised placement. Small and potentially easy to overlook, the Dead Sea Scrolls were thus made absolutely central to the exhibition, with the combined organisational devices constructing the circulation path: 'A small but important artefact carefully placed in a small case can be made to look grand by the shape of the surrounding space' (Royal Ontario Museum 1999: 181). As well as underscoring the informational significance of the objects, the placement of the items also has an impact on representational meanings, as the 'content' conveyed by the core objects of the exhibition – the scrolls themselves – is expanded by relating them to broader issues of history and archaeology. These relations are indicated schematically in Figure 6.2.

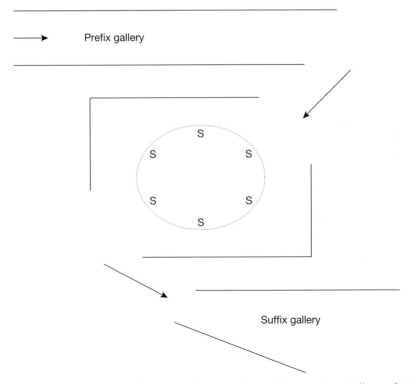

Figure 6.2 Schematic layout of the Dead Sea Scrolls Exhibition, Art Gallery of New South Wales: Centre/Margin structure, with Prefix and Suffix Galleries (not to scale)

Another possible form of placement is dispersal along the vertical axis, although this tends to be exploited more frequently in institutions (which have more than one level, so greater potential to exploit this resource) than in exhibitions (which are frequently single-level). Where the vertical axis is used, it leads to a juxtaposition of 'top' and 'bottom', or 'above' and 'below'. Items placed at the top have the value of the *Ideal*, or generalised 'promise', and items at the bottom have the value of the *Real*, or down to earth, more specific information (Kress and van Leeuwen 1996).[10] While the *space* of the Ideal is often used in exhibitions to place objects up high, placement along the vertical axis is not so frequently used to determine circulation paths within exhibitions, simply because not all gallery and exhibition spaces have multiple levels within them. However, in the double-level '*Te Pasifika*' Gallery at the Melbourne Museum, the vertical axis is exploited to effect. Here, huge sails are suspended from the ceiling, and canoes are raised above the floor on poles and stands. From the viewpoint of the ground floor, the objects are above, in the space of the Ideal, and so are imbued with a sense of wonderment. In contrast, from the position of the next floor up, the same objects are closer to eye-level, in the domain of the Real, and so can be appreciated in terms of their concrete details. The circulation path goes both up and down beside the exhibit and enables the exhibit to be read in two different ways.[11]

Many exhibitions would deploy different organisational devices at the same time, as illustrated by the exhibition of the Dead Sea Scrolls. While only three

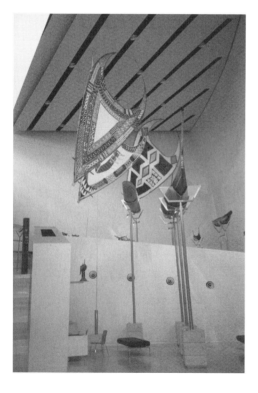

Plate 6.3
Exploiting the Ideal/Real
dimension, *Te Pasifika* Gallery,
Melbourne Museum

core possibilities are suggested here, it is important to appreciate that these (semiotic) values *intersect* with the multiple formal patterns which are possible. Thus, a path which might literally be 'wavy' would still be described in semiotic terms as a 'linear' one, if it is strongly directed, and if it evokes a sense of 'before' and 'after', that is, of directed movement from 'here' to 'there'. Hence, even a 'wavy' path could establish the information values of Given and New. Also, it is important to emphasise that the options are *social-semiotic constructs* – that is, meaning-making resources which have meaning within a particular social context. Why else would institutions debate the preferred way of organising an exhibition, unless important issues of meaning were at stake? One such debate took place at the Australian Maritime Museum (Sydney), where two forms of (potential) organisation were seen to be in tension. The original layout of the museum used an open circulation structure, with centralised placement, to relate different exhibitions to each other. External consultants proposed a renovation, suggesting that exhibitions should be organised in a linear fashion, including placement of exhibits on Aboriginal and Torres Strait Islanders at the beginning of the 'maritime story'. This placement might seem to place the Aboriginal perspective in a positive light, making this view the point of departure for the exhibition. However, the proposed renovation is vigorously critiqued by Witcomb (1994, 2003), who argues that this placement reproduces '. . . an easy temporal narrative in which the Aboriginal maritime experience is relegated to antiquity, before the whites, with no links between the two possible' (Witcomb 1994: 254). Witcomb notes that in fact, 'many of the artefacts and practices referred to in the display were still in use until very recently' (ibid.), and that the original design of the gallery had explicitly attempted to avoid such 'master narratives'. Indeed, the linear model of organisation invokes a strong pedagogic orientation and nineteenth-century classification systems (Witcomb 2003; Bennett 1995). Thus, the organisation itself contributed in important ways to the potential interpretation of the space as a whole, and not all interpretations were equally valued.

This is not intended to suggest that one form of organisation is necessarily better or worse than another. On the contrary, the purpose is to draw attention to the different (cultural) values and meanings attributed to different forms of organisation, and to their potential impact on the 'reading' of an exhibition. Organisation is itself an important resource for making meanings within exhibitions.

Thus, exhibitions make meaning through the relative placement of elements, contributing to particular information values. At the same time, there are other organisational meanings which contribute to an understanding of the exhibition as 'text', including the prioritisation of some elements of the exhibition over others. This prioritisation, or 'salience' (Kress and van Leeuwen 1996) may in fact be constructed by the resource of placement, as in the Dead Sea Scrolls exhibition, where centralised placement gave salience to the Scrolls themselves. The salience of one object or display over another can be achieved in multiple ways; size is one obvious way of achieving this, by virtue of contrast. An object which is significantly larger than any other in an exhibition will necessarily attract attention. Equally, however, the tiniest object can be given the greatest priority, as we have seen. Here, however, such salience needs to be supported by additional design features, such as lighting, contrast, separation from other exhibits, in order for its priority to be realised. Thus, it is the potential to use a spectrum of design features to create a focus, which signals the possible salience of an object or an exhibit. On the website of the Natural History Museum, London,[12] the 'Dinosaurs' Gallery is given salience by having a dynamic, animated dinosaur come to life on the screen, in extreme close-up, with gnashing teeth – quite alarming, really, and certainly attention-grabbing! Generally, salience enables some aspects of a 'text' to be given greater priority than others, suggesting that the salient features are more significant, or alternatively, that all of the features of the text are equal in value, and that none is more important than the other. All those who visit museums and galleries are familiar with the two extremes of these possibilities: having, perhaps, one object or display which dominates a room, or alternatively, having a succession of objects displayed in similar ways, suggesting an equity of value between them.

. . . as interaction

In approaching exhibitions as texts, an equally important part of their meaning potential is the nature of the interaction they enable between exhibition and visitor: what does the exhibition say about the institution? what roles does it enable the visitor to take up? how does it make a visitor feel? In exhibitions, the interactional framework functions to position visitors to behave or respond in certain ways, and can create particular emotive appeals, and an overall air of authority or informality. In particular, the nature of the exhibits within the exhibition contribute to the ways in which visitors are enabled, or prevented, from taking up particular roles and relations within the institution. Consider Plates 6.4–6.7, which represent different types of displays in exhibitions.

Each of these Plates illustrates a different kind of exhibit, and a different kind of interactional potential, reflecting overall shifts in relations between institutions and their visitors. In Plate 6.4, small objects behind glass cases can be perused by visitors as they pass through the corridor; other than the act of stopping to look, visitors are positioned relatively passively in relation to the 'knowledge' displayed; that is, visitors are supposed to absorb this knowledge without questioning it. Similarly, in Plate 6.5, while the mammals on display are not held behind cases, their large size and placement in the position of the *Ideal* mean they are primarily there to be gazed at, in wonderment or contemplation. Plate 6.6 demonstrates a dramatic shift away from this style, inviting the visitor to participate in the display, by answering a general question (What types of sounds might insects make?), absorbing and reflecting on information displayed (linguistically and visually), and interacting by picking up the phones to listen to sounds, and by manipulating associated objects. This interactive potential is carried even further in the display illustrated in Plate 6.7, where visitors are given the opportunity to replicate the construction of an object, a

Plate 6.4 Corridor, glass cases

Plate 6.5 Mammals gallery

Plate 6.6 Panel display

Plates 6.4–6.7
'From contemplating
to creating', Natural History
Museum, London

Plate 6.7 'Make a T-Shirt'

T-shirt. In each instance, the visitor must be involved for any communication to take place (Falk and Dierking 1992: 67): even in the relatively passive exhibit illustrated in 6.4, the visitor must at least stop and look. However, it is the nature of the involvement which varies between the different types of display. Thus, from merely contemplating to actually creating, the positioning, roles and relationships of both the museum and its visitors have changed dramatically. As described in Chapter 4 in relation to language, the variables of power and social distance combine to define relations between institutions and visitors, contributing to the 'persona' of the exhibition and the behaviour potential of visitors (cf. Ravelli 2000; Pang, 2001, 2004). The degree of passivity or interactivity enabled by exhibits, and the degree of control exerted over the navigation of pathways, define the authority of the institution, and contribute to the overall roles a visitor can adopt within an exhibition.[13] 'Interactivity' is not a feature confined to technically interactive displays (Witcomb 2003), but is an aspect of meaning which permeates all displays and exhibitions, being taken up and inflected in different ways.

Interestingly, each of these exhibits is co-present at the one institution, the Natural History Museum, London, demonstrating that these are not historically confined choices, but alternative ways of meaning. Any one exhibition (in this or in other institutions) might make predominant use of just one style of display, or might use a number of different types at the same time. It is interesting to reflect on what the different types represent in terms of 'trends', preferences for one style rather than another at a particular point in time, or within a particular exhibition. As with language, the predominant trend in the past has been for museums to 'present' information to visitors: to make statements, and provide objects to look at. Today, the more predominant trend is to invite interaction, both through language, and through exhibitions which facilitate physical and intellectual engagement with objects and processes. The 'trends' may also be differentiated according not to time, but to an overarching ideology of museum practice: for instance, there is a particularly strong preference today for children's exhibits and exhibitions to be as interactive as possible (Falk and Dierking 1992), as in the children's gallery, 'Launchpad' at the Science Museum, London, where scientific concepts and principles are demonstrated through playfully interactive exhibits. This predominance of interactives for children reflects an ideology that the process of 'doing' is a way to bring together the processes of 'learning' and 'playing', and that it is particularly important to achieve this integration where children are concerned. My point here is not to evaluate this ideology, but to note the way in which an apparently 'simple' choice, such as type of exhibit, can contribute to meanings at this level.

An additional feature of the interactional framework is the general degree of formality or informality, and the overall emotive appeal, constructed in and through the exhibition. The features just discussed play a role here, too; an authoritative, formal exhibition which prohibits close contact will most likely be associated with a (so-called) 'neutral' emotional position, that is, a formal one. Exhibitions which explore other interactional roles are likely to engage other possible emotions, and less formal styles. In addition, other elements of design, such as the connotations provided by colour, lighting, or particular illustrations, can suggest appropriate emotional responses to exhibits, impacting in particular on issues of comfort and security for visitors (Stenglin 2001, 2004a, 2004b); and the general creation of mood (Pang 2001, 2004). Research has suggested that there is an important relationship between *affect* (feelings, attitudes and emotions) and the intrinsic motivations for visitors to learn (Falk and Dierking 2000: 21ff.), and it clearly forms an important part of the overall interactional meanings in an exhibition. Contrast the Plates in 6.8 and 6.9.

In Plate 6.8, the cultural salience of the human face, its exaggerated size, bright, saturated colours, and the humorously presented activity therein, provide a light-hearted backdrop to this display, suggesting that its 'content' will also be fun and engaging. In contrast, in Plate 6.9, the more restrained display, with symmetrical composition and minimal background, suggests that the exhibition of which this is a part is more 'serious', and that a more contemplative affectual response would be appropriate. This is not to say that one of these displays is necessarily 'more interesting' or 'more important' than the other, just that display practices have been used to evoke conventionalised emotional responses. Generally, the overall type of affect ranges from the positive, through to neutral, to negative, and may be emphasised to a strong degree (as in the exaggerated size of the face in Plate 6.8) or only weakly.

The impact of affect on the interaction clearly depends on conventional, and culturally situated, associations of resources such as colour, light, sound, space

Plate 6.9 A restrained display, South Australian Museum

Plate 6.8 A light-hearted backdrop, Melbourne Museum

and so on with particular emotions and responses. Bright colours tend to be associated with (generally) positive emotions; a sense of ease is associated with spaces which allow freedom of movement, without overexposure (Dean 1994: 42), and so on. The strong cultural associations of these resources with particular affectual responses make this a difficult area to pin down; nevertheless, it is still possible to observe variation in the type and degree of affect which is present, as illustrated. For a body of research which has tried to systematically map the ways in which aspects of these interactional meanings are inflected in museum exhibitions, see Stenglin 2004a.

Most importantly, it needs to be emphasised that a so-called 'neutral' affect is still a meaningful choice: it is not that there is *no* interactional meaning being made, but rather, that a particular *type* of interactional meaning, which is culturally accepted as being 'neutral', is being made. As in language, where so-called 'objective' texts still take up a persuasive position, so too in exhibitions. There is nothing emotively neutral about pausing reverently before a static display: this is still a form of emotional and behavioural response, and a way of interacting. In Western culture at this time, such a response tends to be accepted as 'unmarked', whereas other responses (such as laughing) are more 'marked', and so more emotionally evident (cf. Falk and Dierking 1992).

. . . as representation

As well as making meaning through the organisational and interactional frameworks, exhibitions of course make meaning through the representational framework. What is the exhibition 'about'? What view does it present of the subject matter? What does the exhibition 'say'? Such representational meanings are conveyed primarily by what is 'in' the exhibition – the nature of the displays. The very selection of content, the selection of exhibits, is in itself a meaning-making resource (cf. Ravelli 2000) and is one of the key ways in which an overall view of a subject area is established. This selection is significant not only in terms of the literal representation of content – that is, whether the exhibition is about rocks, dinosaurs, steam engines or fashion – but in terms of *the approach to knowledge* which is conveyed by the selection. All collections embody assumptions about 'knowledge and value' (Pearce 1991: 137; 1995). A dinosaur exhibition which consists only of skeletons and scientific models, for example, will suggest that there is a particular way to approach an understanding of dinosaurs as a subject area, and an exhibition which consists of reconstructed, even animated, models, or which consists only of written information, will suggest other ways of understanding.

As noted in Chapter 5 in relation to language, the deeper and more complex representational meanings are constructed through (linguistic) relationships which indicate underlying connections, such as relations of superordination and composition. In three-dimensional space, similar relations are created through the ways in which individual exhibits are brought together in one exhibitionary space: the relationships constructed *between* items or components of a knowledge framework indicate *what that framework is*. 'The beliefs, attitudes and values which underpin the processes of acquisition become embodied in the collections' (Hooper-Greenhill 2000: 23); social and cultural representations are constructed by the processes of bringing objects together; relationships of equivalence are constructed, and these visual statements 'generate their own discourses and act to confirm the discourses with which they are affiliated' (Hooper-Greenhill 2000: 48).

There is a continuum here, ranging from sharp boundaries between content areas, to blurred boundaries, fusing disparate content areas into one, and the endpoints of this continuum tend to coincide with 'old' and 'new' approaches to disciplinary boundaries. 'Old'-style approaches to content are curatorially driven, guided by strong distinctions between subjects and disciplines; thus, an exhibition on 'science' might include sub-sections on chemistry, biology, and physics. Such distinctions are likely to be marked by clear separation of the displays, in terms of both their visual and linguistic content. This is the characteristic approach of the nineteenth-century, modernist museum (Hooper-Greenhill 2000; Witcomb 2003). 'New' style approaches are driven more by an emergence of 'values' or 'themes', in which a range of 'conventional' subject areas are brought together in the service of that value or theme (Hooper-Greenhill 1994). Thus, a contemporary exhibition on science might be characterised as being about 'environmental protection', in which the roles of other 'disciplines' will have some role to play, but where such disciplines will not be a focus in and of themselves. As these multiple perspectives are brought together, the 'new' style is pushed even further in the post-museum, to accommodate polysemous meanings, and to be critical and reflexive of the knowledge being constructed and conveyed (Hooper-Greenhill 2000; Witcomb 2003).

Thus the representational meanings in an exhibition construct an overall approach to knowledge, as well as indicating a basic 'topic'. Here, a range of resources indicate the ways in which representational meanings are shown to be connected, but what connects them is their effect on the relationship between content areas. Simple elements of design, such as the repetition or variation of colour and materials to show continuity or separation of content, may be used to show connections and distinctions between knowledge areas. It is very interesting to note that some of the choices made in the interactional and organisational frameworks have important ramifications for meanings in the representational framework. For instance, the interactional meanings construed through the different types of display, positioning visitors to respond with varying degrees of activity or passivity, have an interesting potential correlation with the approach to knowledge which an exhibit represents. The more static displays suggest a correlation with knowledge as a form of ordering and classification, associated with relational processes in the representational framework ('this rock is a member of the family . . .'), and thus corresponding to a more traditional, taxonomic approach to knowledge. In contrast, the more active displays suggest a correlation with knowledge as a process and activity, associated with material processes which include the visitor ('you can crush the ore with this machine'), and thus presenting a different view of the way in which knowledge can be presented.

Similarly, the information values constructed through the use of pathways and other aspects of layout have implications for the representational framework. The use of a Centre/Margin structure to organise exhibits, for instance, implies that the individual items belong together as some kind of 'whole', thus implying a kind of superordinate relation to the Centre, and a subordinate relation to the Margins. Alternatively, a sequential structuring to the individual components of an exhibition implies that the understanding or experience of one component is a necessary prelude to the next; this can connect with relationships of time in the representational framework ('first this, then that'), or with causal relationships ('because this, then that'). A more random and open placement might imply very few connections between the individual components, and so suggest few explicit representational connections between them. The resource of *framing*, introduced earlier, can also be used to establish these relations, using weak framing practices to suggest connections between content areas, and so, weak classification, or strong framing practices to suggest separation and difference. Together, a range of representational, interactional and organisational resources contribute to the overall *classification* of knowledge (Bernstein 1975), in terms of weak or strong divisions between content areas.

Many museums manage the conflicting implications of these alternatives by integrating a range of perspectives in one exhibition (cf. White 1994). This could be said to speak to the different interests and learning styles of a diverse audience (Gardner 1983, 1996; Cassels 1996), but it also succeeds in presenting complementary perspectives on the 'same' topic, and so constructing a rich and diverse representation of that topic. Whether such a strategy is positive or negative can only be evaluated in relation to institutional goals and visitor feedback. For instance, if the intention is to convey an understanding of classification processes of dinosaur fossils, then a more focussed selection of exhibit types might be preferable. On the other hand, if the intention is to convey an understanding of the way in which ecological and social processes impact on the survival of a species, then a unitary form of display is unlikely to be successful. Either way, the selection of exhibits contributes to representational meanings, both literally and by implication.

. . . as a coherent whole

At the same time as the content areas of an exhibition are signalled as being the 'same' or as 'different', they are also brought together into a coherent whole. As Serrell (1996) notes, all meaning-making practices should refer back to an over-arching 'big idea'. In this way, the representational meanings relate to the *narrative design* or *interplay of genres* of the exhibition (Pang 2001, 2004).[14] Overall, the different components – all the semiotic resources, including language and design – work together to enable the objectives of the exhibition to be achieved. Typically, one exhibition will have a number of different types of display within it, or a number of distinctive sub-sections which approach the topic in different ways – these are the *elemental* genres (meaningful texts on their own, which have their own distinctive structure and purpose) and together, they combine to form a *macro-genre*, an overall structure and purpose for the exhibition as a whole (Martin and Rose 2003). For instance, an exhibition which functions as a *macro-Exposition*, constructing a particular argument, or as a *macro-Directive*, suggesting a particular behavioural response (cf. White 1994; and Chapter 4 in this book), is likely to construct its persuasive point of view through a variety of elements. Think of an exhibition on environmental sustainability, which is fundamentally trying to persuade visitors to change their individual behaviours in relation to environmental issues. The elemental genres of this exhibition might include displays which report on environmental trends; they might include personal recounts of individuals and their experience of engaging in sustainable practices; they might include practical demonstrations of the impact of particular environmental choices, inviting visitors to actively engage in these, and so on. Together, these elemental genres (consisting themselves of language, display and design) work together to build up an overall purpose for the exhibition, ideally persuading the visitor to change their behaviour. At the same time, the presence of the elemental genres enables additional sub-purposes to be achieved, such as raising awareness of environmental issues. While there is a very strong link between representational meanings and genre here, it is important to note that each of the frameworks contributes to an overall sense of genre for the exhibition. For instance, organisational resources, such as the basic pathway types, can support different generic structures. A reasonably clearly defined pathway, giving rise to a linear sequence, will support chronological or linear relations between elements, and so will support such genres as historical recounts, or causal explanations.

Of course, a wide variety of macro-purposes are possible for exhibitions, and it may also be the case that an exhibition might be characterised as having more than one overall purpose – pursuing different paths at the same time. Some notion of narrative design or purpose enables a point of evaluation to be established: it is not necessarily the case that the mere co-presence of different types of displays or sections of an exhibition will make it 'successful'. The different elements need to function cohesively and coherently in relation to some larger whole.

Reviewing the exhibition as text

To return to the discussion of the entrance to the Earth Galleries, at the Natural History Museum, London, we can see in this complex exhibitionary device all the frameworks of meaning operating at once. Perhaps the most startling impact can be seen in terms of the organisational framework. Here, the escalator transfers visitors from the ground to the upper levels; it thus has a linear dimension, and carries visitors from their Given starting point, to the New of the exhibitions. The content of the Galleries is thereby marked as interesting and worth attending to. At the same time, because the escalator moves from bottom to top, the content of the Galleries is marked as Ideal: exciting, full of promise. While the distance between Given and New, and Ideal and Real, is relatively large, the potential divisiveness of this strong framing is undercut by the directional nature of the escalator, thus weakening the overall framing and suggesting that the different states ('before' and 'after') can be brought together. The globe through which visitors pass at the middle of the escalator, as well as the additional framing by the monochromatic walls, marks the Earth and all the knowledge held therein as 'Central' – everything around it, the Galleries, elaborate on this centre, and can be seen to come back to it. Thus, the potentially disparate content of the multiple Galleries is drawn together as one. And of course, through its size and startling novelty, the journey, the central Earth, and the Galleries as a whole, are given Salience.

Simultaneously, the new entrance to the Earth Galleries makes important interactional meanings. The directionality of the journey can be read in different ways: as an invitation to enter, or as a directive to follow the path indicated. While the journey itself, facilitated by the escalator, is in some ways passive, visitors must choose to actively engage with this journey – to make a commitment to engage with and explore what is beyond. The size of the Earth and of the entrance space itself positions the institution authoritatively, and potentially places the visitor in a position of awe; at the same time, the fact that the visitor is taken through the literal heart of the Earth, means that they are enabled to be intimately engaged with all that the Galleries will offer. Different emotional responses are created through other interactional devices. A sense of awe, as in reverence, is enabled by the low lighting and monochromatic walls, which contribute to a cool emotional response. At the same time, a sense of excitement is created by the exaggerated size (relative to individual people!) of the Earth and of the entrance space as a whole.

Representationally, the Earth functions in largely symbolic terms; as previously noted, the journey as a whole stands as a metaphor for what is beyond. The classical figures in the avenue leading up to the Earth, positioned as they are in the space of the Given, allude to the historical precedents of these Galleries, and their links with tradition. Strategically placed portholes in the vast surrounding walls showcase specimens from the Galleries (Bloomfield 2002), and function to hint at the representational content of the as-yet undefined New, beyond the escalator. The consistent use of design resources such as lighting and colour frame the space as one coherent unit, bringing the disparate elements together to function as a whole.

In such ways, this one exhibition device draws together a range of features, to make meanings about the 'text' to be experienced (the galleries and their cohesive relation to each other), the positioning of the visitor in relation to that text (through involvement and wonder) and the nature and role of the content (an exciting promise). As a text, this museum device operates across each of the communication frameworks: organisational, interactional and representational. The meanings created at this level necessarily have implications for the institution as a text also: the startling nature of this entry give great salience and priority to the Earth Galleries and mark them as significant within the institution. The involvement of the visitor implies their potential interaction in subsequent parts of the exhibition, but also, the institution has positioned itself authoritatively by directing the visitors' path, and by creating such a remarkable installation. And through this installation, the institution has declared that its approach to knowledge will be a creative, novel, and contemporary one, albeit linked to well-established traditions. The next part of this chapter will explore other ways in which meanings can be seen to be made at the institutional level.

Being somewhere: institutions

In broadening the lens to consider 'museums as texts', it is of course the institution as a whole which is the ultimate source of meaning making. This is presumably why people visit (and don't visit!) museums: because they are *spaces which speak*. Institutions as a whole make meaning, including, but also going beyond the exhibitions. They construct content and relevance, suggesting what is worthwhile knowledge to learn, and what is an appropriate activity to undertake. They relate to and position visitors in various ways, and they are organised as a 'text', made to cohere as a whole, and function as one unit. At this level, the frameworks combine to build a complex picture of what the museum 'is': what it stands for, how it functions as an institution, its overall persona, and its inter-relations with visitors and communities. I will try and indicate briefly here some of the ways in which each of the frameworks contribute to such meanings at the institutional level.

. . . as organisation

In the first instance, institutions are, of course, complex texts, made up of numerous components, and these are organised in relation to each other. From the moment a visitor steps in to the institution, they engage with the organisation of the space, and that organisation presents the visitor with a particular set of options. For instance, the internal organisation of institutional spaces (different galleries, floors, functional areas) creates a circulation path, or paths, through the institution. Combined with the relative placement of the different spaces, this creates particular information values for those spaces. The moment of 'stepping in' to the institution is a particularly salient one, where the values of *Ideal* and *Real* are typically exploited, especially in the design of (new) museum entries. Here, the fashion is for spacious-as-possible entries, with high ceilings, expansive floor space, and as much light as possible. These design features may have a pragmatic value – an open and airy space is more physically comfortable when large numbers of people may be congregating there – but nevertheless, the use of these features enables the space to function like a 'promise'. Visitors step in, to look up and see (even if there is no physical object there as such, but there often is) the very institution functioning as the Ideal; and that which is about to be experienced – by traversing the horizontal axis – as the Real manifestation of this promise: the exhibitions, the objects, the experience of being in the museum.[15] At the same time, such height functions to evoke the authority of the institution, thus engaging with interactional meanings, and the height also invests its 'contents' with symbolic, as well as literal, value, thus engaging with representational meanings. This then is another instance of the same resource making meaning across the frameworks.

At the institutional level, organisational meanings are particularly important in terms of how they contribute to the general accessibility or complexity of the institution. 'Accessibility' at the institutional level can – and should – encompass many diverse factors, including whether or not there is an entry charge, and how much it is; how the institution engages with diverse local communities, and the range of interpretative activities which take place under the auspices of the institution.[16] But aspects of organisation also contribute to a sense of complexity or accessibility of the institution as a 'text'. This can be interpreted simply in terms of whether it is easy or difficult to find one's way around the institution. When pathways are confusing, signage misleading or absent, and connections too subtle, visitors are less likely to enjoy their experience of visiting the institution, and more likely to feel alienated (Serrell 1996). Clear organisation, in contrast, can greatly enhance the visitor experience. At the new Melbourne Museum, in Australia, the floorplan has a reasonably traditional, linear layout, organised around a main 'corridor' with three perpendicular galleries, all double-levelled. This traditional design (traditional in terms of the floor plan only) could potentially be profoundly frustrating, as it invites dead-ends and back-tracking. However, such problems have been avoided by ensuring multiple connections between different internal spaces – different points of access into and out of galleries, and multiple vertical connections. Hence, rather than being rigid, the interior connections are fluid, and easy to take in and to navigate. Thus, this museum can be quickly navigated as a 'text'; visitors can pick and choose the galleries they wish to visit, and control the pathway of their own visit (Beck and Cooper 2001: 381).

While disorientation is usually a negative experience for visitors, it is not *necessarily* a negative feature. It is negative when it is unintended, when disorientating features interfere with a reading of the institution as text, and when such features undermine other meaning-making processes. However, if disorientation is used *as a meaningful resource*, it can be evaluated differently. Contemporary institutions may wish to disrupt and deliberately challenge conventional notions – of design, of the typical role of such institutions, of the relation of the institution to the community, and it is possible for institutions to exploit this as a resource. An interesting example of this can be seen at the level of the exhibition, in the 'Kaboom! Animation' exhibition at the Museum of Contemporary Art, Sydney (1994–1995). This exhibition attempted to recreate the chaotic and immersive experience of much contemporary animation – it was very loud, visually overwhelming, and potentially disorienting.

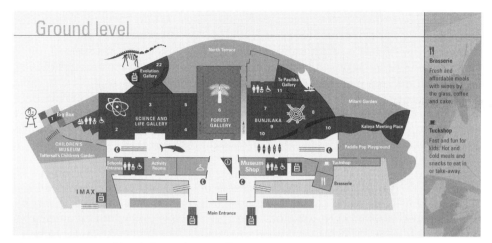

Figure 6.3 Ground-level floor plan, Melbourne Museum

Visitors are alerted to this in the explanatory literature,[17] and so disorientation becomes *part of the meaning* of the exhibition; the experience of it might still be unsettling, but such an experience has a role to play in terms of the goals of the exhibition and the institution.

The organisational framework also contributes to the overall persona of the institution through the connections which are made – or not made – with neighbouring spaces, both in the immediate, physical environment (other buildings, local communities) and in the broader environment of relevant discursive practices (other cultural or public institutions, for instance). Is the institution organised in such a way to suggest similarities and continuities with these other spaces/groups, or to signal difference? Here, the notion of framing helps explain some of the ways in which these relations are created, and an interesting example of this aspect of framing can be seen at the New Art Gallery, Walsall, UK. Here, a crucial part of the design of the gallery was the conceptualisation of its relation to the town as a whole. The gallery was funded in part by the National Lottery, and located in the heart of an industrial, working-class area, at one end of the main shopping district, on an extremely busy thoroughfare. Part of the design brief was to ensure a seamless connection between the gallery and the town, and to integrate the gallery with its local community (cf. O'Neill 1999). The design of the building includes a number of features to help achieve this. Most importantly, access to the functional parts of the gallery – toilets, shop, café – is directly from the street; one doesn't have to 'enter' the institution to use these facilities. One exterior wall can be used as a large projection screen, and so films can be displayed for anyone passing by. Once inside, the necessity for blank wall space and controlled light levels is counter-balanced by many carefully located windows, literally framing views of the town on all sides, and thus reminding visitors that they are always located within this township. The framing provided by these windows thus functions to weaken the potentially divisive barriers of blank, windowless walls, facilitating more

141

open connections between inside and out. Thus, while being a thoroughly contemporary and distinctive civic building, the potential division between everyday city life and the museum is weakened as much as is possible. As with most communication resources, this impacts not only on issues of organisation, but on the interactional and representational frameworks as well. The framing primes visitors to expect a certain kind of positioning within the institution – open, welcoming, relevant – and suggests that the 'knowledge' contained within the institution is perhaps not so separate from everyday experience as might otherwise be thought. The fundamental design of the building thus makes a profound contribution to institutional-level meanings.[18]

Walsall Gallery's attempt to weaken the boundaries between institution and everyday life is in stark contrast to more 'traditional' institutional practices. Location within the centre of cities is not a new phenomenon for museums, but has traditionally been exploited to embody the 'material and symbolic' power of these institutions (Bennett 1995: 87). For instance, the Australian Museum in Sydney, an example of high Victorian architecture, stood out in its time as a major civic building, completely separate from and different to the more ordinary buildings of everyday life. Its design was deemed to be appropriate for such a significant public edifice, and 'symbolised the transformation of New South Wales from a penal settlement to a self-governing colony' (Bridges and McDonald 1988: 35). At the same time, it spoke intertextually with other major civic buildings of the time (the Hospital, the University), and soon became a reference point for other civic buildings, such as the General Post Office in Martin Place. The architecture of the building thus aligned with certain institutional practices – those identified as major civic or cultural practices – and separated itself from others, especially the more *quotidien* aspects of life. To enter the museum was, then, to step into a particular institutional space, strongly framed as separate in relation to everyday practices, slightly more weakly framed in relation to other practices with which the museum was seen to be on a par.

It is also the case that new, contemporary museums are typically designed to be distinctive, to stand out, from the everyday – as did the museums of the Victorian era, only with a different design vernacular. Any distinctive kind of architecture provides strong framing of the institution in relation to its neighbours, by contributing to its perceived salience. Such strong framing is usually achieved architecturally by choosing a distinctive *coding orientation* for the architectural form of the building. A coding orientation represents a set of social values within which, or against which, 'reality' is defined and evaluated (Kress and van Leeuwen 1996).[19] In architecture, buildings which share similar patterns of symmetry, general size and shape, and materials, share the same coding orientation, and so are weakly framed in relation to each other. A building which breaks these conventions makes use of a different coding orientation, and so is more strongly framed. The use of distinctive, often confronting architecture, is a way of strongly framing the institution, and contributing to its perceived salience. The Guggenheim Museum at Bilbao, Spain, is an obvious contemporary example of this practice. Designed by Frank Gehry, its structure consists of steel frames supporting titanium sheathing, enabling a building which appears both solid and curvaceous, free-flowing – in contrast to the rigid and perpendicular designs dictated by conventional building practices.

However, at the same time as creating a distinctive coding orientation, the architecture can be used to weaken the framing between everyday and institutional practice, or between different historical periods, or between co-existing cultures. The Musée Pompidou, which could hardly have been more architecturally distinctive in its time, makes extensive use of glass and open vistas to connect the inside with the outside, and thus to ensure that the separation between surrounding life and the life internal to the museum is not so great after all. In Canberra, the National Museum of Australia combines challenging architectural forms with a site location and other references to significant Indigenous practices, to weaken the otherwise strong separation of Aboriginal and non-Aboriginal communities in Australia (Susskind and the National Museum of Australia 2001).

In such ways, practices of framing and coding orientation facilitate organisational links, highlighting connections or separations between entities. At the same time, these practices contribute to a sense of the overall 'persona' of the institution, creating a particular 'face' for the institution, and priming visitors for the institutional roles to be enacted within. Thus, these resources also contribute to interactional meanings at the institutional level.

Plate 6.10 A new coding orientation, Guggenheim Museum, Bilbao, Spain

. . . as interaction

The interactional framework is an intrinsic part of the meaning potential of an institution: how does an institution position visitors to behave and to respond? What impact does the physical makeup of an institution, or its policies and actions, have on its visitors? Interactional meanings are conveyed both by choices in aspects of design, and by choices in relation to policy. The impact of meanings conveyed by design are clearly evident: we respond emotionally – both positively and negatively – to buildings and what they contain, and physical spaces both enable and constrain our behaviour. Interactional meanings at the level of institution encompass some of the ways in which power relations are evoked, and the sort of 'face' which is created for the visiting public (O'Toole 1994; O'Toole and Butt 2003). Above all, in terms of the interactional framework, institutions create an overall 'persona' (O'Toole 1994): a persona which is generally welcoming, or which effectively excludes. This is achieved in a number of ways, particularly in terms of the ways the variables of power and social distance are inscribed and combined in the institution. As also discussed in relation to exhibitions, these define the role relations and behaviour potential of visitor and institution. One of the most evident signals of these variables is the sheer physicality of the building, and the impressions it makes on those who enter, especially in terms of the sense of 'authority' which the museum projects. Authority, as an issue of power, is usually signified in buildings through overall size and verticality (O'Toole 1994; Kress and van Leeuwen 1996): larger size indicates greater status, although status can also be signalled by other markers of exclusivity, such as specialised materials. In the interior, foyers replicate this status with spaces which are as large and as light as possible. It is not surprising that the majority of museums, reflecting their role as major cultural icons, are constructed to reflect the status of their times. However, here we can see how power and social distance can become contradictory variables for museums. Museums signal the significance of their socio-cultural presence with impressive exteriors and foyers which are as light and as large as possible, but they also need to counter-balance this with some way of inviting visitors 'in' and making them feel welcome. Thus, on large and potentially over-awing exteriors, smaller doors exist to signal a more human scale (Doyle 1991) or more intimate spaces are created within a larger one, through a change in colour, lighting or ceiling height. A balance is found between the need to make visitors comfortable, and the need to make them feel secure (cf. Stenglin 2001, 2004a, 2004b).

There are also other design decisions that can impact on the roles and relations enabled by the institution. The re-thinking of physical accessibility at the New Art Gallery, Walsall, reduces some of the perceived exclusionary status of such an institution: social contact is facilitated, and so the power differential between the museum and its potential visitors is lessened. By being less protective of its status, the museum lessens the division between itself and its local communities. While few institutions get to start with such a blank slate, new exhibitions and new activities provide an opportunity to rethink interactional relations with visitors and community in fundamental ways.

144

Of course, these choices are not made 'once' and then applied uniformly across all levels; there is rarely only one manifestation of power or social distance within any institution. Rather, these variables are revisited again and again at all levels, and may be combined in complex ways. The point in reflecting on these dimensions of the interactional framework is not to produce some 'measure' of power or social distance, but to recognise when these resources are being deployed, and their probable effects.

Another major way in which museums can change their relations with visitors is through the enactment of policy-level decisions. Some of the most fundamental changes in interactional meanings can be seen in the policies informing museum practice: the extent to which community consultation is invited in the conceptualisation and formation of exhibitions is one instance of this, as is the extent of visitor feedback which is both sought and incorporated into exhibition design and development. While such practices can be time-consuming and potentially controversial, they are also likely to be very successful, so long as they are supported institutionally, and are more than an occasional and ad hoc gesture (Hooper-Greenhill 1994: 22–23). The significance of these practices is that they change the fundamental power relations between institution and visitor: the opportunity to contribute to important decisions is shared, thus to some extent, the balance of power is shared. There is, thus, some potential for co-construction of knowledge, or some reciprocity in behaviour potential: it is no longer just the museum and relevant disciplinary communities which get to define what counts as 'knowledge'; other forms of knowledge, and other opinions, are made materially relevant in terms of choices about exhibition content and interpretation.

It is still the case that this 'reciprocity' is rarely, if ever, truly equal: institutions retain the right to 'invite' consultation and feedback, and the right to act, or not act, upon it. However, it is also the case that if museums take their new interactional relations seriously, their own behaviours must shift in relation to that of their visitors. If visitors are actively and creatively engaged in the co-construction of knowledge, the museum can no longer play a role such as 'arbiter' or 'determiner' of information, but needs to be something more like 'provider' or 'facilitator'.

The relevant interactional relations are not just between museum and visitor, however, but also between museum and community, especially where that community has a special interest in exhibition content. Access to the broadest possible definition of community is central to new interactional relations; not just in terms of physical understandings of accessibility, but also in terms of political understandings. Processes which invite the inclusion of non-traditional groups in decision-making processes, in exhibition development and content, redefine the overall interactional roles available to museums and visitors/communities. In Australia, inclusion of Indigenous communities in the conceptualisation, design and development of exhibitions has helped make these more relevant to these specific communities, and more representative and respectful of their own knowledge-based practices. In addition, institutions now

145

have the opportunity to reflect critically on their involvement in other social practices, such as colonial practices of appropriation, and to adjust their response to this, as noted in Chapter 4. In such ways, the interactional framework is central to the fundamental concerns of institutions, as engagement with communities and with the visiting public is an inherent part of the contemporary museum agenda.

. . . as representation

A further dimension to the institutional-level meanings can be seen in the representational framework. Representational meanings are at least partly about what is literally represented in the institution: how, for example, functional elements such as ticket purchase or toilet facilities are indicated (O'Toole 1994; Pang 2001). These are fundamental, pragmatic features which every institution must address. Beyond this, however, representational meanings have far deeper implications: as well as the indication of function, there are additional meanings, attributed to more abstract levels and connections, such as the broader taxonomic frameworks discussed in relation to language in Chapter 5 and in relation to exhibitions, in the earlier part of this chapter. These combine to give a sense of what the institution 'stands for', or what it is 'about'.

As already noted, while the selection of content is the primary resource for indicating representational meanings (an exhibition on rocks versus an exhibition on dinosaurs, for example), the nature of the selection and display also carries additional meanings. For instance, that the process of selecting and displaying rocks is a valid activity, that it is a way of 'doing' science. Where the rocks are kept behind glass: that the exhibit is too important for ordinary people to touch, and that only those in specialised positions (e.g. curators) can have full access. Or, where the rocks are part of an interactive exhibit that allows them to be smashed: that experience is part of the process of learning, and is as valuable as the object itself. Again we see constant interaction between the frameworks: the interactional meanings constructed around the content area contribute to a sense of what the institution is 'for', and what visitors 'can do', when they enter that institution. Similarly, organisational meanings contribute to these processes. The relation of exhibitions to each other adds further layers of meaning: are the exhibitions coherently related themselves to some larger 'big idea' which the institution is promoting? Are particular interests and subjects marginalised within that picture, addressed but somehow not made central? Here, the resources of pathways, framing, salience and other organisational features contribute to these institutional-level meanings. For instance, the ways in which pragmatic and other functions are addressed, as with the location of toilets and café at the New Art Gallery, Walsall, makes a statement about the accessibility of the institution. So, not only are there toilets, but their location is part of a larger institutional stance towards community relations.

Sometimes, the representational meanings made at institutional level can be only indirectly concerned with the actual 'content' of exhibitions, and yet, they nevertheless add substantially to a sense of what the museum is 'about'. For instance, consider the possible ways in which children can be catered for in terms of exhibits and displays. There tends to be a continuum in framing practices here: on the one hand, exhibits designed for children can be presented as an integrated part of all exhibitions (and so, weakly framed), or on the other hand, as a separate, clearly identified 'section' (and so, strongly framed). There are arguments for both solutions, but both have implications for what it 'means' to be a child in a museum. At the Melbourne Museum, as is the case for many institutions, a special section for children has been identified, both from within and from without, as being a distinct and purpose-specific space. From the outside, the children's gallery is a skewed, multi-coloured cube, in contrast to the restrained minimalism of the remainder of the building (see Plate 6.11). From within, its exhibits are designed for children, and are not found elsewhere within the institution. Exhibits for children could have been dispersed throughout all of the other galleries, which would constitute a weak framing between adult and child experiences. However, previous institutional experience had suggested that the strong framing provided by a separate children's wing was especially attractive to potential family visitors,[20] and so strong framing was preferred. While neither weak nor strong framing is an inherently better strategy, each has implications for what it 'means' to be a child in the museum. Strong framing, where the children's exhibits are separate, suggests that childhood is a specialised experience, that it needs to be nurtured; whereas weak framing suggests that the childhood experience is a more integrated part of adult experiences. While the subject matter of the exhibition may have nothing to do with childhood per se, the institution, through its practices, nevertheless conveys meanings about childhood, and what it means to be a child visitor, through such choices. In this way, the 'subject matter' of an exhibition is only part of the representational meanings created within an institution as a whole.

Many other features within an institution can contribute to these more abstract representational meanings. For instance, the degree of permanence of exhibitions reflects on the values and significance of the institution, though the evaluation of such permanence will vary according to the framework of values within which it is interpreted. In the past, more permanent displays were generally seen to be a sign of the significance and the authority of the institution, with less permanent displays relegated to topics deemed to be less central to the institution's agenda (MacDonald 1998). Today, permanence can be evaluated negatively, as an indicator of an inability to respond to the ongoing change of the modern world, and rapidly changing exhibitions can be seen as a sign of an institution's ability to keep up with constantly changing domains of knowledge.

Plate 6.11 Children's Museum, at the Melbourne Museum

In such ways, the representational framework contributes to a sense of what the institution 'is', and what it is 'about'. But the other frameworks also contribute to the overall picture: the behaviour potential enabled for visitors, the persona created for the institution, the general accessibility of the institution and the prioritisation of some messages over others: all these are part of the meanings of the institution.

Conclusions

This chapter has attempted to indicate how the basic communication frameworks for language can be extended, to account for a broader, more comprehensive understanding of 'museum as text'. The initial focus was on the level of the exhibition, followed by the level of the institution. What I have provided here is an indication of the potential of this approach, a way of seeing that 'communication' is more than just language, and that all sorts of other practices – of architecture, of design, of display, of policy – are part of the meaning package that is a contemporary cultural institution. Each of the frameworks, the organisational, interactional and representational, contribute to meanings at the level of both the exhibition and the institution, using distinct resources to make meanings, and combining in complex and powerful ways. In the next chapter, I will try and draw the frameworks together, showing some of the ways in which language and the broader issues of design are integrated.

7

Conclusion

Integrating the frameworks

Review

This book has provided a set of frameworks for understanding communication, via language, and via resources of design and display, which enable processes of meaning-making in museum texts to be more fully understood. Museum texts have been interpreted both in terms of *texts in museums*, especially its written texts, and in terms of *museums as texts*, through the ways in which diverse resources are integrated at the level of the exhibition and the institution. Communication has been explained as a socially contextualised, semiotic resource, that is, one which actively constructs meanings, rather than passively transmitting them. The frameworks provided are those of organisational, inter-actional and representational meanings – different facets of communication, each related to particular issues of social context, and invoking their own particular communicative resources.

The majority of the book has focussed on the language of museum texts, using each of the frameworks to explore the relevant meaning-making resources. Chapter 2 examined organisational meanings, demonstrating some of the ways in which organisational resources – from the macro to the micro level – contribute to issues of purpose, cohesion, and information flow in texts. In Chapter 3, the particular connection between the organisational framework and issues of context was examined further, showing that organisational meanings are closely related to issues of *Mode* in the context. Here, aspects of the com-plexity of texts were explained, and related to issues of accessibility in museum texts. While museum communicators need to understand what contributes to a well-organised and effective text, it was also highlighted that it is important to be wary of simplistic advice, especially when it comes to rules and formulae about grammar.

The interactional framework was introduced in Chapter 4, highlighting the relationship between the *Tenor* of the context – the roles and relations holding between interactants – and their meaning potential as construed in text. Issues of style and stance were also canvassed here, acknowledging that texts need to be relevant and engaging for visitors, but not facile. In Chapter 5, the examin-ation of the representation framework was related to issues of *Field* in the context, demonstrating the ways in which 'content' is actively constructed through choices in language, and highlighting the range of ways in which 'one' subject could be communicated. As well as being aware of appropriate ways to convey technical meanings, museum communicators also need to be critically aware and self-reflexive, acknowledging that there is no 'necessary' or 'natural' way to convey the content of a particular subject area.

The frameworks established for language were re-examined in Chapter 6, which adopted an extended sense of communication, in terms of the ways in which whole exhibitions, and whole institutions, can be seen to make meaning. An extension of the frameworks to this level demonstrated that here, meaning is an equally complex, multi-functional resource. While this chapter provided only a snapshot of the potential of this approach, it highlights the ways in which a range of resources, such as spatial organisation, or content selection, can contribute to communication at this level. This text-based, social-semiotic approach does not mean that meaning is 'fixed within the text' (Witcomb 2003: 146); rather, meaning depends on the social and cultural contexts with which the text negotiates. This approach does mean, however, that meaning is constructed and interpreted in relation to *text-based resources*: meanings do not arise from thin air; they are textual products and represent a complex set of resources. Explicit engagement with these resources enables more specific reflection on issues of meaning.

Overall then, the approach of this book has been to *pull apart* communication; to recognise it as a coherent whole, but to explore it as a complex of resources, each with particular relations to context. This perspective enables a strategic focus on texts; it should be possible to take any text, and examine it in terms of each of the three frameworks, as the frameworks operate simultaneously. Given that the approach has been to separate the frameworks and examine them individually, it is important now to see how it is that they operate together, in an integrated way.

Integrating the frameworks

There are three different ways in which the frameworks introduced in this book can be seen to be integrated. First, each of the frameworks is always present in every text. In this book I have focussed on them separately, in order to highlight their individual specificities, but they are always co-present in text, and any one example can be examined from multiple viewpoints, reflecting the contributions of the different frameworks. It is not the case, for instance, that a particular text 'doesn't have' interactional meanings, although it might be the case that we are so used to a particular interactional style that its effects can go unnoticed. The same is true for organisational and representational meanings; they are all always co-present.

The second way in which the frameworks are integrated is through the fact that a specific communicative resource can have multiple effects, across the frameworks. In this book, when particular resources have been introduced and examined, they have usually been related primarily to one framework, but they can also have implications for the other frameworks. For example, the resource of nominalisation, introduced in Chapter 3 as a resource which impacts on organisational meanings, also has an impact on interactional and representational meanings. A text which has a high proportion of nominalisations is likely to be organisationally complex, interactionally impersonal (because human agents are removed from the text) and representationally technical. Similarly, a design resource, such as the type of circulation path used, can have multiple effects. In organisational terms, a circulation path creates organisational relations between multiple elements within an exhibition; this contributes to interactional meanings, by positioning visitors in terms of their behavioural potential, and to representational meanings, by invoking a particular narrative design. These are just some of the ways in which a singular resource can be seen to have an impact across the frameworks, and this is another way in which the frameworks need to be seen and understood as an integrated resource, as well as being individual strands of meaning.

A third sense of integration arises when the two emphases of the book – texts in museums, and museums as texts – are brought together. Clearly, texts in museums do not exist apart from their exhibitionary or institutional context, and exhibitions and institutions themselves are complex, *multi-modal texts –* texts which make their meaning through a combination of resources across various semiotic systems, which often includes language. Language and other communicative resources operate together to make meanings within museum contexts, and are integrated in complex and interesting way.

It is important to try and understand how the meanings arising from individual semiotic systems (language, layout, interactivity . . .) are able to work together to create 'one' text. It is not the case that the different resources are 'added' together, to produce another text; rather their effect is to 'multiply' meaning – to produce something more than the sum of the parts (Lemke 1998). This effect arises through *intersemiosis*. Intersemiosis is the co-ordination of semiosis across different sign systems (Ravelli 2000: 508), akin to Eco's explanation of 'text' in architecture deriving from a 'system of systems' (Eco 1977: 308). The process of intersemiosis creates the overall 'experience' that a visitor takes away from a museum, arising from the *interaction* of the different semiotic modes which constitute the exhibitionary or institutional space. It is intersemiosis which draws together the individual constituents of the space and brings them together as a meaningful whole.

The 'meaningful whole' of a multimodal text arises from the patterning of patterns. In the first instance, each semiotic system makes its own meanings: sentences, paragraphs and texts produced in language; arrangements of objects, rooms and buildings produced via layout, and so on. Meanings at this level are 'first order' meanings. However, these meanings can be re-patterned, giving rise to second-order meanings: the level of symbolic articulation. It is here that more general levels of meaning, 'themes' in the conventional sense, are found (Hasan 1989).

Let's look schematically at some of the ways this meaning-making occurs in museums. Figure 7.1 maps out some of the first- and second-order meanings across the different meaning frameworks. The first-order meanings are noted in terms of the main language and design features addressed in relation to each of the communication frameworks; together, these resources create second-order meanings for the exhibition and the institution.

In this map, the communication frameworks – organisational, interactional and representational meanings – are located down the left-hand column. Across the top are two columns, first-order and second-order meanings. The first-order meanings are those made through the systems of language and of a range of 'design' elements. The second-order meanings are those made in exhibitions and institutions as a whole, where individual effects of particular resources combine with others, to produce holistic effects. Intersemiosis is the process that re-patterns the various first-order meanings into another, more complex layer of meaning.

This map necessarily condenses a lot of information and so is selective and partial, but it indicates the ways in which meanings across different frameworks and different modalities can combine together. Thus, the boxes within the map are indicative of the sort of features which are relevant, and are not necessarily comprehensive. The 'first order' meanings of language are the issues discusssed in Chapters 2 to 5. This includes the ways in which organisational meanings are created through a selection of (grammatical) Theme, generic structure, and details of language complexity. Interactional meanings are created through the range and predominance of speech functions, type of voice and address used, and the use of modality and Appraisal to indicate a stance towards material.

	First-order meanings (resources)		Second-order meanings (effects)	
	← Intersemiosis →			
	Language	Design	Exhibition	Institution
Organisational meanings	Generic structure Grammatical Theme Complexity	Pathways Framing Placement	Narrative design Information flow; Information values Accessibility	Purpose Access
Interactional meanings	Speech function Voice, Address Mood, Modality and Appraisal	Interactive potential affect	Behaviour potential Stance Formality Objectivity	Visitor and community relations Positioning Persuasiveness
Representational meanings	Defining Taxonomising Process type Participant roles Circumstances	Selection Framing Coding orientation	Knowledge type	Disciplinary Boundaries and connections, Validation, Critique

Figure 7.1 Intersemiosis between language and design

Representational meanings are created through the selection and inter-relation of Process type, Participant role and Circumstances, with relations built between concepts through defining and taxonomising.

Similarly, the first-order meanings of design are those addressed in Chapter 6, however with the label 'design' indicating a range of modalities here, not just one (for instance, it might be colour, lighting, spatial layout, item selection . . .), and remembering that this might be operational at the level of the exhibition or the institution. Organisational meanings here relate items to each other and create pathways between them, aligning or separating areas through resources of framing, and creating information values through resources of placement. Interactional meanings facilitate certain kinds of activity and forms of participation, as well as creating emotional and emotive responses. Representational meanings are created through the selection and relationship of content items, with framing and coding orientation contributing to a sense of boundaries. Such first-order meanings, in both language and design, combine together to produce second-order meanings for both exhibition and institution. For the exhibition, an overall narrative design or generic purpose can be discerned, facilitating a particular behaviour potential for visitors, and creating a certain approach to knowledge. For the institution, this relates to policy-level issues of purpose, accessibility, visitor and community relations, and disciplinary boundaries, and roles of validating or critiquing those boundaries.

In such ways, then, a complex 'text', such as an exhibition or a whole institution, makes meaning across the frameworks, and by drawing on a range of resources. One piece of this puzzle remains, however, and that is the question of how it is that many potentially diverse meanings, arising from different sources, can be brought together as 'one' text[1] – how does intersemiosis, as opposed to a meaningless jumble of effects, arise? This depends on the notion of *foregrounding* – that is, features which 'stand out' from others and which relate to the meaning of the whole text (Halliday 1973). Features may be foregrounded either because they create a 'norm' in the text, that is, establish a pattern which guides the reading of other features, or because they break a norm, that is, contradict an established pattern. The 'norm' is defined according to the perspective of the observer, and this is an additional way in which the 'same' text can be read differently. The norms of a curator, reading a text, are likely to be different from those of a visitor, so the text is understood and evaluated in relation to different expectations. The principle remains, however, that foregrounding brings disparate meanings together, through a 'consistency' of patterning (Hasan 1989: 98); it is a kind of 'integrative principle' (Pang 2004). What then, might be an example of foregrounding? Pang proposes that the language of evaluation (judgements, appreciation, cf. Chapter 4) might be one of these integrative principles, and I would agree, with the corollary that the integrative principle might derive from *any* of the frameworks. That is, it could be interactional meanings which guide the integration of the text (for example, guiding a visitor to evaluate a certain subject matter in a positive or negative light); or the integration could be via organisational meanings (for example, structuring the text so that it achieves a particular social purpose) or the integration could be via representational meanings (for example, creating a novel relationship between conventionally separate disciplines).[2]

Such integration is most likely to arise through, and be made evident in, choices in language – titles, headings, key points in written texts, consistent patterns across written texts. It is not *reliant* upon language – integration and foregrounding could be achieved by other semiotic resources – but where language is used as a resource, it is likely to be used both as a basis for explanation, by the developers of the exhibition, and as a basis for interpretation, by visitors.[3] Language can be seen to have a macro-discursive function, providing the coherent thread which links disparate elements of an exhibition together (Jacobi and Poli 1995). However, this does not have to be the case, and the relationship between language and other semiotic resources can be partially explained in terms of Barthes' (1977) notion of *anchorage*, where the meanings of one semiotic system elaborate meanings in another. Where a visual image and verbal text are related, the image may illustrate the verbal text, or the verbal text may anchor the meanings of the verbal image. In making use of this notion, it is important to bear in mind the corollary of Kress and van Leeuwen (1996: 16–17) who stressed that this does not mean that one system is dependent on the other; rather, each system is an independent semiotic system with its own organisation, structure and affordances.

Foregrounding and its role in intersemiosis leads to a basis for evaluating exhibitions as 'text', that is, evaluating the sense in which the various resources operate successfully to achieve exhibition aims. Typically, one would expect some consistency of foregrounding across semiotic resources – that is, for all signs to point in the same direction. For instance, the grammatical Theme of an explanatory label should be consistent with the salient element of an image or display (Ferguson *et al.* 1995). In an exhibition, (linguistic) invitations to actively participate in and engage with exhibition content should be consistent with the learning and activity experiences enabled by the exhibition. Similarly, an abstract, scientific model of a dinosaur should not be accompanied by a narrative about hunting them! For the institution, claims about inclusivity and desired community relations should be realised in actual community relations and reflected in appropriate exhibition content. The goals and objectives for institutions, exhibitions and exhibits need to be realised consistently, across the levels, and across the meaning frameworks. In general, where signs do 'point in the same direction', a depth of purpose is achieved through the consistent realisation of goals across levels and spaces.

Occasionally, however, symmetry and consistency are not the only ways to achieve intersemiosis. Very rarely, dissonance might be used as an organising principle, as discussed in Chapter 6 in relation to the 'Kaboom!' exhibition, where part of the intention was to create an atmosphere of chaos. Here, then, chaos, and a lack of consistency, were part of the desired aims of the exhibition, and so this becomes the point for evaluating its success. Slightly more frequently, especially today, is the principle of *critical disruption* – not a complete absence of consistency across the semiotic resources, but an intentional disruption of 'comfortable' or familiar messages, used to punctuate an exhibition and so critique its own content. Such a rhythm can be found in the 'Bunjilaka' exhibition in Melbourne, referred to a number of times throughout this book, where conventional and critical approaches to the 'same' material are juxtaposed at various points. This juxtaposition brings into question the whole role of the museum in relation to the 'collection' and interpretation of Indigenous knowledge and artefacts. These disruptions are foregrounded against the 'norms' established elsewhere in the exhibition, and against the norms of established curatorial practices in Western museology.

In these ways, dissonance and disruption can be used to effect. On the whole, however, consistency and symmetry are more likely to be the integrative principle, and departures from such a principle are likely to be evaluated negatively. In many ways, this is saying what museum professionals already know: that an exhibition, and a visit to an institution, should be an 'experience', and that all semiotic resources impact upon this experience in some way. Exhibitions and institutions should be able to function to some extent successfully, even if they are only partially taken in, and this can only occur where there is some degree of redundancy across the resources. Through foregrounding then, as a principle of intersemiosis, the communication frameworks are integrated as meaning-making resources.

Using the frameworks

There are a number of practical implications arising from the frameworks proposed in this book. In the first instance, the frameworks proposed here have two slightly contradictory implications: they enable texts to be seen as an integrated whole, and at the same time, they enable texts to be pulled apart. As integrated wholes, it is important to use the frameworks to appreciate that meaning is complex and multifunctional, and cannot be limited to a transparent notion of 'content'. Texts need to be consistently re-visited and interrogated from multiple viewpoints, to try to appreciate the range of meanings they make. This means that texts also need to be pulled apart – considered in terms of each of the frameworks – what content is being created? what roles and relationships are enabled by the text? how does the organisation contribute to the structure and coherence of the text? The advantage of the frameworks is that they enable both a *holistic* view of texts, considering them as complex and multifunctional in meaning, and a *strategic* view of texts, enabling particular aspects of meaning to be focussed on as needed. For example, it might be important in the development of an exhibition to reflect in depth on interactional meanings, and so this book has provided some guidelines as to which resources will have the most impact on interactional meanings. Importantly, the frameworks have been explored in relation to both the language of texts in museums, and the design aspects of museums as texts, with both perspectives addressed at a number of levels, from micro-level issues of particular grammatical constructions, to macro-level issues of the overall shape and purpose of text. These complex perspectives also facilitate a strategic examination of texts – not every aspect of a text, nor every level, can be considered simultaneously, and it is possible to use the frameworks to identify those levels, resources, and aspects of meaning, which need most work.

Importantly, then, the frameworks need to be considered as an integral part of exhibition development. The complex view of meaning explained here indicates that the writing of texts cannot be some 'add-on' feature of exhibition development, nor can editing be relegated to a *post hoc* process of error-checking (cf. Blais 1995). While final polishing and checking for basic errors is always required, text production is itself a meaning-making process and needs to be integrated as a fundamental component in the development of an exhibition. Thus, the frameworks should be used from the outset to establish clear goals – what general level of complexity is to be aimed at? what sort of relationship is to be established? what view of content is to be presented? Similarly, issues of design are also meaning-making resources, and cannot be *post hoc* add-ons to the development process. The fundamental contributions to meaning of design resources, such as the selection and relative placement of items, needs to be considered from the start of exhibition development. Design is more than something which is just 'aesthetically pleasing'; it makes meanings of its own, and it is the strategic manipulation of language and design resources which enables exhibitions and institutions to be the meaningful texts which they are.

The frameworks proposed here can also make a useful contribution to issues of evaluation. While this area has not been specifically addressed in this book, the strategic focus on meanings which is enabled by the frameworks, can be used to highlight issues which are relevant to the evaluation of an exhibition's communication systems, in both front-end, formative and summative terms (Belcher 1991). Representationally, issues of content can be addressed – what did the visitor understand? which concepts were clear? do some need to be re-explained? is one view presented of the subject matter, or several? In interactional terms, an exhibition might be evaluated in terms of the extent of involvement or engagement a visitor felt they had with exhibition content – were they able to engage with the content? what did they perceive as the source and relative status (authority) of the content? what feelings were evoked for them? In organisational terms, evaluation can address the effectiveness and coherence of texts – is the overall purpose of the text clear? are visitors able to follow the whole text? can visitors choose which level they wish to focus on? are they able to manage the level of detail within the text? These are just some of the ways in which the frameworks enable some strategic directions for evaluation to be developed.

In addition, and perhaps most importantly of all, the frameworks enable some strategic reflection on the overall agendas and purposes of cultural institutions. What is it that the institution is trying to achieve, in terms of making meanings about a particular content area, about their role and relationships with visitors and communities, about appropriate and effective ways to communicate?

Communication agendas are most likely to go astray when there are mis-alignments or gaps in perceptions of context. For instance, if exhibition texts are prepared by writers who are most used to writing for their scholarly peers, and thus producing texts which suit that context, adjustments need to be made to adapt to the actual context of the exhibition. If museums create one set of roles and relationships for visitors, but visitors seek others, then dis-comfort and unease will arise. If a particular level of knowledge is presumed of visitors, but not shared by them, then confusion will result, and similarly, if a particular approach to knowledge is presumed but not shared, then controversy and rejection will result. The frameworks encompass the many ways in which institutions make and enable meanings, and go to the core of their communication agendas.

Of course, even the most careful design and preparation of text, and the deepest reflection on institutional agendas, is not able to fully account for or control all of the ways in which that text might be responded to. For instance, a text which is designed to engage an explicit response from visitors might simply be bypassed by someone who is not interested – such as a mother chasing her wayward toddler. Or, for reasons completely beyond the control of the museum, a visitor might go through the motions of engaging with and reading a text, but be too distracted to focus. Such factors cannot be controlled, and indeed, control is not the point. The point is to try and understand those factors which are *most likely* to enhance or detract from the communication, and to try and understand the ways in which a text is *most likely* to be responded to: there will always be provisional and contingent aspects to meaning.

Expanding the frameworks

All of the areas addressed in this book could be revisited and pursued in more depth, and there are a number of ways in which such explorations could be pursued. First, a number of resources introduced in this book demand imme-diate attention and further research, such as the nature and variety of genres of exhibition texts, as well as further exploration of exhibitions themselves as genres. This could be done in terms of the elemental genres which are used, and in terms of the overall macro-genres which characterise an exhibition. Such an exploration would highlight issues of purpose more clearly, and could be very revealing about new directions in contemporary museum practices. In addition, given the refined perceptions of interactivity being developed in museo-logical theory (cf. Witcomb 2003), it would be interesting to explore further the resources which are used to enable interaction and influence perceptions, for example through resources such as the attitudinal lexis (Appraisal) discussed in Chapter 4. Here, it would be interesting to explore how different appraisal values are played out in different types of museum texts: the art gallery versus the natural history museum, for example; the texts which introduce whole exhibitions, versus the texts which explain an object; different types of exhib-itions within the one institution. And generally, the intersemiosis between the many resources of language and design could be explored further, in terms of how these resources are integrated, and how they contribute to institutional-level meanings.

A second way in which an understanding of the frameworks can be expanded, is by focussing on particular meaning-making practices in more depth, and interrogating these meanings in relation to museological developments. Here, the practices of critical disruption, characteristic of the post-museum, stand out as meriting most attention. How does an exhibition succeed in creating and enabling polysemy? Where and how do exhibitions and institutions close down such potential? What do such critical practices say about museology, and the relationship of museology to disciplinary discourses?

As meaning is always relational, an additional area of further exploration is that of locating museum practices in relation to other contemporary practices of meaning making (cf. Bennett 1995; Witcomb 2003). Where and how do the meaning-making practices of museums intersect with the discourses of education, of regulation, of mass media, of entertainment? How are they the same, or different? These are already well-established areas of exploration in museum studies, but the frameworks introduced in this book offer an additional range of analyses, to further explore the ways in which the social significance of contemporary cultural institutions are constructed.

In an ideal world . . .

In an ideal world, all of the decisions made in museums would be based on an understanding of meaning. However, museums are not ideal worlds; they are subject to the constraints of time, of limited budgets, and competing political agendas. Thus, decisions made in the construction of an exhibition might be made as much because of the type of display that can be produced with the available resources, as because of a given communication objective. As someone who sees communication at the heart of everything, I am naturally inclined to think that everyone should have communication at their heart. But as Witcomb (2003) rightly argues, the demand for 'everyone' to be reflexive of communication has implications for the very role of museums today. The contested boundaries between potentially competing agendas, such as research versus public engagement, cannot be ignored. Nevertheless, all decisions, whatever their source and motivation, inevitably do have implications for meanings, and are open to criticism and evaluation on that basis. Perhaps it is too much to expect curators to also be expert public communicators, but *institutions* need to be fully reflexive and aware of the impact of communication, and able to implement appropriate strategies. This book, then, is one resource which enables critical reflection on these issues. Some of it can be used to provide very simple principles for particular aspects of text production (such as how to clarify the organisation of information within a text); other aspects go to the heart of institutional agendas and should contribute to vigorous debate about issues of meaning.

One outcome of this book is that it debunks some cherished 'rules' about language (such as to 'avoid the passive voice'), and it highlights language as a complex, elastic resource, which constantly adapts to and is adapted by context. However, my claims that language is both complex and eternally elastic, and that the appropriateness of communicative choices needs to be evaluated in context, is not a sop to excuse textual ills. Nothing excuses self-delusion. A museum (or government, or public interest group) that believes there is one view of a subject matter that is 'neutral' or 'fair', and another which is 'political' or 'biased', is simply denying huge swathes of intellectual thought and research, from multiple disciplinary perspectives, which make such a claim patently absurd. An art gallery that clings to its high-art discourse, pasted on the wall in dense texts printed in size 12 font, is choosing to speak to a very restricted audience. A modernist museum which nods its head towards superficial markers of interaction, while retaining firm control of the communicative agenda, is changing little in terms of institutional relations. Language, and all forms of communication, are complex resources. There may be no simple rules, and it is certainly not possible to control all aspects of meaning making, but that does not mean that there is not a clear obligation on the part of those who have the privilege to be in influential communicative positions, to attempt to understand at least some of the complexity and diversity of those resources, and to attempt to evaluate the context and their communicative choices critically, and realistically. This is the least we can do.

Notes

1 Introduction: texts, frameworks and meanings

1 Halliday's terms are *ideational* (equating with representational); *interpersonal* (equating with interactional) and *textual* (equating with organisational). I have chosen terms which I hope will be more transparent in the museum context, but intend them to be largely co-extensive with Halliday's original terms. Within SFL and related approaches, there is some variation in the specific terms used, but general overlap in their meanings; cf. Lemke's terms, *presentational, orientational,* and *organisational* (Lemke 1998) and also Kress and van Leeuwen's terms, *representation, composition* and *interaction* (Kress and van Leeuwen 1996).

2 In Halliday's SFL model, an initial upper case is used to signal functional terms, which are semantically oriented; initial lower case is used to signal class terms, which are formally oriented, hence *Field, Theme, Participant,* vs *clause, noun,* etc.

3 As noted, this equates with Halliday's 'interpersonal' meanings. However, note that this does not simply mean 'when people are communicating directly'. For instance, Hooper-Greenhill (1994: 142) differentiates 'mass communication' from 'interpersonal communication'. The former arises where communication is indirect, and where there is no actual interaction. The latter arises where people are literally engaged with each other in the process of communication. In this book, interactional meanings arise in *all* forms of communication, and relate to those meanings in text which establish interpersonal relations, whether these are direct or indirect.

4 For useful introductions to systemic-functional linguistics and detailed advice on how to do text analysis, see Eggins 2004; Butt *et al.* 2001; Droga and Humphrey 2002. Bear in mind that these resources are targeted at students of linguistics and are relevant only for those wishing to pursue actual technical detail.

5 The technical name for this is *rank*; see discussions of the *rank scale* in the textbooks just mentioned.

6 Technically, *morphemes* are an additional building block that make up words, but these generally do not impinge on the discussions of meaning to be canvassed in this book, and so are ignored here.

7 I am aware that the alternative terms here are not necessarily co-extensive, but for the sake of simplicity, will largely use 'exhibition' and 'exhibit' throughout the book.

8 And see also a more elaborate description of levels in Pang 2004.

9 There are many books which do attempt to cover these issues; see for example Dean 1994; Serrell 1996.

10 cf. Halliday and Matthiessen 2004.

2 Organisation as a way of making meaning: using language to organise, shape and connect

1 Again, this refers to 'organisation' as a means of manipulating and shaping text, not 'organisation' as a synonym for the museum or institution.

2 '... the textual component has an enabling function with respect to the other two (i.e. the ideational and interpersonal metafunctions, or representational and interactional frameworks; LR); it is only in combination with textual meanings that ideational and interpersonal meanings are actualised' (Halliday 1978: 113).

3 Many of the points and examples in this chapter are closely based on the guidelines presented in Ferguson *et al.* 1995. I am grateful to the Australian Museum for permission to reproduce these points and examples.

4 This text is accompanied by explanatory diagrams, which model the events explained in the text. Thus, the participants (*the egg, the embryo* ...) seem to be specific, because they refer to the elements represented in the diagram; these are, however, intended to stand for all instances of this process.

5 Indeed some writers, such as Jacobi and Poli (1995), would argue that the venture is inevitably fruitless, although I would suggest that it could in fact be highly revealing.

6 See Macken-Horarik 2004, for additional examination and analysis of Art Express texts, using a complementary framework.

7 For example, the 2002 winner, Nicholas Harding, in his painting of the popular local actor, John Bell, employed an unusual technique of a particularly thick application of oils, which became the subject of much interest.

8 Management Brief, Aboriginal and Torres Strait Islander Cultures Centre, Museum of Queensland, 2004; courtesy of Richard Cassels.

9 Technically, this is called a 'hyper-Theme' in linguistics; later we will see that 'Themes' operate as points of departure at the level of the sentence; hyper-Themes operate as points of departure for larger sections of text (Martin 1992; Martin and Rose 2003).

10 This is called a 'macro-Theme', and is the point of departure for the text as a whole.

11 More technical information about Themes and how they are identified can be found in Ferguson *et al.* 1995. See also the introductory linguistic texts referred to in Chapter 1.

12 The boundaries of the New are less precise than those of the Theme; the New is more an 'area' of the clause, rather than a specific element as such; see Halliday 1994, Halliday and Matthiessen 2004, or Martin and Rose 2003, for further details.

13 Technically, these are referred to as Circumstances, and give background information about time, place, manner and so on; see Halliday 1994 or Halliday and Matthiessen 2004 for further discussion.

14 It is in fact the correlation between visual and linguistic structure which explains some of the possible problems in Ekarv's proposals for chunking texts. (Ekarv 1999; Gilmore and Sabine 1999). Following this method, texts are broken down so that 'the end of each line would coincide with the end of a natural phrase or idea' (McManus 2000: 106). This has the advantage of 'chunking' the text into meaningful sections, and so helping to focus readers on issues of meaning. However, a problem with this method is that readers feel it 'slows down' their reading (McManus 2000). This arises because the chunking of the text means that the start of each new line is also the start of a new phrase or idea; this phrase or idea may be in the middle of a clause, but if it appears at the beginning of a new line, it is given some visual emphasis which it would not otherwise have. Thus, layout *seems to be being used as an additional semi-otic resource* (to the eyes of the visitor); that is, the layout is imposing the weight of grammatical Theme onto an element which would otherwise be buried in Rheme, without receiving prominence. It is this which 'slows' the text down and gives it its 'poetic' feel.

3 Focus: making texts accessible: adjusting the level of complexity

1 The fact that the literature addresses these issues does not, sadly, mean that they are always attended to in exhibition production; I am still amazed at how many times I have to peer and squint at a text on the wall, just because it is presented in 12 point font, that is, the font used for reading a book in the comfort of one's own home.

2 The continua represented here for Mode complement a more basic distinction between 'natural' and 'mass' communication methods (Hooper-Greenhill 1994). 'Natural' communication, occurring directly between individuals, lies at the more spoken end; 'mass' communication generally lies towards the more written end. However, as the examples show, within that broad category, there can still be distinct variation in Mode in terms of the continua of contact/feedback and the role of language.

3 One way in which such choices impinge on meaning-making is in the overall values attached to the choice of medium. For example, and especially in art galleries, there is often a curious split between that which is presented orally, by a guide, and that which is displayed on the wall in written form. In some institutions, greater access is provided to basic and introductory information via the guide, including more personalised and opinionated information, and more explicit evaluation of the artwork. Such tours are typically taken by novice visitors. At the same time, the guides may well have an 'amateur' status – they are volunteers, even if pseudo-professionalised with in-house training. Thus, such institutions suggest that 'real' art-goers do not need access to interpretation; a little written text is all that is needed. In such ways, basic choices of medium can be very significant. See further discussion of the complex place of written text in art institutions in Dobbs 1990; McManus 2000; O'Neill 1999; Ravelli 1998; the role of audio guides in Lamarche 1995 and Decrosse and Natali 1995, and the role of audio tours in heritage sites in Bath 2000.

4 There are some notable exceptions to this, especially the language of the law, infamous for its wealth of sub-clauses and dependent clauses.

5 I am not advocating either of these examples as 'better' or 'worse' than the other, nor am I advocating either as an example of what 'should' be written in a museum context. They each illustrate differences in Mode, the first being more spoken, the second being more written.

6 Readers would need to learn how to accurately identify clause boundaries, and to describe logical relations between clauses, for instance. See Halliday 1994 or Halliday and Matthiessen 2004 if interested!

7 Baños (1995: 208–212), discussing Richaudeau, correctly draws attention to the meanings contributed by grammatical items.

8 Halliday (1998) shows that nominalisation tends to be built up in a text as the text unfolds.

9 Personal communication: Jane Bywaters, Museum of London.

4 Interacting in and through language: using language to relate, engage and evaluate

1 As explained in Chapter 1, interactional meanings are equivalent with Halliday's interpersonal meanings (Halliday 1978, 1994; Halliday and Matthiessen 2004). Note however that in existing museum literature, the term 'interpersonal meaning' has been referred to with a related, but different sense, namely, those involving active engagement with people as individuals, as opposed to, for instance, mass forms of communication (cf. Hooper-Greenhill 1994). In this book, the interactional framework encompasses both mass communication and (this second use of) interpersonal communication. See also Note 3 in Chapter 1.

2 Of course at stake here is neither power nor social distance in an absolute sense; I am not suggesting that an institution can force any subject (visitor) into any particular behaviour; rather, at stake are 'power' and 'social distance' as resources for making meaning – a set of resources for opening up or closing down the potential for various forms of interaction.

3 Material exchanges are in fact primary in the development of language: children first ask for things – milk, juice, mummy, etc., not the time of day or the state of your health!

4 Such as the forthcoming Aboriginal and Torres Strait Islander Cultures Centre, at the Queensland Museum, as noted in Chapter 2.

5 http://www.tepapa.govt.nz/TePapa/English/AboutTePapa/CommunityRelationships/.

6 Melbourne Museum, Visitor Guide

7 In a number of cases, where bi- and multi-lingual options exist, the overall choice of language itself has a fundamental impact on interactional meanings also: whose language is allowed to speak? cf. Falk and Dierking 2000.

8 Again the issue is not what is 'really' going on in the world, but how linguistic resources are used *to construct a picture of what is going on*. In museums, the degree of actual contact is a very important variable in the way visitors are able to learn from museums (Falk and Dierking 2000), but what is of interest to us here is how museums convey a particular style – one which appears to be friendly and intimate, or one which appears to construct a great social distance.

9 The case of docents, guides, and curators leading tours and answering questions is another matter altogether. Such interaction, via the spoken medium, is likely to coincide with a more personal and less formal approach, but even here there can still be wide variation in the type of language used and the nature of the interaction that results. Some guides will be more formal, more 'written' in their style of language, others less so. Discussion of this aspect of museum texts requires separate treatment, which is beyond the scope of this book, but see Bennett 1998b for some historical contextualisation of the role of guides.

10 Note that 'voice' is used in two ways. 'Grammatical voice' refers to a particular grammatical form of a clause, such as the active or passive voice. General 'voice' refers to an overall interactional effect created in a text (such as an 'institutional' voice, or a 'personal' voice) through a range of resources, which may include, but which is not limited to, grammatical voice.

11 As Derewianka notes (1990), high modality is often used in argumentative (expository) texts, to assert a point of view and persuade the reader that something must be done (it is a problem; it must be stopped . . .), and low modality is used to open up discussion and debate (it seems we have a problem with . . .).

12 These are classified as 'metaphors' because, instead of using just a modal verb to express the modality (*the eyes may imitate . . .*), a whole clause structure is used (*It is thought that . . .*). See Eggins 2004: 174–175.

13 Martin and Rose (2003) following White (2003) call these different kinds of attribution 'hetereglossia' and 'monoglossia', drawing on Bakhtin's (1981) notion of the dialogic nature of text. A heteroglossic voice is one where the source is other than the writer; a monoglossic voice is one where the writer is the source.

14 'Affect' here refers to instances of language which convey explicit expressions of emotional reaction (to laugh, cry, be happy, etc). The use of this term should not be taken to imply a split between cognitive and emotional responses (see, for example, Belcher 1991: 187). The term reflects the systematic inscription of emotion in textual choices, not mental states as a response to the text.

15 Exhibited at the Museum of Contemporary Art, Sydney, in 1996. Examples are taken from the brochure accompanying the exhibition. For full descriptions of the Appraisal categories cited here, see Martin and Rose 2003.

16 Even when community groups are invited to contribute to exhibitions, it is usually still the institution which issues the invitation, and which vets the final product. Radical revisions of these relations, where power is actually given over, are rare.

5 Representing the world through language: using language to portray, interpret and construct

1 In many respects, it is difficult to separate these processes: the language is as much a part of the display as anything else; the methods of display communicate in their own ways. However, for practical reasons, I will address language here as a separate resource, and consider its integration with other design elements in the following chapter.

2 Despite the fact that the we may have a very firm belief that our representations 'reflect' the real world. The whole point is to recognise that textual products construct a picture of the 'real' world.

3 To be fair, this text is around 30 years old, and is not typical of contemporary texts in the museum.

4 These are not necessarily conscious choices, but reflect the choices that are available to us as part of our complex linguistic system; this is the insight provided by Halliday's model of systemic linguistics, e.g. Halliday 1994; Halliday and Matthiessen 2004.

5 This is related to, but nevertheless different from, the traditional distinction of transitive and intransitive verbs. In the case of in/transitive verbs, the relevant variable is one of extension: was the action extended to another Participant, or not? (Hence, *the lion ran*: intransitive; *the lion chased the tourist*: transitive.) The distinction described here is one where the relevant variable is one of causation: which Participant brought about the Process? Here the relevant contrast would be between *the lion chased the tourist* (external cause) and *the tourist ran* ('internal' cause). Technically this perspective on causation is called *ergativity*. See further these examples and discussion in Halliday 1994: 161ff.; Halliday and Matthiessen 2004: 284ff.

6 Emmanuel de Roux, writing for *Le Monde*, reviewing the exhibition 'Aborigènes, Les Couleurs du Rêve, Lyon', cited by Peter Hill, *Sydney Morning Herald*, 8.5.2004, p. 8; this is not therefore an exhibition text as such, but illustrates an interesting point about representational meanings.

7 They are also different in terms of the other communication frameworks. Each has a different textual organisation, with different Themes or 'points of departure' and different methods of developing the Themes. Similarly, each is different in interactional terms: 'Mission Infossible' and 'More than dinosaurs' are more interactionally engaging; 'Triceratops' adopts a conventionally 'neutral' scientific voice, while 'Velociraptor' is terse with its authoritative, scientific voice.

8 These examples originally discussed in Ferguson *et al.* 1995: 47ff.

9 As noted in Ferguson *et al.* 1995, this version has implications for Theme development, as it has a different Theme from the original example.

6 Extending the frameworks: understanding exhibitions and museums as texts

1 But see Pang (2001, 2004) for descriptions here, and Stenglin 2004a, who has attempted to account for the 'grammar of space', particularly as it is realised in museum exhibitions. At the time of writing, Stenglin 2004a was not available for circulation, but it does make use of a systemically informed, social-semiotic approach, and is complementary to the frameworks proposed here, while pursuing them in more depth.

2 Also, the focus on 'museums as texts' might be even more localised: considering how one exhibit, whether two- or three-dimensional, might make meaning across the three communicative frameworks, for instance, in terms of the relative placement of visual image and written text. These localised meanings are certainly important and contribute to related meanings in an exhibition as a whole, but I will not focus on them here. See Kress and van Leeuwen (1996) for analyses of two and three-dimensional visual texts; and Pang (2001, 2004) and Hooper-Greenhill (2000) for some discussion of this in museum contexts.

3 There are many other contributions to the analysis of multi-modal text beyond these. This selection highlights some of the work which has focussed on museums or similar three-dimensional texts.

4 Pang (2001, 2004) locates issues of Circulation Path (and related traffic flow, etc.) under the 'interpersonal' metafunction, or what I am calling here the interactional framework. Clearly this is not inappropriate, as the circulation path positions the visitor to interact with an exhibition/the institution in a particular way. At the same time, Stenglin (2004a, 2004b) addresses similar issues in relation to the experiential metafunction, or what I am calling here the representational framework. This also is appropriate, as the way in which a text 'unfolds' creates basic representational meaning (e.g. serial unfolding will be seen to equate with a sequence in time, leading to a recount-like structure for

the text). However, following Kress and van Leeuwen's (1996) location of 'reading path' in relation to issues of composition, I prefer to speak of pathways first in relation to the textual metafunction, referred to here as the organisational framework, drawing an analogy between reading and navigation. Like most choices, however, the impact is plurifunctional: navigation relates to both organisation, interaction and representation. A pathway creates coherence for the separate components of a text (and so is organisational); it positions visitors to move through the text in a certain way (and so is interactional) and it creates a particular structure for that text (and so is representational). The difference in these descriptions is one of starting point, and of emphasis.

5 In fact Pang (2001, 2004) combines descriptions of traffic flow (basic formal patterns) with descriptions of flow rate (constant, variable or stopped) to produce a combined systemic description of circulation path. Stenglin (2004a, 2004b) describes similar features in terms of a combination of 'path' (as in pathway) and 'venue' (as in a place to stop along the way).

6 Of course, even with only 'one' pathway, visitors can subvert these choices, by backtracking, for example, or by skipping whole sections. It is the 'apparent' nature of this choice, open or closed, which is at issue here.

7 It is important to note both the relationship with and difference from the same term used in Bernstein's discussion of discourse and pedagogy (e.g. Bernstein 1975). For Bernstein, framing 'refers to the degree of control teacher and pupil possess over the selection, organisation, pacing and timing of knowledge transmitted and received in the pedagogical relationship' (Ellis 2004: 212, citing Bernstein 1975: 88–89 and Atkinson 1985: 136). 'Weak framing means that there are more options available to the learners during learning and strong framing means less options/control are available' (Ellis ibid.). Bernstein's use of framing co-exists with practices of *classification*, that is 'the degree of boundary maintenance between contents. It does not refer to what is classified but to the relationships between contents. Strong classification insulates the contents by strong boundaries. Weak classification blurs the boundaries between the contents. (Ellis ibid.). Thus, Kress and van Leeuwen's use of the term 'framing' represents a slight but important adaptation. For them, framing is about (more or less) literal boundaries – the extent to which 'contents' are indicated as being part of the 'same' text or part of 'different' texts, through a variety of realisations. It thus overlaps in some ways with Bernstein's 'classification'. The coverage of Bernstein's original use of the term, 'framing', relates more closely to what we are discussing here in terms of the degrees of freedom afforded visitors in their navigation of exhibition pathways and their interaction with exhibits (see further the discussion on interactional meanings in exhibitions, p. 130 and Note 4 above). I will continue to use the term 'framing' here in the sense in which Kress and van Leeuwen have established it, and note that it has implications for our understanding of classification, which relates to representational meanings.

8 A similar instance of coercive positioning via linear organisation is discussed by Witcomb 2003 (pp. 136ff.) in relation to the Beit Hashoah Museum of Tolerance, Los Angeles.

9 'For something to be presented as Centre means that it is presented as the nucleus of the information on which all the other elements are in some sense subservient. The Margins are these ancillary, dependent elements' (Kress and van Leeuwen 1996: 206).

10 'For something to be Ideal means that it is presented as the idealised or generalised essence of the information, hence also as its, ostensibly, most salient part. The Real is then opposed to this in that it presents more specific information (e.g. details), more 'down to earth' information . . . or more practical information . . . This is of course no less ideological' (Kress and van Leeuwen 1996: 193).

11 'The soaring walls of the East Superspace provide the majestic ambience for the sails flying above the canoes, themselves floating below on a sea of subdued light', *Te Vainui O Pasifika*, Te Pasifika Gallery, Melbourne Museum.

12 http://www.nhm.ac.uk/museum/floorplans.

13 This is close to Bernstein's (1975) use of the term 'framing', to indicate the ways in which teachers and students can control the pacing, timing, and sequencing of information in a pedagogical context. However, as observed in Note 4 above, the term 'framing'

is used in this book in a slightly different sense, in relation to borders and boundaries between elements in a spatial composition, following Kress and van Leeuwen 1996.

14 Note that 'narrative design' here is a generalised sense of the term, equating with the sense of 'generic structure' established in Chapter 2. It does not necessarily mean a literal 'narrative' – it can do, but can also encompass other genres, such as Explanation, Exposition, Directive, and so on. Note also that 'narrative design' does not necessarily equate with a linear 'master narrative' (Witcomb 2003). A master narrative is one kind of narrative design, though there can also be many others.

15 'The horizontal plane is the plane of activity, or of the floorplan . . . The vertical plane . . . is the plane of the spectacle, or of the façade of the building . . .' (van Leeuwen 1998: 5; cf. Kress and van Leeuwen 1996: 260). See also Witcomb (2003: 39), and her discussion of historical trends in the overall organisation of museums (ibid., p. 115ff.).

16 One example where technology enables a redefinition of accessibility is in the way in which replicas of rare and fragile objects can be made physically accessible, for instance the New British Library has computer representations of rare, ancient documents, which unfold in real time before the reader, enabling some approximation of the process of accessing these texts.

17 Unfortunately the signalling of this intention could have been more effective. The brochure accompanying the exhibition stated, among other things, that 'The Rooms on Level 1 are designed for fleeting, random and casual encounters: visitors are overwhelmed by sights and sounds, and experience the intensity of and craziness of animation "on-the-run".' This all-important information, however, was buried in the second column of an A4 brochure, and would have been more effective if it had been foregrounded in some way.

18 A similar effect is achieved at the new Melbourne Museum, where windows are used within the building so that visitors can glimpse inside the 'working' spaces of the institution – offices and so on (and also presumably vice versa!). See some description of this in Beck and Cooper 2001.

19 For example, within a naturalistic coding orientation, images which have natural, well differentiated colours, various shades in the colours, and a reasonably high level of representational detail, are 'most real', and have 'high modality'. Within such a coding orientation, images which use just a few colours, without shading, and with a low level of representational detail, are 'less real', and have a 'low modality'. In contrast, however, within a scientific coding orientation, naturalistic images would have a low modality, and black-and-white technical diagrams would have the highest modality. Such correlations are culturally and historically situated; Lemke, for instance (1998, 2002) points out that the 'naturalistic' conventions for scientific representations in books and journals are changing.

20 Penny Morrison, Carolyn Meehan; personal communication.

7 Conclusion: integrating the frameworks

1 Note again that this does not mean that there is one reading of the text; as emphasised throughout, readings can diverge, and the 'one' text is still complex in meaning.

2 Kress and van Leeuwen (1996) suggest rhythm and composition as integrative principles in multi-modal texts.

3 Again it needs to be stressed that even if visitors totally *ignore* all the language of an exhibition – and research suggests that they do not – that language has still informed the shared communication objectives of the exhibition team, and has contributed to its *raison d'être*.

Bibliography

Ambruster, B. (1984) 'The problem of "inconsiderate" text' in G.G. Duffy, L.R. Roehler and J. Mason (eds) *Comprehension Instruction*, New York: Longman: 202–217.

Atkinson, P.A. (1985) *Language, Structure, and Reproduction: An Introduction to the Sociology of Basil Bernstein*, London: Methuen.

Bakhtin, M.M. (1981) *The Dialogic Imagination*, translated by C. Emerson and M. Holquist, Austin: University of Texas Press.

Baños, Hélène (1995) 'Writing exhibition texts' in Andrée Blais (ed.) *Text in the Exhibition Medium*, La Société des Musées Québécois; Musée de la Civilisation: 205–228.

Barthes, R. (1977) *Image – Music – Text*, London: Fontana.

Bath, Brian (2000) 'Audio-tours at heritage sites' in Paulette M. McManus (ed.) *Archaeological Displays and the Public: Museology and Interpretation*, 2nd edn, London: Archetype Publications: 157–163.

Beck, Haig and Cooper, Jackie (2001) 'Melbourne Museum: a new architectural identity' in Carolyn Rasmussen (ed.) *A Museum for the People: A History of Museum Victoria and its Predecessors 1854–2000*, Melbourne: Scribe Publications: 381–384.

Belcher, Michael (1991) *Exhibitions in Museums*, Leicester and London: Leicester University Press.

Bennett, Tony (1995) *The Birth of the Museum: History, Theory, Politics*, London: Routledge.

—— (1998a) *Culture: A Reformer's Science*, London: Routledge.

—— (1998b) 'Speaking to the eyes: museums, legibility and the social order' in Sharon MacDonald (ed.) *The Politics of Display: Museums, Science, Culture*, London and New York: Routledge: 25–35.

—— (1999) 'That those who run may read' in Eilean Hooper-Greenhill (ed.) *The Educational Role of the Museum*, 2nd edn, London and New York: Routledge: 241–254.

Bernstein, B. (1975) *Class, Codes and Control 3: Towards a Theory of Educational Transmissions*, London: Routledge & Kegan Paul.

Bitgood, S. (1989) 'The ABCs of label design' in S. Bitgood, A. Benefield and D. Patterson (eds) *Visitor Studies: Theory, Research, and Practice*, Volume 2, Jacksonville, AL: Center for Social Design: 115–129.

Blais, Andrée (1995) 'Writing, a critical process' in Andrée Blais (ed.) *Text in the Exhibition Medium*, La Société des Musées Québécois; Musée de la Civilisation: 193–204.

Bloomfield, Robert M. (2002) 'Making the earth move for you: the earth galleries at the Natural History Museum, London' in Barry Lord and Gail Dexter Lord (eds) *The Manual of Museum Exhibitions*, Walnut Creek: Alta Mira Press: 387–392.

Blunden, Jennifer and Slam, Anne (1997) *Label Manual: Communication Briefs; Information Hierarchies; Procedures; Formats*, 2nd edn, Haymarket: Powerhouse Museum.

Bridges, Peter and McDonald, Don (1988) *James Barnet: Colonial Architect*, Sydney: Hale and Ironmonger.

Brown, K. and Solomon, N. (1992) *What is Plain English* and *Writing Plain English Workplace Documents*: Training manuals, University of Technology, Sydney: Centre for Workplace Communication and Culture.

Brown, R. and Gilman, A. (1960) 'The pronouns of power and solidarity' in T. Sebeok (ed.) *Style in Language*, Cambridge, MA: MIT Press: 253–276.

Butt, D., Fahey, R., Feez, S. *et al.* (2001) *Using Systemic Functional Grammar: An Explorer's Guide*, 2nd edn, Macquarie University: NCELTR.

Cameron, D. (1995) *Verbal Hygiene*, London and New York: Routledge.

Campbell, Leo J. and Holland, V. Melissa (1982) 'Understanding the language of public documents because readability formulas don't' in Robert J. Di Pietro (ed.) *Linguistics and the Professions: Proceedings of the Second Annual Delaware Symposium on Language Studies*, Norwood: Ablex: 157–171.

Carter, James (1999) 'How old is this text?' in Eilean Hooper-Greenhill (ed.) *The Educational Role of the Museum*, 2nd edn, London and New York: Routledge: 211–214.

Cassels, Richard (1996) 'Learning styles' in Gail Durbin (ed.) *Developing Museum Exhibitions for Lifelong Learning*, London: The Stationery Office: 38–48.

Chouliaraki, Lilie and Fairclough, Norman (1999) *Discourse in Later Modernity: Rethinking Critical Discourse Analysis*, Edinburgh: Edinburgh University Press.

Christie, F. and Martin, J.R. (1997) (eds) *Genre and Institutions: Social Processes in the Workplace and School*, London: Cassell.

Coxall, Helen (1991) 'How language means: an alternative view of museums text' in Gaynor Kavanagh (ed.) *Museum Languages: Objects and Texts*, Leicester: Leicester University: 85–100.

—— (1996) 'Writing for different audiences' in Gail Durbin (ed.) *Developing Museum Exhibitions for Lifelong Learning*, London: The Stationery Office: 196–199.

—— (1999) 'Museum text as mediated message' in Eilean Hooper-Greenhill (ed.) *The Educational Role of the Museum*, 2nd edn, London and New York: Routledge: 215–222.

Cranny-Francis, Anne (1992) *Engendered Fiction: Analysing Gender in the Production and Reception of Texts*, Kensington: University of New South Wales Press.

Crystal, David (2001) *Language and the Internet*, Cambridge: Cambridge University Press.

Dean, David (1994) *Museum Exhibition: Theory and Practice*, London and New York: Routledge.

Decrosse, Anne and Natali, Jean-Paul (1995) 'The oral text as a singular form of the written text in an exhibition' in Andrée Blais (ed.) *Text in the Exhibition Medium*, La Société des Musées Québécois; Musée de la Civilisation: 157–180.

Derewianka, Beverly (1990) *Exploring How Texts Work*, Newtown: Primary English Teaching Association.

Doyle, Peter (1991) 'The Sociosemiotics of electricity substations' *Social Semiotics*, Vol 1, No. 1: 81–98.

Droga, L. and Humphrey, S. (2002) *Getting Started with Functional Grammar*, Sydney: Target Texts.

Durbin, Gail (ed.) (1996) *Developing Museum Exhibitions for Lifelong Learning*, London: The Stationery Office.

Eagleson, R.D. (1990) *Writing in Plain English*, Canberra: AGPS.

Eco, Umberto (1977) *A Theory of Semiotics*, London: Macmillan.

Eerdmans, Susan (2003) 'Sharing an experience: Claude Monet's Bathers at La Grenouillère' in Paola Nobili (ed.) *Camminare per quadri: il linguaggio divulgative dell'arte*, Bologna: CLUEB (Cooperative Libraria Universitaria Editrice Bologna): 109–120.

Eggins, Suzanne (2004) *An Introduction to Systemic-Functional Linguistics*, 2nd edn, London: Pinter Publishers.

—— and Slade, Diana (1997) *Analysing Casual Conversation*, London and Washington: Cassell.

Ekarv, Margareta (1999) 'Combating redundancy: writing texts for exhibitions' in Eilean Hooper-Greenhill (ed.) *The Educational Role of the Museum*, 2nd edn, London and New York: Routledge: 201–204.

Ellis, Robert A. (2004) 'Supporting genre-based literacy pedagogy with technology – the implications for the framing and classification of pedagogy' in Louise J. Ravelli and Robert A. Ellis (eds) *Analysing Academic Writing: Contextualised Frameworks*, London: Continuum: 210–232.

Fahy, Anne (1995) 'New technologies for museum communication' in Eilean Hooper-Greenhill (ed.) *Museum, Media, Message*, London and New York: Routledge: 82–96.

Fairclough, N. (1995) *Critical Discourse Analysis: The Critical Study of Language*, London: Longman.

Falk, John H. (1993) 'Assessing the impact of exhibit arrangement on visitor behaviour and learning' *Curator* 36(2): 133–146.

—— and Dierking, Lynn D. (1992) *The Museum Experience*, Washington DC: Whalesback Books.

—— and —— (2000) *Learning from Museums – Visitor Experiences and the Making of Meaning*, Walnut Creek, CA: AltaMira Press.

Ferguson, L., MacLulich, C. and Ravelli, L. (1995) *Meanings and Messages: Language Guidelines for Museum Exhibitions*, Sydney: Australian Museum.

Flesch, Rudolf (1949) *The Art of Readable Writing*, New York: Harper & Row.

Fowler, R., Hodge, B., Kress, G. *et al.* (1979) *Language and Control*, London: Routledge & Kegan Paul.

Gardner, Howard (1983) *Frames of Mind*, London: Paladin Books.

—— (1996) 'Multiple intelligences' in Gail Durbin (ed.) *Developing Museum Exhibitions for Lifelong Learning*, London: The Stationery Office: 35–37.

Gee, J. P., Hull, G. and Lankshear, C. (1996) *The New Work Order: Behind the Language of the New Capitalism*, St Leonards, NSW: Allen and Unwin.

Gieryn, Thomas F. (1998) 'Balancing act: science, *Enola Gay* and History Wars at the Smithsonian' in Sharon MacDonald (ed.) *The Politics of Display: Museums, Science, Culture*, London and New York: Routledge: 197–228.

Gilmore, Elizabeth and Sabine, Jennifer (1999) 'Writing readable text: evaluation of the Ekarv method' in Eilean Hooper-Greenhill (ed.) *The Educational Role of the Museum*, 2nd edn, London and New York: Routledge: 205–210.

Griffin, Des (1996) 'Previous possessions, new obligations: a commitment by Australian museums' *Curator* 39/1 1996: 45–62.

Gunning, Robert (1968) *The Technique of Clear Writing*, New York: McGraw-Hill.

Halliday, M.A.K. (1973) *Explorations in the Functions of Language*, London: Edward Arnold.

—— (1978) *Language as Social Semiotic: The Social Interpretation of Language and Meaning*, London: Edward Arnold.

—— (1985) 'It's a fixed word order language is English' *ITL Review of Applied Linguistics*: 67–68.

—— (1989) *Spoken and Written Language*, Oxford: Oxford University Press.

—— (1994) *An Introduction to Functional Grammar*, 2nd edn, London: Edward Arnold.

—— (1998) 'Things and relations: regrammaticising experience as technical knowledge' in J.R. Martin and Robert Veel (eds) *Reading Science: Critical and Functional Perspectives on Discourses of Science*, London: Routledge: 185–235.

—— (2001) 'Literacy and linguistics: relationships between spoken and written language' in A. Burns and C. Coffin (eds) *Analysing English in a Global Context: A Reader*, London and New York: Routledge: 181–193.

—— (2002a) 'Categories of the theory of grammar' in Jonathan Webster (ed.) *On Grammar*, London and New York: Continuum: 37–94. First published in *Word* 1961, 7(3): 241–292.

—— (2002b) 'Spoken and written modes of meaning' in Jonathan Webster (ed.) *On Grammar*, London and New York: Continuum: 323–351.

—— and Hasan, Ruqaiya (1976) *Cohesion in English*, London: Longman.

—— and Matthiessen, Christian M.I.M. (2004) *An Introduction to Functional Grammar*, 3rd edn, London: Arnold.

Hasan, Ruqaiya (1989) *Linguistics, Language and Verbal Art*, Oxford: Oxford University Press.

Hein, George E. (1996) 'Constructivist learning theory' in Gail Durbin (ed.) *Developing Museum Exhibitions for Lifelong Learning*, London: The Stationery Office: 30–34.

—— (1998) *Learning in the Museum*, London and New York: Routledge.

—— (1999) 'The constructivist museum' in Eilean Hooper-Greenhill (ed.) *The Educational Role of the Museum*, 2nd edn, London and New York: Routledge: 73–79.

—— and Alexander, Mary (1998) *Museums: Place of Learning*, Washington DC: American Association of Museums.

Hewings, Ann (1999) Disciplinary engagement in undergraduate writing: An investigation of clause-initial elements in geography essays, unpublished Ph.D. thesis, Department of English, University of Birmingham.

Hirschi, Kent D. and Screven, Chandler (1996) 'Effects of questions on visitor reading behaviour' in Gail Durbin (ed.) *Developing Museum Exhibitions for Lifelong Learning*, London: The Stationery Office: 189–192.

Hodge, Robert (n.d.) 'A semiotic analysis of the Australian museum's *Indigenous Australians: Australia's First Peoples*' Exhibition' Australian Museum: internal document.

—— and D'Souza, Wilfred (1999) 'The museum as a communicator: a semiotic analysis of the Western Australian Museum Aboriginal Gallery, Perth' in Eilean Hooper-Greenhill (ed.) *The Educational Role of the Museum*, 2nd edn, London and New York: Routledge: 53–66.

—— and Kress, Gunther (1988) *Social Semiotics*, Cambridge: Polity Press.

Hooper-Greenhill, Eilean (1991) 'A new communication model for museums' in Gaynor Kavanagh (ed.) *Museum Languages: Objects and Texts*, Leicester: Leicester University: 49–61.

—— (1994) *Museums and their Visitors*, London: Routledge.

—— (ed.) (1995) *Museum, Media, Message*, London and New York: Routledge.

—— (ed.) (1997) *Cultural Diversity: Developing Museum Audiences in Britain* (Contemporary Issues in Museum Culture Series), London: Leicester University Press.

—— (ed.) (1999) *The Educational Role of the Museum*, 2nd edn, London and New York: Routledge.

—— (2000) *Museums and the Interpretation of Visual Culture*, London and New York: Routledge.

Iedema, R. (2003) *Discourses of Post-Bureaucratic Organization*, Amsterdam: Benjamins.

Jacobi, Daniel and Poli, Marie Sylvie (1995) 'Scriptovisual documents in exhibitions: some theoretical guidelines' in Andrée Blais (ed.) *Text in the Exhibition Medium*, La Société des Musées Québécois; Musée de la Civilisation: 48–78.

Johns, A.M. (1997) *Text, Role, and Context*, Cambridge: Cambridge University Press.

Karp I. and Lavine S.D. (eds) (1991) *Exhibiting Cultures: The Poetics and Politics of Museum Display*, Washington: Smithsonian Institution Press.

Kavanagh, Gaynor (ed.) (1991) *Museum Languages: Objects and Texts*, Leicester: Leicester University.

—— (ed.) (1996) *Making Histories in Museums*, London and New York: Leicester University Press.

Kelly, L. (1995) 'Museum audiences: what do we know? what we don't know; how can we find out' Australian Museum Internal Document. Kaplan, Flora E.S. (1995) 'Exhibitions as communicative media' in Eilean Hooper-Greenhill (ed.) *Museum, Media, Message*, London and New York: Routledge: 37–58.

Kress, G. (1989) *Linguistic Processes in Sociocultural Practice*, Oxford: Oxford University Press.

—— and van Leeuwen, T. (1996) *Reading Images: The Grammar of Visual Design*, London: Routledge.

—— and van Leeuwen, T. (2001) *Multimodal Discourse: The Modes and Media of Contemporary Communication*, London and New York: Arnold.

Labov, W. and Waletzky, J. (1967) 'Narrative analysis: oral versions of personal experience' in J. Helm (ed.) *Essays in the Verbal and Visual Arts*, American Ethnological Society, Proceedings of Spring Meeting, Washington, DC: University of Washington Press: 12–44.

Lamarche, Hélène (1995) 'The audio guide as an aid to understanding in an exhibition' in Andrée Blais (ed.) *Text in the Exhibition Medium*, La Société des Musées Québécois; Musée de la Civilisation: 181–190.

Lehmbruck, M. (1974) 'Psychology: perception and behaviour' in *Museum* 26 iii–iv: 191–204.

Lemke, J.L. (1998) 'Multiplying meaning: visual and verbal semiotics in scientific text' in J.R. Martin and R. Veel (eds) *Reading Science*, London: Routledge: 87–113.

—— (2002) 'Multimedia genres for scientific education and science literacy' in M.J. Schleppegrell and C. Colombi (eds) *Developing Advanced Literacy in First and Second Languages*, Mahwah, NJ: Lawrence Erlbaum Associates: 21–44.

Luke, Timothy W. (2002) *Museum Politics: Power Plays at the Exhibition*, Minneapolis: University of Minnesota Press.

MacDonald, Sharon (1998) 'Exhibitions of power and powers of exhibitions: an introduction to the politics of display' in MacDonald, Sharon (ed.) *The Politics of Display: Museums, Science, Culture*, London and New York: Routledge: 1–24.

—— (ed.) (1998) *The Politics of Display: Museums, Science, Culture*, London and New York: Routledge.

Macken-Horarik, Mary (2004) 'Interacting with the multimodal text: reflections on image and verbiage in *ArtExpress: Visual Communication*, Vol. 3; No. 1: 5–26.

MacLulich, C. (1991) 'More than meets the eye – new perspectives on text writing and editing in museums' in *Doing Time – Museums, Education and Accountability*, MEAA conference proceedings: 51–59.

—— (1992) *Text Production Project: An Outline of a New Project for 1993*, Australian Museum: internal document.

—— (1994a) 'Off the wall: theory and practice in the language of exhibition texts', unpublished M.Litt. thesis, University of Sydney.

—— (1994b) 'Off the wall: new perspectives on the language of exhibition texts' in *Evaluation and Visitor Research in Museums – Towards 2000 (Conference Proceedings)*, Sydney: Powerhouse Museum: 105–115.

McManus, Paulette M. (1989a) 'Oh, yes, they do: how museum visitors read labels and interact with exhibit texts' *Curator* 32(2): 174–189.

—— (1989b) 'What people say and how they think in a science museum' in David L. Uzzell (ed.) *Heritage Interpretation* Volume 2 *The Visitor Experience*, London and New York: Belhaven Press: 156–165.

—— (1991) 'Making sense of exhibits' in Gaynor Kavanagh (ed.) *Museum Languages: Objects and Texts*, Leicester: Leicester University: 35–46.

—— (2000) 'Written communications for museums and heritage sites' in Paulette M. McManus (ed.) *Archaeological Displays and the Public: Museology and Interpretation*, 2nd edn, London: Archetype Publications: 97–112.

Martin, J.R. (1989) *Factual Writing: Exploring and Challenging Social Reality*, Oxford: Oxford University Press.

—— (1992) *English Text: System and Structure*, Philadelphia and Amsterdam: Benjamins.

—— (1993) 'Literacy in science: learning to handle text as technology' in M.A.K. Halliday and J.R. Martin *Writing Science: Literacy and Discursive Power*, London: The Falmer Press: 166–202.

—— (2001) 'Language, register and genre' in A. Burns and C. Coffin (eds) *Analysing English in a Global Context: A Reader*, London: Routledge: 149–166.

—— and Rose, David (2003) *Working with Discourse: Meaning Beyond the Clause*, London: Continuum.

Miller, Steven (1990) 'Labels' *Curator* 33(2): 85–89.

O'Halloran, K.L. (ed.) (2004) *Multi-modal Discourse Analysis*, London: Continuum.

O'Neill, Mark (1999) 'Museums and their communities' in Gail Dexter Lord and Barry Lord (eds) *The Manual of Museum Planning*, 2nd edn, London: The Stationery Office: 21–38.

O'Toole, Michael (1994) *The Language of Displayed Art*, London: Leicester University Press.

—— and Butt, David (2003) 'Interdisciplinary principles of "textual" analysis: the matter and meaning of buildings' *21st Century COE Program, Studies for the Integrated Text Science Proceedings of the Second International Conference, June 2003*, Nagoya: 23–29.

Pang, Kah Meng Alfred (2001) Disciplining history – a multimodal analysis of the museum exhibition 'From colony to nation', unpublished master's thesis, National University of Singapore.

—— (2004) 'Making history in *From Colony to Nation*: a multimodal analysis of a museum exhibition in Singapore' in K.L. O'Halloran (ed.) *Multi-modal Discourse Analysis*, London: Continuum: 28–54.

Pearce, Susan M. (1991) 'Collecting reconsidered' in Gaynor Kavanagh (ed.) *Museum Languages: Objects and Texts*, Leicester: Leicester University: 135–154.

—— (1995) 'Collecting as medium and message' in Eilean Hooper-Greenhill (ed.) *Museum, Media, Message*, London and New York: Routledge: 15–23.

Peers, Laura and Brown, Alison K. (2003) *Museums and Source Communities: A Routledge Reader*, London and New York: Routledge.

Poynton, C. (1989) *Language and Gender: Making the Difference*, Oxford: Oxford University Press.

Purser, E. (2000) 'Telling stories: text analysis in a museum' in E. Ventola (ed.) *Discourse and Community: Doing Functional Linguistics*, Tübingen: Gunter Narr Verlag: 169–198.

Ravelli, Louise J. (1988) 'Grammatical metaphor: an initial analysis' in E.H. Steines and R. Veltman (eds) *Pragmatics, Discourse and Text: Some Systemically Inspired Approaches*, London: Pinter: 133–147.

—— (1996) 'Making language accessible: successful text writing for museum visitors' *Linguistics and Education* 8: 367–387.

—— (1998) 'The consequences of choice: discursive positioning in an art institution' in A. Sanchez-Macarro and R. Carter (eds) *Linguistic Choice Across Genres: Variation in Spoken and Written English*, Amsterdam: Benjamins: 137–153.

—— (2000) 'Beyond shopping: constructing the Sydney Olympics in three-dimensional text' *Text* 20(4): 489–515.

Reddy, M. (1979) 'The conduit metaphor – a case of frame conflict in our language about language' in A. Ortony (ed.) *Metaphor and Thought*, Cambridge: Cambridge University Press: 285–324.

Rothery, J. and Stenglin, M. (1997) 'Entertaining and instructing: exploring experience through story' in F. Christie and J.R. Martin (eds) *Genre and Institutions: Social Processes in the Workplace and School*, London: Cassell: 231–263.

Royal Ontario Museum, Communications Design Team (1999) 'Spatial considerations' in Eilean Hooper-Greenhill (ed.) *The Educational Role of the Museum*, 2nd edn, London and New York: Routledge: 178–190.

Samson, Denis. (1995) 'Reading strategies used by exhibition visitors' in Andrée Blais (ed.) *Text in the Exhibition Medium*, La Société des Musées Québécois; Musée de la Civilisation: 135–153.

Sandell, Richard (ed.) (2002) *Museums, Society, Inequality*, London and New York: Routledge.

Saumerez Smith, Charles (1989) 'Museums, artefacts and meanings' in Peter Vergo (ed.) *The New Museology* London: Reaktion Books: 6–21.

Scheeres, H. (1999) 'Restructured work, restructured worker' *Literacy and Numeracy Studies*, Vol. 9, No. 1: 27–38.

Schiele, Bernard (1995) 'Text in the exhibition medium' in Andrée Blais (ed.) *Text in the Exhibition Medium*, La Société des Musées Québécois; Musée de la Civilisation: 33–48.

Screven, G. (1992) 'Motivating visitors to read labels' *ILVS Review: A Journal of Visitor Behaviour* Vol. 2 No. 2: 183–211.

—— (1995) 'Motivating visitors to read labels' in Andrée Blais (ed.) *Text in the Exhibition Medium*, La Société des Musées Québécois; Musée de la Civilisation: 97–134.

Serrell, Beverly (1996) *Exhibit Labels: An Interpretive Approach*, Walnut Creek, CA: AltaMira Press.

Simpson, Moira G. (1996) *Making Representations: Museums in the Post-Colonial Era*, revised edn, London and New York: Routledge.

Solomon, N. (1996) 'Plain English: from a perspective of language in society' in R. Hasan and G. Williams (eds) *Literacy and Society*, London: Longman: 279–307.

—— and Brown, K. (1995) *Plain English: Best Practice in the Public Sector*, Australian Language and Literacy Council, NLLIA.

Specht, Jim and MacLulich, Carolyn (2000) 'Changes and challenges: the Australian Museum and Indigenous communities' in Paulette M. McManus (ed.) *Archaeological Displays and the Public: Museology and Interpretation*, 2nd edn, London: Archetype Publications: 39–63.

Spencer, Hugh A.D. (1999) 'Exhibition development' in Gail Dexter Lord and Barry Lord (eds) *The Manual of Museum Planning*, 2nd edn, London: The Stationery Office: 155–173.

Stenglin, Maree (2001) 'Comfort and security: a challenge for exhibition design' in Linda Kelly and Jennifer Barrett (eds) *Uncover Vol. 1: Proceedings of the Uncover Graduate Research in the Museum Sector Conference*: 23–30.

—— (2004a) Packaging curiosities: Towards a grammar of three-dimensional space, unpublished Ph.D. thesis, Department of Linguistics, University of Sydney.

—— (2004b) 'Space Odyssey: a guided tour through the semiosis of three-dimensional space' Systemic-Functional Linguistics Research Seminar, University of Sydney.

Stevenson, Jane (2003) 'Looking at paintings, looking at language: art and art texts for the language learner' in Paola Nobili (ed.) *Camminare per quadri: Il linguaggio divulgative dell'arte*, Bologna: CLUEB (Cooperative Libraria Universitaria Editrice Bologna): 121–148.

Susskind, Anne, and the National Museum of Australia (2001) *Building History: The National Museum of Australia*, Canberra: National Museum of Australia.

Swiecimski, Jerzy (1989) 'Truths and untruths in museum exhibitions' in David L. Uzzell (ed.) *Heritage Interpretation* Volume 2 *The Visitor Experience*, London and New York: Belhaven Press: 203–211.

Unsworth, L. (1997) ' "Sound" explanations in school science: a functional linguistic perspective on effective apprenticing texts' *Linguistics and Education*, 9(2): 199–226.

Uzzell, David L. (ed.) (1989) *Heritage Interpretation* Volume 2 *The Visitor Experience*, London and New York: Belhaven Press.

van Leeuwen, Theo (1998) 'Textual space and point of view', paper presented to the Museums Australia State Conference, *Who Sees, Who Speaks – Voices and Points of View in Exhibitions*, Australian Museum, 21 September.

Wallace, M. (1995) 'The battle of the Enola Gay' *Museum News* 74(4).

White, Peter R. (1994) 'Images of the shark: Jaws, gold fish, or cuddly toy? An analysis of the Australian Museum's 1994 *Shark* exhibition from a communicative perspective', unpublished manuscript, Department of Linguistics, University of Sydney.

—— (2003) 'Beyond modality and hedging: a dialogic view of the language of intersubjective stance' *Text* 23(2), special issue, edited by M. Macken-Horarik and J.R. Martin: 259–284.

Witcomb, Andrea (1994) 'Post-modern space and the museum – the displacement of "public" narratives' *Social Semiotics* 4(1/2): 239–260.

—— (2003) *Re-Imagining the Museum: Beyond the Mausoleum*, London and New York: Routledge.

Index

Pages containing illustrations are indicated in **bold** type.

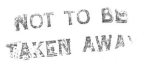